W9-DJE-920

Key to Government
in Chicago and
Suburban Cook County

352.07781 K44f

AUG 1 4 2002

Researched and written by volunteers from
    The League of Women Voters of Chicago
    The League of Women Voters of Cook County
    Cook County Court Watchers
    Citizens Information Service of Illinois

Editor: Barbara Page Fiske
Research Editors: Jacqueline Brown, Elinor Elam, Renee Hansen, Beth Kink
Picture Editor: Oswelda Badal
Contributors: Mary Allan, Oswelda Badal, Gwen Barnett, Katherine Bowe, Eleanor Byman, Betty Cameron, Verlaine Carnell, Evanne Carvlin, Doreen Crewe, Leon Despres, Patricia Dixon, Anne Evans, Mary Farquhar, Wilfred Gadsden, Verna Hill, Robert C. Howard, Dina Lawrence, Donna Moore, Marni Ohsman, Edna Pardo, David Patt, Phyllis Peara, Jean Peterson, Jeanne Quinn, Charlotte Senechalle, Winifred Slusser, Eleanor Vaughan, Alice Vaught, Cecile Vye, Dolores Wagner, Doris Wallace, Irvana Wilks, Betty Willhoite, Ann Wolff

Technical Assistance: Everett Conner, Susan Elam, Emily Ellison, Alan Fiske, Donald Fiske, Susan Fiske-Emery, Florence Goold, Theresa Goss, Dan Levin, John Lucy, Kathryn Mason, Chris Van Brunt

Advisory Committee: Jan Brooks, Toni Hartrich, Alice Jurica, Patricia Lynn, Julie Montague, Carolyn Moore, Bob Slayton

Columbia College Library
600 South Michigan
Chicago, IL 60605

KEY
to Government in
Chicago
and
Suburban
Cook
County

Edited by
Barbara Page
Fiske

DISCARD

The University of Chicago Press

Chicago and London

352.07731 K4 2

Key to government in Chicago
and suburban Cook County

The University of Chicago Press, Chicago 60637
The University of Chicago Press, Ltd., London

© 1989 by The University of Chicago
All rights reserved. Published 1989
Printed in the United States of America

98 97 96 95 94 93 92 91 90 89   54321

Library of Congress Cataloging-in-Publication Data

Key to government in Chicago and suburban
   Cook County.

   Rev. ed. of: Key to our local government :
Chicago, Cook County, metropolitan area.
4th ed. 1978.
   Includes index.
   1. Chicago (Ill.)—Politics and government.
2. Cook County (Ill.)—Politics and government.
I. Fiske, Barbara Page. II. League of Women
Voters of Chicago. III. Key to our local
government.
JS708.K49   1989   352.0773'1   88-29574
ISBN 0-226-25194-2

Contents

ILLUSTRATIONS

TABLES

Foreword

The *Key to Government in Chicago and Suburban Cook County* is the successor to a former publication, *The Key to Our Local Government: Chicago, Cook County, the Metropolitan Area*. The editors wish to express their gratitude to the University of Chicago Press for advice, encouragement, and expertise, as we undertook a new approach to presenting local government structure. We also thank our advisory committee and hope they will feel we have listened carefully to their advice.

Citizens Information Service gratefully acknowledges the support of Amoco Foundation, the Illinois Bar Foundation, and the Bowman C. Lingle Trust for the costs of preparation of the book.

This version of the *Key* builds on the work of previous researchers and editors and on the studies of local government conducted by the League of Women Voters, Cook County Court Watchers, and Citizens Information Service of Illinois, who have published various guides to specific aspects of government from which the editors have borrowed freely, with permission.

To collect the information in this book, research editors assigned individual researchers to cover agencies with which they were familiar; the research editors also did a great deal of the research. Resources used were statutes, ordinances, budgets, comptroller reports, program reports and publications of the agencies, and telephone and personal interviews. The sections on each agency were sent to the agency for review and correction. We are enormously grateful to the busy people in those agencies who took time to review and supplement our information, though we could not, in view of limitations of space, always include all they would have liked to have had in the book. They are proud of the work of their agencies.

Students of government may be interested to know that out of more than 150 separate agencies we asked for help, very few had to be pursued with follow-up calls, and that was usually because we had not identified correctly the person in the agency whose job it would be to review the material. This illustrates the fact that you have to knock on the right door to get the answers you need, and we hope this book will help you do so.

Fig. P. 1. Chicago flag and seal. Four red stars on the flag commemorate Fort Dearborn, the Great Fire, the World Columbian Exposition, and the Century of Progress. Two blue stripes represent the Chicago River and its two branches, and three white stripes represent the North, South, and West sides of the city.

Source: Chicago Mayor's Office

Fig. P. 2. Cook County flag and seal. The large star symbolizes Chicago as the county seat, and the 38 stars represent the 38 townships in the county.

Source: Cook County Board

Preface

HOW TO USE THIS BOOK

This book is intended to be a guide to the structure of local government in Cook County, Chicago, and municipalities and special service areas within the County. We also refer to the state and federal governments as their laws, regulations, funding, and services affect local government.

All levels of government constantly change, especially the responsibilities assigned to particular departments, their budgets, and the number of their employees. Figures given here are accurate at the time of publication but are mainly intended to give some idea of the size of the various agencies, especially as compared to the size of their assignments. If you need to know the most recent figures on budgets, numbers of employees, or salaries, references are given as to where to find them.

Agency addresses and telephone numbers also change. The Chicago telephone directory includes a set of blue pages listing numbers for the United States, Illinois, Cook County, and city of Chicago governments, and an additional directory of services ranging from Alcoholism to Zip Codes. Many suburban directories have similar pages. Note that beginning on November 11, 1989, all suburban numbers will have the area code 708, while Chicago numbers will retain the 312 area code.

Government can be examined from two viewpoints within the purview of this book. One is the structure of government: that is, what the designated responsibilities of each governmental body and official are, what the laws provide as to the authority to carry out these responsibilities, how they are financed, and how the citizen can affect them. These aspects are described in chapters 1 through 9. If you are gathering information on government and encounter obstacles, the section Your Rights to Know, in this preface, will be helpful.

The second way of looking at government is from the point of view of services, such as education, recreation, health, transportation, welfare and employment. Responsibilities for providing these and other services often are divided among various levels of government and agencies. In procedures for enforcement of criminal law, for instance, responsibility is divided among municipal, county, state, and federal agencies: the police of a municipality have the power to arrest and provide lock-ups to hold prisoners for court appearance; county officials prosecute and provide a public defender; the court system is that of the state of Illinois (though judges are elected locally); and the prison system is county and state. Enforcement of federal criminal law is carried out by entirely separate federal law enforcement and prosecuting agencies, the federal courts and the federal prison system.

If you seek information about a governmental body or department, the statement it prepares for budget hearings or its annual report will generally tell you what that particular agency does. Its budgets for its various funds and the relevant appropriation ordinances (if you examine all of them) may tell you what funds it obtains from other levels of government. But one agency will not usually report what services other agencies provide and whether they are in any way coordinated with its own. Chapter 10 attempts to show how the functions of government are divided and what agencies provide the various governmental services.

We hope the book will be useful to concerned citizens. We would welcome suggestions for the next edition.

YOUR RIGHTS TO KNOW

Many people believe it is difficult to obtain information from governmental bodies. In fact, this has not been our experience in gathering information for this book. Most agencies have publications which describe their services and how they function. State statutes setting forth governmental powers are available at libraries, and budget documents and comptrollers' reports are available and informative. The number of individual reports and descriptions of services, ranging from multicolor glossy publications to simple single sheets, can become almost overwhelming.

If you do encounter difficulties in getting information, several Illinois laws protect your right to know what actions have been taken or are being discussed by governmental bodies. Others are designed to disclose any personal financial interest an official might have in a governmental decision. In general, these laws protect the privacy of individuals in personnel decisions; they also protect sensitive negotiations (such as those on purchase of real estate, collective bargaining, law suits, and investments) until decisions are final and formally acted upon.

In the case of inquiries about economic interests of individual officials or candidates, the laws entitle the official or candidate to know that you are making the inquiry.

ILLINOIS OPEN MEETINGS ACT

The Open Meetings Act was passed in 1957. As amended several times since then, it can be found in Chapter 102, 41-46, of the Illinois Revised Statutes. The office of the Illinois attorney general publishes a *Guide to the Illinois Open Meetings Act.*

The act applies to legislative, executive, administrative, and advisory bodies of state and local governments, except for the General Assembly and its committees. A further exception is made in the case of municipalities organized under the commission form of local government: executive and administrative discussions of a mayor and commissioners under that form of government are exempt. The act, however, applies to committees or other subdivisions of any other public body. It requires the bodies to which it applies to hold open meetings, with the public given notice of the times and places of the meetings. A meeting is defined as "any gathering of a majority of a quorum of the members of a public body held for the purpose of discussing public business." A quorum is the number of members of a body required by law or the rules of the body to be present for official action to be taken. (Thus, if a ten-member board has a quorum requirement of five, a meeting of three members of that board to discuss public business would fall under the requirement to give public notice of the meeting.)

The governmental body is required to give public notice of its regularly scheduled meetings at the beginning of each calendar or fiscal year. Ten days notice must be given of a change in the regular meeting date. If a special meeting or a reconvened meeting is to be held, public notice including the meetings's agenda must be given at least 24 hours before the meeting. For emergency meetings notice must be given as soon as practical before the meeting to any news medium which has filed a request for notice, and notice of the emergency meeting must be posted at the governmental body's office.

Meetings or parts of meetings to discuss certain topics may be closed to the public, but notice of closed meetings must still be given and minutes must be kept. Meetings may be closed to discuss certain sensitive issues, such as personnel matters, salaries, collective bargaining, law suits, law enforcement activities, acquisition of real estate, or certain investment decisions. No final action may be taken at a closed meeting.

Minutes of meetings open to the public must be available for public inspection within seven days of the approval of the minutes. Minutes of closed meetings are to be made available when the public body decides there is no need to keep them confidential.

Anyone who believes that a public body is not in compliance with the act may bring suit in the circuit court within 45 days of the meeting in question. The court may declare that any action taken at a closed session in violation of the act is null and void. Violation of the act is punishable by a fine up to $500 and imprisonment for up to 30 days.

ILLINOIS FREEDOM OF INFORMATION ACT

This act took effect July 1, 1984 and applies only to records prepared or received after that date. The act can be found in Chapter 116, 201-11, of the Illinois Revised Statutes. The Illinois Attorney General's Office publishes *A Guide to the Illinois Freedom of Information Act*.

The act applies to the legislative, executive, administrative, and advisory bodies of state and local governments and requires that they must make their records available to be read or copied. The body may charge for the actual cost of reproduction of such records. There are 28 exemptions listed in the law, including records which would represent an invasion of personal privacy, criminal history records, negotiations on contracts or collective bargaining or purchase of real estate, test questions and scoring keys.

If you make a written request for a public document, the governmental body must respond in writing within seven working days after it receives your request. If your request is denied, you must be notified of the reasons for the denial and who made the decision. You may appeal to the head of the public body. If that appeal is denied, you may bring suit. If the court decides the act was violated, it may order disclosure of the records. The court may award you attorney fees if it finds that the records were of significant public interest and the governmental body had no legal basis for withholding the record.

LOBBYIST REGISTRATION ACT

Illinois law (Chapter 63, 171-82) requires the registration of persons who (for pay or on behalf of others) promote or oppose passage of legislation by the Illinois General Assembly or approval or veto by the governor. Lobbyists are required to report lobbying expenditures, and these reports are open to public inspection.

ILLINOIS LOCAL RECORDS ACT

The Freedom of Information Act described above applies to records prepared after July 1, 1984. The Local Records Act, as amended in 1986, applies to records prepared before July 1984 of the obligation, receipt, and use of public funds. It requires local governments and school districts to make their records available for public inspection, provided that the person asking to see the records gives advance notice. Copies may be made, and a fee may be charged for the copies. The act specifically protects against the invasion of any person's right to privacy. This act is in Chapter 116, 43.101 of the Illinois Revised Statutes.

DISCLOSURE OF INTEREST

Municipal office-holders are not by law permitted to have a direct or indirect interest in any contract on which they may be expected to vote. This act, however, permits a governing body to make contracts worth up to $25,000 a year with a firm in which a member of that governing body has an interest, under certain conditions: the member must have less than a 7.5% share in the ownership of the firm (local banks and savings and loan institutions are excepted); the member must disclose that interest before the vote and must abstain from voting. Violation of this act is a felony, and the office becomes vacant on conviction of a violation. This act is in Chapter 24, 3-14-4, and Chapter 102, 3, of the Illinois Revised Statutes. The act as amended became effective October 4, 1981.

DISCLOSURE OF ECONOMIC INTEREST

Certain officials and candidates for office must file statements of their economic interests and those of their spouses. Included are all elected officials and candidates for office, appointed members of Zoning Boards of Appeals and Plan Commissions, and all employees earning $35,000 or more a year in government pay. An exception is made for teachers employed by the state but not for teachers employed by a local school or community college district. The statements must be filed with the county clerk by May 1 of each year. Candidates must file such a statement at the time they file for election.

The statements must be available for reading and copying. To examine a statement, you must fill out a form giving your name, occupation, address, telephone number, and the reason for the examination. A copy of the form you fill out is sent to the person whose statement you have examined.

Under the Illinois Constitution, a candidate who fails to fill out the form is ineligible to run for the office, and an officeholder who fails to do so must forfeit the office. Conviction of willfully filing a false statement is subject to a $1,000 fine or a maximum of a year in jail. The law is in Chapter 127, 604A of the Illinois Revised Statutes. It became effective January 24, 1972.

CAMPAIGN FINANCING DISCLOSURE

The Campaign Financing Disclosure Act, passed in 1974, sets reporting requirements for candidates for public office and political committees who receive more than $1,000 in loans or contributions (including in-kind contributions such as free rent or free printing).

A candidate or a political committee must disclose the names and addresses of all those who contribute $150 or more. Anonymous contributions may not be accepted; if received, they must be turned over to the state. Records must also be kept of all expenditures of $20 or more. A state political committee files with the state Board of Elections, a local committee with the county clerk.

Under the law, the public may view all records required to be filed. To examine a statement, you must fill out a form giving your name, occupation, address, telephone number, and the reason for the examination. A copy of the form is sent to the candidate or political committee whose records you have examined. Complaints may be filed with the general counsel of the state Board of Elections. The penalty for willfully filing a false complaint is a fine of up to $500 and/or imprisonment of up to six months.

If the state Board of Elections decides that a complaint appears to be justified, a public hearing is held. If the board decides after the hearing that a violation has occurred, the general counsel of the board notifies the state attorney general and the state's attorney of the county. Either one may prosecute. The penalty for violation is the same as that for filing a false complaint. This law is in Chapter 46, 9-11, of the Illinois Revised Statutes.

CHICAGO GOVERNMENTAL ETHICS ORDINANCE

The Chicago Governmental Ethics Ordinance (Chapter 26.2 of the Chicago Municipal Code) which became effective on August 1, 1987 requires financial interest reports from elected and appointed officials of the city and employees earning $40,000 or more a year. Exceptions are appointed officials of advisory agencies which have no authority to make binding decisions or to make expenditures other than those incurred for research. Reports must be filed with the Board of Ethics by May 1 of each year.

The statements must be available for reading and copying at the office of the Board of Ethics (see chapter 5). To examine a statement, you must fill out a form giving your name, occupation, employer, address, telephone number, and the reason for the examination. A copy of the form you fill out is sent to the person whose statement you have examined.

The ordinance forbids city officials and employees to participate in governmental decisions in which they have economic interests. Officials or employees (except aldermen) who have a financial interest in matters pending before a city agency must disclose the nature of any conflicts of interest to the Board of Ethics. Members of the city council must disclose the nature of any conflicts of interest and abstain from voting in such a case. The ordinance restricts officials and employees with respect to the employment or award of contracts to their relatives. It forbids officials and employees to coerce other officials and employees to make (or not make) political contributions.

The ordinance also sets limits on the activities of former city officials and employees in representing others before city agencies.

Lobbyists whose pay or expenditures total $5,000 a year or more must register. They must report their city agency lobbying activities and expenditures by January 20 and July 20 each year. These reports must be made available to the public by the Board of Ethics.

The Board of Ethics has the power to receive and to initiate complaints. Such complaints are confidential. The board may investigate complaints (except those against aldermen, which must be referred to a city council committee). The board reports to the corporation counsel and to department and agency heads, the mayor, or the council, as appropriate.

Penalties for violation of the ordinance include discharge and fines of up to $500.

CHICAGO BOARD OF EDUCATION BUSINESS AND FINANCIAL INTEREST STATEMENT

In addition to the form required by the state Disclosure of Economic Interest Act, an additional form must be filled out by members of the Chicago Board of Education and certain employees of the Chicago public school system. Employees included are those in the Bureau of Purchases, those otherwise involved in purchases and contracts, and all employees earning $35,000 or more a year without overtime.

A conflict-of-interest policy, forbidding members, officers, and employees of the board to have a financial interest in any board purchase, was passed in 1980 (Board Report 80-256-6A). The Business and Financial Interest Statement requirement was established in 1987 for the 1986 year (Board Report 87-0225-FN2).

The form asks for information about board members' or employees' own interests and those of their family members. It covers real estate and business interests, fees, honoraria, gifts, loans, and possible interest in contracts or purchases made by the school system.

Forms are to be filed by April 30 with the Department of Internal Audit of the school system. Statements are available for reading and copying. To examine a statement, you must fill out a form giving your name, address, telephone number, employer, and reason for examining the form. A copy of the form you fill out is sent to the person whose statement you have examined.

LEGAL NOTICE
NOTICE OF A PUBLIC HEARING
ON AN APPLICATION TO UNDER-
TAKE ACTIVITIES REGULATED BY
THE LAKE MICHIGAN AND CHI-
CAGO LAKEFRONT PROTECTION
ORDINANCE.
PUBLIC NOTICE IS HEREBY GIVEN
THAT A PUBLIC HEARING WILL
BE HELD BEFORE THE CHICAGO
PLAN COMMISSION ON THURS-
DAY, THE FOURTEENTH (14TH)
DAY OF APRIL, 1988, AT 1:00
P.M., IN THE CITY COUNCIL
CHAMBER, SECOND FLOOR, 121
NORTH LASALLE STREET, CHI-
CAGO, ILLINOIS ON THE FOL-
LOWING:
The application submitted by
Daniel N. Epstein, 35 East
Wacker Drive, Chicago, Illinois for
the construction of 14 two-story
townhouses and 14 attached
garages for the property located
at 5224-36 South Cornell, Chi-
cago, Illinois.
Dated at Chicago, Illinois, this
twenty-eighth (28th) day of
March, A.D. 1988.
Elizabeth L. Hollander
Secretary
Chicago Plan Commission
E. Wayne Robinson
Chairman
Chicago Plan Commission

LEGAL NOTICE
Sealed Proposals will be accepted
by the Secretary of The City
Colleges of Chicago until 10:00
A.M., THURSDAY JUNE 16, 1988
for the following:

BROADCASTING EQUIPMENT
FOR
WYCC-TV/CHANNEL 20
CHICAGO CITY-WIDE
COLLEGE

Bid specifications may be obtained at the office of The
Director of Purchasing, 12th
Floor, 226 West Jackson Blvd.,
Chicago, Illinois (312-855-3080)
prior to MONDAY JUNE 13,
1988

Laurence B. Stanton
Associate Vice Chancellor
City Colleges of Chicago
Board of Trustees of
Community College
District No. #508

NOTICE OF PUBLIC HEARING
CITY OF CHICAGO
PROPOSED HIGHWAY PROJECT
BRYN MAWR AVENUE
EAST RIVER ROAD TO
CUMBERLAND AVENUE
Notice is hereby given to all
interested parties that a Public
Hearing will be held regarding
the improvement of Bryn Mawr
Avenue from East River Road to
Cumberland Avenue.
The subject Public Hearing will be
held Thursday evening, April 21,
1988, 7:00 to 9:00 p.m. at the
Salvation Army Church 8354 W.
Foster Avenue. The meeting will
be fully accessible to the handicapped.
The purpose of the Public Hearing is to receive comments from
any individual or organization
interested in the proposed
improvement. After the City's
presentation, residents and other
interested persons may make
oral statements as well as submit
written statements regarding
the improvement. Personnel
from the Illinois Department of
Transportation and the City of
Chicago Department of Public
Works will be present. Written
statements and/or exhibits will
be accepted at the Department
of Public Works until May 31,
1988.
The purpose of the proposed
improvement is to provide additional capacity and traffic safety
to the section of Bryn Mawr
Avenue between East River Road
and Cumberland Avenue. The
proposed improvement will
involve widening Bryn Mawr
Avenue from two to five lanes to
accommodate the existing and
anticipated traffic volumes due
to development in this area. The
alignment of the improvement
will generally remain as it is. The
center lane of the improvement
will be a dual left turn lane. An
exclusive right turn lane will be
added to southbound Cumberland Avenue to the north of
Bryn Mawr Avenue. No additional right-of-way acquisition
will be required for this project.
The Project Development Report,
as well as maps, drawings, written correspondence resulting
from coordination with other
agencies, organizations, and individuals, and other pertinent
information, will be available for
public inspection and copying
upon publication of this notice at
the Department of Works,
Bureau of Transportation Planning and Programming, 320
North Clark Street, Room 411,
Chicago, Illinois 60610. These
materials will be available for
inspection at the Hearing as well.
Information is also available by
contacting Ms. Candace Tesler at
744-7843.
By order of David Williams, Jr.
Acting Commissioner of Public
Works

LEGAL NOTICE

NOTICE OF THE BOARD OF
APPEALS OF COOK
COUNTY OF THE TIME
AND PLACE FOR FILING
COMPLAINTS RELATING TO
THE REAL ESTATE AS-
SESSMENT FOR THE YEAR
A.D. 1987, FOR ALL NON-
CARRIER RAILROAD PAR-
CELS IN ALL TOWNS AND
TOWNSHIPS OF COOK
COUNTY.

NOTICE IS HEREBY GIVEN THAT
DURING THE PERIOD OF May 27,
1988 thru June 16, 1988, the Board of
Appeals of Cook County will accept
the filing of Valuation Complaints for
the revisions and corrections of the
1987 Real Estate Assessment for all
Non-Carrier Railroad parcels in all
towns and townships of Cook County

All complaints will be considered by
the Board in Room 601 of the County
Building, 118 North Clark Street,
Chicago, Illinois, in accordance with
the Laws of Illinois, under the
provisions of the Revenue Act of
1939, as amended.

Call 443-5542 for a complaint form
and further information.

This will be the final period for filing
Exemption Complaints in all towns
and townships of Cook County.

Approved by the Board of Appeals,
of Cook County, Illinois in said
County, this 25th day of May, 1988.

Wilson Frost   Thomas A. Jaconetty
Commissioner   Commissioner

PUBLIC NOTICE
Notice is hereby given that the
Department of Urban Renewal
as agent for the City of Chicago
will hold a public meeting at the
Richard J. Daley Center, 2nd floor
Conference Room, 50 West
Washington Street, Chicago, Illinois on Tuesday, May 17, 1988
at 2:00 P.M., for the purpose of
considering proposals submitted
by proposed redevelopers and to
accept such proposals as it deems
to be in the public interest and in
furtherance of the purpose of
the Consolidation Act of 1961
(subject to approval of the City
Council of the City of Chicago).
For information regarding
matters that will appear on the
Meeing's Agenda, please call
922-7922, Extension 707.
Equal Housing Opportunities.
Bess Donaldson, Chairman
Department of Urban Renewal

Fig. P. 3. Public notices required by law often appear in the classified sections of newspapers of general circulation. These are examples.

Introduction

WHERE WE ARE

When Illinois became a state in 1818, the city of Chicago and the county of Cook did not exist. Now sections of the city that were farmlands a century ago are old neighborhoods; villages, towns, and cities have arisen in Cook County on what was farmland at the end of World War II.

Chicago lies on a plain approximately 600 feet above sea level on the western shore of Lake Michigan, at the confluence of the Chicago River, a part of the Mississippi river system. The river runs through the city, dividing it into three "sides," south, north, and west. What would otherwise be the "east side" is generally referred to as the Lakefront. The city resembles a semicircle, stretching about 10 miles north, 15 miles south, and 10 to 15 miles west of the mouth of the river, and has an area of almost 213 square miles. In population (3,009,530, according to 1986 U.S. census estimate), it is the third-largest city in the United States.

Within the city, there are 77 community areas, recognized as such by the U.S. census, sociological studies, some city planning agencies, and some community organizations. These neighborhood names often reflect former townships, now used only as tax assessment districts, or former independent municipalities now part of the city. Many Chicagoans will tell you they live in (for instance) Rogers Park, Uptown, West Garfield, or Hyde Park; they are referring to traditional neighborhoods, not to suburban towns.

Cook County includes Chicago and 129 other towns, cities, and villages. It extends for 34.5 miles along the lakefront and as far as 31 miles west from Lake Michigan, an area of 956 square miles. The 1986 U.S. census estimate of its population was 5,297,900.

The name of the city is thought to have come from the Indian word Checagou, which has been translated both as wild onion and as skunk; its site was originally a marsh. The first Europeans known to have been in the area were the French explorers Joliet and Marquette in 1673. By 1679 there

1

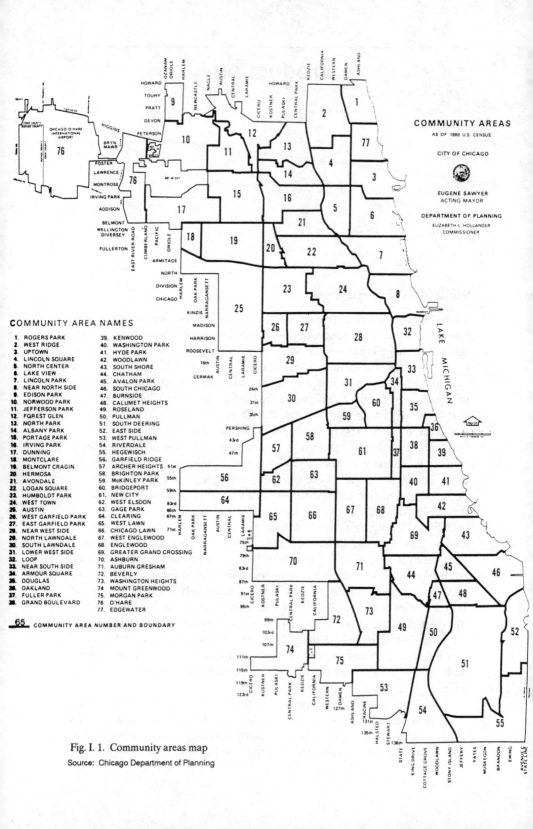

COMMUNITY AREAS
AS OF 1980 U.S. CENSUS

CITY OF CHICAGO

EUGENE SAWYER
ACTING MAYOR

DEPARTMENT OF PLANNING
ELIZABETH L. HOLLANDER
COMMISSIONER

COMMUNITY AREA NAMES

1. ROGERS PARK
2. WEST RIDGE
3. UPTOWN
4. LINCOLN SQUARE
5. NORTH CENTER
6. LAKE VIEW
7. LINCOLN PARK
8. NEAR NORTH SIDE
9. EDISON PARK
10. NORWOOD PARK
11. JEFFERSON PARK
12. FOREST GLEN
13. NORTH PARK
14. ALBANY PARK
15. PORTAGE PARK
16. IRVING PARK
17. DUNNING
18. MONTCLARE
19. BELMONT CRAGIN
20. HERMOSA
21. AVONDALE
22. LOGAN SQUARE
23. HUMBOLDT PARK
24. WEST TOWN
25. AUSTIN
26. WEST GARFIELD PARK
27. EAST GARFIELD PARK
28. NEAR WEST SIDE
29. NORTH LAWNDALE
30. SOUTH LAWNDALE
31. LOWER WEST SIDE
32. LOOP
33. NEAR SOUTH SIDE
34. ARMOUR SQUARE
35. DOUGLAS
36. OAKLAND
37. FULLER PARK
38. GRAND BOULEVARD

39. KENWOOD
40. WASHINGTON PARK
41. HYDE PARK
42. WOODLAWN
43. SOUTH SHORE
44. CHATHAM
45. AVALON PARK
46. SOUTH CHICAGO
47. BURNSIDE
48. CALUMET HEIGHTS
49. ROSELAND
50. PULLMAN
51. SOUTH DEERING
52. EAST SIDE
53. WEST PULLMAN
54. RIVERDALE
55. HEGEWISCH
56. GARFIELD RIDGE
57. ARCHER HEIGHTS
58. BRIGHTON PARK
59. McKINLEY PARK
60. BRIDGEPORT
61. NEW CITY
62. WEST ELSDON
63. GAGE PARK
64. CLEARING
65. WEST LAWN
66. CHICAGO LAWN
67. WEST ENGLEWOOD
68. ENGLEWOOD
69. GREATER GRAND CROSSING
70. ASHBURN
71. AUBURN GRESHAM
72. BEVERLY
73. WASHINGTON HEIGHTS
74. MOUNT GREENWOOD
75. MORGAN PARK
76. O'HARE
77. EDGEWATER

65 COMMUNITY AREA NUMBER AND BOUNDARY

Fig. I. 1. Community areas map

Source: Chicago Department of Planning

was a trading post, abandoned by 1700 because of Indian hostility. In 1795 the western Indian tribes gave the United States six square miles at the mouth of the Chicago River. In 1779 Jean Baptiste Point du Sable had settled on a site near the lake just north of the river, and he has become known as Chicago's first citizen. The trading post he established was sold to John Kinzie in 1804. Fort Dearborn had been built the previous year; during the War of 1812 the fort was attacked by Indians and the settlers were massacred. The fort was rebuilt in 1816.

A county was formed in 1831, which extended from the Wisconsin state line to the Indiana state line. It was named for Daniel P. Cook, a pioneer lawyer and judge and the state's first attorney general, and the small village of Chicago was selected as the seat of the county government. In 1833 the village was incorporated; it covered one square mile. Just four years later Chicago was incorporated as a city. The present boundaries of Cook County were established in 1839.

Because of the opening of the Illinois-Michigan canal and the development of Chicago as a rail center, the city's population grew from 4,417 in 1840 to 29,963 in 1850. By 1871, when the city was leveled by a fire that raged for 27 hours, its population was over 300,000. More than 300 people died in the fire, and 90,000 were left homeless. Rebuilding began almost at once, and the population continued to grow.

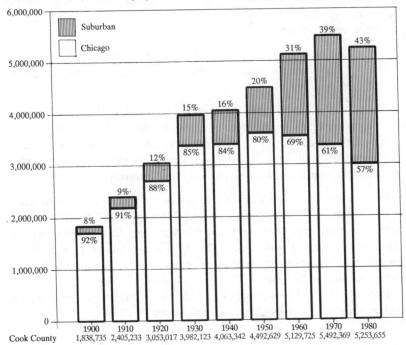

Fig. I . 2. Chicago population as percent of Cook County

Source: U.S. Census

The growth of Cook County followed a pattern typical of that of many areas around large American cities. There were settlements in the county long before the city reached out into it, and many community areas in Chicago which retain their names were villages annexed to the city. The spurts of growth in the county outside of the city were chiefly in residential communities. Population growth and later commercial and industrial development tended to follow the suburban railroads and the building of expressways, in what has been called a "finger" development. Areas between the fingers filled up more slowly.

THE METROPOLITAN AREA

For administrative purposes and for U.S. census data, the Chicago metropolitan area is defined in several different ways. In considering population trends and other statistical data, it is important to know which area is being reported.

The Northeastern Illinois Metropolitan Area was defined in 1957 by the Illinois legislature as including the six counties of northeastern Illinois: Cook, DuPage, Kane, Lake, McHenry, and Will. Within it there are nearly 1,200 local governments. Two units of government, the Northeastern Illinois Planning Commission (NIPC) and the Regional Transportation Authority (RTA) have these six counties as their service area. The U.S. census no longer recognizes the above six counties as a metropolitan area for providing metropolitan statistics.

The Chicago Primary Metropolitan Statistical Area (PMSA) is now defined by the census as including the three Illinois counties of Cook, DuPage, and McHenry.

The Consolidated Metropolitan Statistical Area (CMSA) now combines six PMSAs to make up the larger unit of the Illinois-Indiana-Wisconsin CMSA. This includes eight Illinois counties (Cook, DuPage, Kane, Lake, McHenry, and Will, as well as Grundy and Kendall), Lake and Porter Counties in Indiana, and Kenosha County in Wisconsin.

Both of these census definitions are different from those formerly used by the census: the Chicago Standard Metropolitan Statistical Area (SMSA) was the same six counties as the Northeast Illinois Metropolitan Area described above, and the Chicago-Northwestern Indiana Consolidated Statistical Area consisted of those six counties plus Lake and Porter Counties in Indiana.

The federal definitions apply to a number of federal programs and may be changed at any time by Congressional action.

1   **Levels of Government**

In Cook County, we live under several layers of government, each with a defined geographic area and legal responsibilities. If you are a citizen of the United States and have registered to vote, you are entitled to elect officials of the nation, the state, the county, and (unless you live in an unincorporated area) your municipality. Whether or not you are a citizen, you are subject to the laws of those governments and must pay taxes to them.

But local government in Cook County is more complex than that. For historical and political reasons, a large variety of other local governmental bodies overlap municipalities and sometimes county lines. One reason for the multiplication of local governments is that, before passage of the 1970 Illinois Constitution, local governing bodies could issue bonds only up to the amount of 5% of the assessed valuation of property within their boundaries. But park districts, education districts, or other kinds of special districts could be set up as separate bodies, within the same or an overlapping area, and could issue bonds of their own.

These nonmunicipal governmental entities in both Chicago and suburban Cook County include elementary school, high school, junior college, library, transit, and sewage districts, and other special-purpose authorities. All of these local governmental bodies can exist because of state laws; some also had to be approved by vote of the people in the area they serve, through a referendum. Many, but not all, have the power to levy taxes. Though they are usually governed by elected officials, some are managed by officials appointed by elected officials. This book describes the many local government bodies which provide services to the residents of Cook County and, more briefly, services provided by the federal and state governments.

FEDERAL GOVERNMENT

The federal government touches our lives in many ways; collection of the federal income tax, recruitment for military service, and the postal service are three of the most familiar. Social Security is paid directly to the individual by the federal government. Federal law is enforced through the United States court system, which is separate from the state court system. States and local governments must conform with the U.S. Constitution as interpreted by the U.S. Supreme Court.

Sixty federal departments and agencies have regional, zone, or area offices in Chicago, including the Immigration and Naturalization Service, the Social Security Administration, the Public Health Service, the Veterans Administration, and many others. They are listed in the blue pages in the front of the Chicago telephone directory.

The federal government provides funds for programs administered by local governments in such areas as housing, welfare, transportation, and environmental problems. When it does so, Congress sets requirements for how these funds are to be spent, and the federal agencies which administer the funds set rules which are published in the *Federal Register*. Some federal funds available to local governments go directly to them, while others are distributed by the state.

Federal Court Decisions. Federal courts sometimes restrict the actions of local governments. For instance, use of water from Lake Michigan is limited by a 1967 U.S. Supreme Court decision which permits total diversion to Illinois for all purposes, including water supply and maintenance of navigation levels in the Sanitary and Ship Canal, of no more than 3,200 cubic feet per second. The state legislature has designated the Illinois Department of Transportation to apportion the diversion water.

Shakman Decisions. Two federal court orders (known as the Shakman decisions, for the attorney who initiated the case) affect the powers of specific government bodies in Cook County to hire, assign, promote, and fire employees on the basis of political contributions or political party work. The first, a consent decree in 1972, affects existing employees. It provides that no local or state governmental employee (or contractor or supplier) in the Federal Northern Court District of Illinois can be required to make political contributions and no employee can be required to do political work as a condition of employment.

The second, a court order in 1979, affects hiring, providing that employees may not be hired on political grounds. As of June 1988, local government bodies and offices bound by this court order include the city of Chicago, the Chicago Park District, the Cook County Sheriff, and the Clerk of the Cook County Circuit Court. Other government bodies and offices, along with the Cook County Democratic Central Committee, are not bound by this second order, having successfully appealed it (the U.S. Supreme Court declined to hear a further appeal). In addition to the Democratic party committee, offices not bound by the restrictions on hiring are those of the president of the Board of County Commissioners, the Cook County clerk, the Cook County assessor, and the Forest Preserve District.

STATE GOVERNMENT

All powers not specifically granted to the federal government in the U.S. Constitution remain with the states and the people. At the other end of the scale of size, local governments in Illinois are creatures of the state, governed by the Illinois Constitution and state law.

Like the federal government, the state deals directly with Illinois residents in a number of areas, and branches of many state agencies have been established in Cook County for this purpose. The Illinois Department of Public Aid administers public assistance for Cook County and general assistance for Chicago. The Illinois Department of Children and Family Services provides direct services through its field offices. There are employment service offices in the city and suburbs under the Illinois Department of Labor; automobile license plates can be purchased from a branch of the office of the Illinois Secretary of State; the Illinois Department of Agriculture maintains inspection divisions; and the principal public mental health facilities are state institutions. A complete listing of state agencies with local offices is in the blue pages of the Chicago telephone directory.

LOCAL GOVERNMENT POWERS

Municipalities. Cities, villages, and towns (but not townships) are municipalities. Under the state constitution, those which are not home rule units (see below) have only the powers granted to them by state legislation, with the following additional powers: (1) to make local improvements by special assessment; (2) by referendum, to change their form of government (within the forms provided by state law) and the way their officials are selected and their terms; (3) to incur debt and levy taxes within the provisions of state law.

Home Rule: Cook County and Home Rule Municipalities. Until 1971 all local governmental units had only those powers given to them by the state legislature under the authority of the state constitution. The 1970 state constitution grants home rule to all counties with an elected chief executive officer, such as the president of the Cook County board. Home rule status is granted automatically to any municipality with a population of 25,000 or more. Smaller municipalities may choose by referendum to become home rule units. A municipality may also opt out of home rule status by referendum. Cook County home rule municipalities are listed in chapter 2.

HOW A BILL IS PASSED

A bill may originate in either the House or the Senate, and the procedure is almost identical. If it originates in the House:

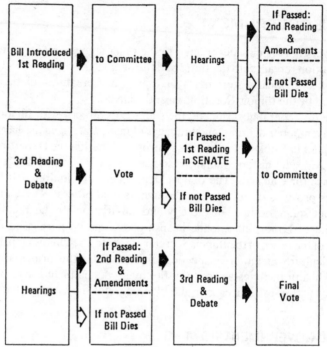

Each bill must be read by title on three different days in each house before it is passed. The first reading introduces the bill to the houses. The second reading allows for amendments of the bill. When a bill is called for its third reading, it is voted on for passage.

When the Senate does not amend an original House bill, the bill goes to the Governor for final action. The Governor may sign the bill, allow the bill to become law without·his signature or veto the bill.

If the Senate amends the bill, it goes back to the House. If the House concurs with the Senate amendments, the bill goes to the Governor. The House may refuse to accept the Senate amendments, however. If the Senate withdraws its amendments, the bill goes to the Governor for his action. If the Senate will not withdraw its amendments, the bill goes to conference committee where differences may be worked out. If agreement is reached by both houses, the bill will go to the Governor for action.

If the amended bill is rejected by the House, and either the House or the Senate fails to approve the first conference committee report, the bill may go to a second conference committee. If either the House or the Senate does not approve the second conference committee report, the bill is dead.

Fig. 1. 1. How a bill is passed

The state legislature (the General Assembly) acts on many matters of concern to local governments, including funding of their operations and restrictions of their powers.

Source: 1987-1988 Handbook of Illinois Government, Jim Edgar, Secretary of State

Home rule is a legal division of power between the state and certain local governments. Article VII, Section 6(a) of the 1970 Illinois Constitution provides that a home rule unit "may exercise any power and perform any function pertaining to its government and affairs, including, but not limited to, power to regulate for the protection of public health, safety, morals, and welfare; to license; to tax; and to incur debt."

A home rule municipality may issue general obligation bonds without referendum in amounts depending on the population of the unit: (1) if its population is 500,000 or more, it may borrow an amount equal to 3% of the assessed value of its taxable property; (2) if its population is more than 25,000 and less than 500,000, an amount equal to 1%; and (3) if its population is 25,000 or less, an amount equal to 0.5%. (Additional general obligation bonds may be issued if approved by referendum.)

Limitations are set, however: a home rule unit may not enact any tax based on income or license for revenue (as opposed to licensing for regulation). It may not issue general obligation bonds maturing more than 40 years from the time of issuance. It may not define and provide for the punishment of a felony. (Violation of a municipal ordinance is a misdemeanor.) The state may limit or remove home rule powers by a three-fifths vote of each house of the legislature. By majority vote of each house, the state may pre-empt a home rule power and has done so, notably in licensing: if the state and local government both exercise a power, such as licensing, the legislature can limit the local government's power or declare the state's exercise of it to be exclusive.

Townships, School Districts, Special Purpose Districts. Under the state constitution, townships, school districts, and special purpose districts have only the powers granted by state law. The constitution sets further limitations on what laws may be passed governing them: the legislature is to provide by law for the selection of their officers, but their officers may not be appointed by anyone in the judicial branch of government; they may incur debt to be paid by property taxes only when the bonds mature within 40 years from the time the debt is incurred; they do not have the power to make special assessments unless they had that power before July 1, 1971.

REGIONAL AGENCIES

NORTHEASTERN ILLINOIS PLANNING COMMISSION (NIPC)
400 W. Madison St., Chicago 60606; *phone 454 0400*

In many situations, the decisions of one municipality or special purpose district will affect others, for example in flood control, sewer extensions, major zoning changes, and transportation extensions. The Northeastern

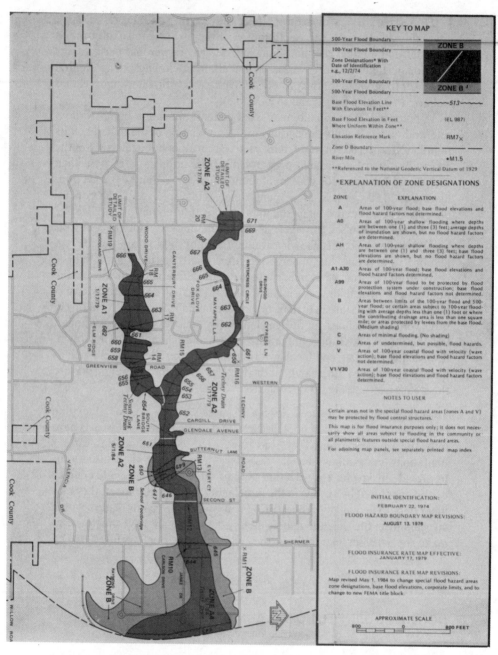

Fig. 1. 2. Portion of flood plain map, used for planning and for flood insurance. Maps are available from the Northeastern Illinois Planning Commission.

Source: Northeastern Illinois Planning Commission.

Illinois Planning Commission (NIPC) was created by state legislation in 1957 to devise a comprehensive general plan that would guide and coordinate development in the counties of Cook, DuPage, Kane, Lake, McHenry, and Will. By law its powers are advisory only and are not binding upon units of local government or state and federal agencies.

The legislature gave NIPC three statutory charges: to conduct research and collect data for planning; to prepare and recommend plans and policies to local governments and prepare zoning and building ordinances for them; and to prepare comprehensive plans and policies to guide the development of the six counties. It is also designated by the governor of Illinois as the area-wide planning and development clearinghouse for federally-financed projects, to be sure they conform to plans for the area. (This is still often called A-95 review; A-95 is the federal Office of Management and Budget circular describing these duties, although the federal government has not required such review since 1983.)

Publications. NIPC has an extensive publications department, a publications list, a newsletter mailed upon request, and a variety of reports and plans available to the public. Its major efforts for 1987-88 included implementation of its recently adopted Waste Management Policy Plan. It also published "Comparative Guide to Northeastern Illinois and 25 Other Metropolitan Areas," revised population and household forecasts to the year 2005, and preliminary population and household forecasts to 2010.

Commissioners. A 1983 amendment to the original NIPC act provides for 30 commissioners. The governor appoints 5, who must reside in the six-county area. The mayor appoints 5 commissioners, 3 of whom must be members of the city council. Cook County has 3 representatives on the commission, appointed by the president of the county board with the concurrence of the board. Each of the other five counties is represented by a county board member, appointed by the respective county board chair. The Chicago Transit Authority (CTA), the Regional Transportation Authority (RTA), the Metropolitan Sanitary District (MSD), the Illinois Association of Park Districts, and the Chicago Park District each appoint 1 commissioner. The other 7 commissioners are elected by an assembly of suburban mayors and village presidents; these commissioners must be elected municipal officials, 2 from Cook county (1 from north and 1 from south of Roosevelt Road), and 1 from each of the other five counties.

The term of office of a commissioner is four years. Chicago's appointments are staggered, but all others are concurrent. The assembly of suburban mayors and village presidents which elects 7 commissioners was first convened in 1973 and by law is convened every four years. Voting in the assembly is weighted in proportion to the population of the respective municipalities. In case of a vacancy among the 7 elected commissioners, the assembly is reconvened to fill the unexpired term. Appointing authorities may make replacements.

NIPC has neither taxing authority nor any other assured sources of revenues; its funding comes from voluntary contributions or contracts for services. For fiscal 1987, its budget was $2,200,000, approximately 13% from federal funds, 44% from state funds, and 43% from local funds and contributions.

NIPC sets its regular meeting dates at its December meeting. The full board meets four times a year, at noon on the third Thursday of March, June, September, and December. The Executive Committee meets as necessary. The Governmental Services Committee, which reviews requests

Fig. 1. 3. Railroad Lines in Cook County.
Source: Northeastern Illinois Planning Commission.

for federal funding, meets at noon on the fourth Thursday of every month. The Planning and Policy Development Committee meets at 9:30 A.M. on the first Wednesday of every month. The Areawide Water Quality Steering Committee meets at 11:30 A.M. on the first Wednesday of every month.

CHICAGO AREA TRANSPORTATION STUDY (CATS)
300 W. Adams St., Chicago 60606;   *phone 793 3456*

The Chicago Area Transportation Study was created in 1955 by agreement among federal, state, county, and Chicago governments to coordinate transportation planning and programming. Its area has since been expanded to include the six-county area of northeastern Illinois. It collects data on transportation needs and is responsible for determining whether transportation planning is consistent with air quality control planning.

CATS is responsible for allocating federal and state highway and mass transportation funds within its area. In its fiscal year 1988 it allocated $958,538,000 to local government agencies.

Policy Committee. The CATS 20-member Policy Committee is chaired by the state secretary of transportation and is composed of the chair of the Council of Mayors, the executive director of the state Toll Highway Authority, the commissioner of the Chicago Department of Public Works, and representatives of the six county governments, the Regional Transportation Authority, the Chicago Transit Authority, Metra, railroad companies, mass transit districts, providers of private transportation, the Northeastern Illinois Planning Commission, the Federal Highway Administration, and the Urban Mass Transportation Administration.

Funding. The Policy Committee appoints the executive director at an annual salary in 1988 of $58,740. In 1988 CATS had 54 employees and a budget of $2,815,000. Its budget is funded by federal, state, and local governmental agencies; for federal highway planning, 85% comes from the federal government and 15% from state and local governments; the proportions for mass transportation planning are 80% and 20%. The portions paid by the state and local governments are allocated by agreement. A part of CATS income derives from work on contract for local agencies and private concerns.

Council of Mayors. In 1965 CATS organized a Council of Mayors to provide local input for transportation planning. The council is made up of 11 subregional councils, plus the city of Chicago. It establishes priorities among locally initiated projects which use federal aid funds for urban systems. These funds, for roadway projects, are allocated by population. The individual programs of the Council of Mayors are incorporated into a regional transportation program and approved by the CATS Policy Committee. There are 6 subregional councils in Cook County, based on geography, and each of the other five counties constitutes a council. In fiscal year 1988, a total of $1,029,000 was allocated to Chicago and the 11 councils for planning under the Unified Work Program.

SUBREGIONAL ASSOCIATIONS

In northeastern Illinois there are hundreds of intergovernmental agree-ments; some are for establishing boundary agreements, but most are for sharing or transferring functions or services. In addition there are a number of interlocal associations by which local governments contract for planning, jointly perform a function, or share common concerns and interests. These kinds of intergovernmental cooperation have been encouraged by the 1970 Illinois constitution and the Intergovernmental Act of 1973. Federal funding of certain programs, such as CETA and the Housing Act of 1954, encouraged local governments to work together on specific projects and plans. Many of these associations of governments lie wholly or partly within Cook County.

The Barrington Area Council of Governments (BACOG) (132 W. Station St., Barrington 60010, *phone 381 7871*) serves eight municipalities with planning and growth management, joint services, and citizen education

The Northwest Municipal Conference (Mount Prospect Library, 10 S. Emerson St., Mount Prospect 60056, *phone 253 6323*) is the oldest intergovernmental organization in the state. Organized in 1958 to discuss the future of commuter rail stations along the Chicago and Northwestern lines, the conference has 32 municipalities and 7 townships as members, re-presenting a population of over 950,000 Cook, DuPage, and Lake County residents.

The South Suburban Mayors and Managers Association (1154 Ridge Road, Homewood 60430, *phone 957 6970*) provides technical and joint services to municipalities in the southern suburbs in Cook County (and a few in Will County). It covers a geographic area with more than 550,000 residents.

The West Central Municipal Conference (740 Hillgrove, Western Springs 60558, *phone 246 4614*) provides a medium for joint study and solution of problems of municipal governments. It has 22 member municipalities in west suburban Cook County and 1 associate member, the Brookfield Zoo. The population served is more than 311,000.

2   Forms of Local Governments

Chapter 1 gave an overview of the responsibilities and the limitations of powers of local governments. This chapter describes the varieties of local governmental bodies, which are generally dependent on property taxes for support. These include municipalities, suburban townships and road districts, community college and school districts, library districts, mosquito abatement districts, and other smaller special purpose districts. The voters elect the officials of all but a few of these governmental bodies.

MUNICIPALITIES

The Illinois Constitution defines municipalities as cities, villages, and incorporated towns; there are 129 in Cook County. Before the 1870 constitution, municipalities had to be chartered by the state legislature, but that constitution prohibited any further charter municipalities. The 1970 constitution provides that incorporated towns have the powers granted to cities and villages. All other municipalities in the county are cities or villages. The Illinois Municipal Code (Chapter 24 of the Illinois Revised Statutes), formerly known as the Cities and Villages Act, is the state law that provides for the forms and powers of municipalities, within the special grants of power given by the constitution to home rule municipalities. In the following lists the 50 home rule municipalities in Cook County are indicated by (H).

Manager Form. Any city, village, or town (except Chicago) may, by referendum, adopt the manager form of government, with or without changing its structure otherwise; 47 Cook County municipalities have managers. A municipality with a population of over 500,000 (Chicago) may not adopt the manager form. The council or board adopts ordinances specifying the manager's duties and appointing the manager, who becomes administrative head of all departments and appoints their heads. The manager may be removed by a majority vote of the council. Municipalities

15

with the manager form of government are indicated in the following lists by (M).

Administrator Form. The administrator form is not a form described in state law but is a method of centralizing administration without passing a referendum to hire a manager. An ordinance is passed to create the office of administrator, to be responsible for day-to-day operations. An administrator does not have the power a manager does to appoint department heads. The 19 Cook County municipalities with the administrator form of government are indicated in the following lists by (A). Two villages have administrative assistants; they are indicated by (AA).

Aldermanic Cities. The governing body of an aldermanic city is the city council; there may be one, two, or three aldermen elected from each ward. The number of wards depends on the population of the city. The chief executive is the mayor. The mayor presides over the council and is responsible for enforcing the ordinances enacted by the council. The council passes on most appointments made by the mayor. The following 18 Cook County municipalities are aldermanic cities:

Berwyn (H)	Hickory Hills
Blue Island	Hometown
Burbank (H A)	Northlake (M)
Calumet City (H)	Oak Forest (H A)
Chicago (H)	Palos Heights
Countryside (H A)	Palos Hills
Des Plaines (H A)	Park Ridge (H M)
Elgin (H M)	Prospect Heights (A)
Evanston (H M)	Rolling Meadows (H M)

Strong Mayor Cities. The strong mayor form of government was added to the Illinois statutes in 1969. The mayor and from 8 to 20 aldermen are elected from wards. The mayor has broad powers, including those of a municipal manager. The mayor appoints department heads and board and commission members, except those covered by civil service, without needing council approval. Two Cook County municipalities are strong mayor cities:

Country Club Hills (A)	Markham

Trustee Villages. The legislative body of a trustee village is a board of six trustees elected at large and presided over by a president. The board performs the same functions as a city council and mayor. Villages with populations over 25,000 may choose by referendum to elect trustees from districts. The following 104 Cook County municipalities are trustee villages:

TRUSTEE VILLAGES

Alsip (AA)
Arlington Heights (H M)
Barrington (M)
Barrington Hills
Bedford Park (H)
Bellwood
Bensenville (M)
Berkeley
Bridgeview
Broadview
Brookfield
Buffalo Grove (H M)
Burnham (H)
Burr Ridge (A)
Calumet Park (H)
Chicago Ridge
Crestwood
Dixmoor
Dolton (H)
East Hazel Crest
Elk Grove Village (H M)
Elmwood Park (H M)
Evergreen Park (H A)
Flossmoor (M)
Ford Heights
Forest Park
Forest View (A)
Franklin Park
Glencoe (M)
Glenview (H M)
Glenwood
Golf (H)
Hanover Park (H M)
Harwood Heights
Hazel Crest (M)
Hillside
Hinsdale (M)
Hodgkins
Hoffman Estates (H M)
Homewood (M)
Indian Head Park
Inverness
Justice
Kenilworth (M)
LaGrange (M)
LaGrange Park (M)
Lansing (H)
Lemont (A)
Lincolnwood (A)
Lynwood (AA)
Lyons (A)
Matteson (A)

Maywood (H M)
McCook (H)
Melrose Park
Merrionette Park
Midlothian
Morton Grove (H A)
Mount Prospect (H M)
Niles (H M)
Norridge (H)
Northbrook (H M)
Northfield (M)
North Riverside (M)
Oak Lawn (H M)
Oak Park (H M)
Olympia Fields
Orland Hills (A)
Orland Park (H M)
Palatine (H M)
Park Forest (H M)
Phoenix
Posen
Richton Park (M)
Riverdale
River Forest (A)
River Grove
Riverside (M)
Robbins
Roselle (M)
Rosemont (H)
Sauk Village (M A)
Schaumburg (H M)
Schiller Park
Skokie (H M)
South Barrington (H)
South Chicago Heights (A)
South Holland (H)
Steger
Stickney (H)
Stone Park (H)
Streamwood (M)
Summit
Thornton (H)
Tinley Park (H M)
University Park (H M)
Westchester (M)
Western Springs (M)
Wheeling (H M)
Willowbrook (A)
Willow Springs
Wilmette (H M)
Winnetka (M)
Worth

Commission Cities or Villages. The form of commission city or village is permitted only for a municipality with a population under 200,000. The council consists of a mayor and four other commissioners elected at large. There are five departments to conduct municipal business: public affairs, finance, health and safety, streets and improvements, and public property. The mayor is commissioner of public affairs, and the other commissioners by majority vote of the council are assigned executive control over individual departments. The following are commission cities:

Chicago Heights (H)   Harvey (H)

The following are commission villages:

Forest Park   Palos Park

Special Charter Municipalities. Incorporated towns and villages that retain the structure established by charters issued before 1870 are special charter municipalities. Each special charter village elects its president and clerk. The following are special charter municipalities:

Village of Barrington (Trustee village)
City of Chicago (Aldermanic city) (H)
Town of Cicero (Incorporated town) (H)
City of Des Plaines (Aldermanic city) (H)
Village of Glencoe (Trustee village)
Village of Winnetka (Trustee village)

TOWNSHIPS AND ROAD DISTRICTS

Townships were originally subdivisions of the county but are now units of government within the county which have powers and responsibilities defined by state law. In Chicago, the only vestige of townships is the definition of property tax areas. Outside of Chicago, except for Evanston and Oak Park, municipal boundaries do not often coincide with township boundaries. Several municipalities and unincorporated areas may lie within a township, and a municipality may be in as many as four townships. There are three kinds of townships: congressional, school, and civil. Their boundaries do not necessarily coincide.

Congressional Townships. A congressional township is simply a geographic area established by Congress in 1795 to identify public lands in the North- west Territory. Congressional townships were six-mile-square sections, and such survey townships are still sometimes used to demarcate school districts, road districts, and election districts.

School Townships. School townships, which have responsibilities for suburban school systems, are described below in the section, Suburban Public Schools.

Civil Townships. The organization of civil townships in Illinois reflects the New England background of many early settlers who brought with them ideas of local government based on citizen participation in town meetings. Towns or townships were a traditional form of local government in which the citizens, or "electors," rather than their representatives, acted as the governing body. Laws still on the books reflect the rural background of this form of government, in which citizens themselves have the power to regulate peddlers, provide for public wells, and prohibit cattle from running at large.

There are 17 commission-form counties in Illinois. These reflect another tradition which spread from the South, where counties were a form of regional government, and municipalities were the units that performed strictly local services.

Cook County combines these two forms of local government: 8 townships within the city of Chicago became inactive after 1870 (except as property tax assessment areas), but 30 civil townships remain units of local government in suburban Cook County. The Illinois legislature under the 1970 constitution provides for the structure, officers, functions, and powers of townships; the citizens have the power to create or abolish townships through referendum.

Township responsibilities. In suburban Cook County, townships have three responsibilities: general assistance to the needy who do not qualify for programs funded by state and federal governments; maintenance of roads and bridges where there are four or more miles of roads in unincorporated areas; and limited responsibilities, under the direction of the county assessor, for property assessment. Townships may provide additional services in addition to carrying out these reponsibilities.

Powers of electors: As defined in the statutes, electors means "legal voters." At most township meetings, however, no check is made as to whether those present and voting are registered voters of the township. Powers of the electors present at a town meeting include the following:

* Purchase, sale, or lease of corporate property (a referendum is required if the purchase entails a new tax or a tax rate above limits set by the legislature)
* Transfer of funds for roads and bridges to a city or village that entirely incorporates the area of the township
* Provision of liability insurance for officers and employees
* Order of an audit of accounts
* Authorization for participation in a municipal retirement fund
* Contracts with municipalities for fire protection or with the county for additional police protection in unincorporated areas

* Provision of mental health services
* Authorization of tax levies for senior citizen services or housing, for libraries, or for cemeteries
* Authorization of tax levies for public assistance, not to exceed tax rates set by the legislature

Town meeting. The powers of the electors are exercised at the annual town meeting, held on the second Tuesday of April. (If this conflicts with the celebration of Passover, the meeting is held on the first Tuesday following the last day of Passover.) The meeting place is fixed by the board of trustees of the township, and 10 days notice must be given. Special town meetings are held if the board calls one or if at least 15 voters file a statement with the town clerk that a special meeting is necessary; the objects of the meeting must be set forth, and the meeting's business is limited to those objects.

ELECTED TOWNSHIP OFFICIALS. The elected officials of a township are the board of trustees, which is made up of the supervisor, four trustees, and the town clerk (who has no vote); an assessor; a collector; and, in townships with road districts, a highway commissioner. All are elected in the consolidated municipal elections the first Tuesday in April, every four years (1989, 1993, etc.).

The Board of Trustees, formerly the Board of Auditors, has the responsibility for auditing all town funds. It prepares the town budget and appropriation ordinance and designates the depository for town funds. It sets the pay for township officials and must do so in election years before the last Tuesday in March. The board may contract for mental health services, for nursing home care, or for services to youth. It may appoint committees on services for youth or for senior citizens, and it may appoint three-member boards to contract for police or fire-protection services for unincorporated areas. It also may transfer non-tax funds to museums and historical societies.

The Township Supervisor is the chief executive officer, chair of the board of trustees, supervisor of general assistance, and treasurer of town funds and of Road and Bridge funds. The supervisor may not transfer general assistance funds to any other fund and must obtain approval of the board of trustees or the electors at the annual town meeting to transfer other monies from one fund to another.

A major responsibility of the supervisor is for general assistance, which is aid, often temporary, for people who do not qualify for federal or state categorical assistance. (See chapter 10 for a description of general assistance.) The supervisor is responsible for establishing policies and written standards, determining eligibility, keeping records, and informing applicants of their rights. The supervisor may provide social services, education and training, child care, housekeeping services, home and financial management, housing improvements, essential medical care (not including preventive care or psychiatric services), and a drug abuse program. An applicant for township general assistance must be a resident of the township; or if not, the township of origin can be billed for reimbursement. If a township receives state public aid funds, it must follow rules set by the Illinois Department of Public Aid (IDPA); as of 1987, no Cook County township used state funds to administer its general assistance program. All townships are required to institute a workfare program or a Job Search, Training, and Work Program, or both.

The Town Clerk keeps records for the Board of Trustees. If there is a township road district, the clerk serves also as district clerk for the highway commissioner. The clerk gives notices of meetings, keeps minutes, and (under supervision of the county clerk) registers voters and administers absentee voting procedures for township residents.

The Township Collector is a position with no responsibilities in Cook County. State law requires the election of a collector in each township, but under a 1970 Illinois Supreme Court decision the duties of the office now are carried out by the county collector.

The Township Assessor in Cook County acts as a deputy for the county assessor, keeping property assessment cards for real property in the township and recording changes and exemptions.

The Highway Commissioner is elected only in the 21 townships in Cook County that have at least four miles of roads in unincorporated areas. The road district is the unincorporated area, and the highway commissioner has responsibility for construction, maintenance, and equipment for roads in that area. An annual report to the township board is required on the Wednesday immediately preceding the annual town meeting.

FUNDING. The local property tax is the main source of funds for townships and road districts, with tax rate limitations set by the state legislature. In 1972 townships as well as counties and municipalities became recipients of federal revenue sharing funds, and many townships used those funds for additional projects. (As of 1988, revenue sharing no longer existed.)

Tax Rate Limits: Townships. The tax rate limit for townships is 0.25% of the equalized assessed valuation (EAV) of property in the township, where the EAV is $36,000,000 or more. Since the EAV in Cook County ranges from $94,000,000 in Calumet Township to over $1,000,000,000 in Elk

Grove, Niles, and Schaumburg Townships, this limitation is the only one that applies. In addition, the board may levy a tax of up to 0.1% of EAV for general assistance; it may not exceed this amount, and it must levy this amount to qualify for state public aid funds (note, above, that no Cook County township as of 1987 received such state funds). Other small rates are allowed for particular activities, such as 0.1% for a senior citizens' service committee.

Tax Rate Limits: Road Districts. The tax rate limit for township road districts is 0.125% of EAV of the township, or 0.165% with approval of the township board. In addition, a levy may be extended up to 0.033% for damages and 0.05% for projects undertaken jointly with the county. Regardless of how many miles of unincorporated roads there are, collected road district taxes are divided equally between the township and the municipalities within the township.

COMMUNITY COLLEGES IN SUBURBAN COOK COUNTY

Chicago is a community college district, and there are seven community colleges in suburban Cook County. Each was established by the Illinois Public Community College Act and is governed in accordance with that act and with policies adopted by the Illinois Community College Board. The Chicago City Colleges are described in chapter 7; the following describes the suburban districts.

Each college offers credit and noncredit courses in five general areas: baccalaureate-transfer, awarding associate's degrees; vocational education, awarding associate's degrees or certificates; remedial-development studies; continuing education; and public service. Residents of the district served by each college pay its in-district tuition rates, which vary from one college to another. When students' home institutions do not offer the curricula in which they are interested, they can take courses at other community colleges.

Boards. Each college is governed by an unpaid seven-member local board elected at large, in November of odd-numbered years, for staggered six-year terms. The board appoints the president of the college, determines tax rates and the annual budget, and makes policies subject to state law and rules. Advisory committees assist each college in developing curricula in vocational fields that are responsive to the needs of community residents and area employers. Board meetings are open to the public.

Funding. Funding for each college is derived chiefly from local property taxes, state reimbursements, tuition and fees. The Illinois Community College Board publishes *Illinois Community College System Data and Characteristics*, providing information about each college, in April of each year. Tuition and fee amounts listed below are for full-time students who live in each college's district.

WILLIAM RAINEY HARPER COLLEGE
Algonquin and Roselle Roads, Palatine 60067;   *phone 397 3000*

Community College District 512 serves an area of 218 square miles, with a 1986 population of 425,725. Its 1986 expenditures were $24,967,296; it had 809 employees and 15,954 students. Tuition and fees for in-district residents were $810.

MORAINE VALLEY COMMUNITY COLLEGE
10900 S. 88th Avenue, Palos Hills, 60465-0937;   *phone 974 4300*

Community College District 524 serves an area of 139 square miles, with a 1986 population of 341,960. Its 1986 expenditures were $19,085,692; it had 585 employees and 12,776 students. Tuition and fees for in-district residents were $768.

MORTON COLLEGE
3801 S. Central Avenue, Cicero 60650;   *phone 656 8000*

Community College District 527 serves an area of 16 square miles, with a population of 122,241. Its 1986 expenditures were $5,709,172; it had 175 employees and 3,287 students. Tuition and fees for in-district residents were $570.

OAKTON COMMUNITY COLLEGE
1600 E. Golf Road, Des Plaines 60016;   *phone 635 1600*

Community College District 535 serves an area of 102 square miles, with a population of 361,565. Its 1986 expenditures were $18,030,909; it had 485 employees and 10,804 students. Tuition and fees for in-district residents were $536.40.

PRAIRIE STATE COMMUNITY COLLEGE
202 S. Halsted Street, Chicago Heights 60411; *phone 756 3110*

Community College District 515 serves an area of 165 square miles, with a 1986 population of 192,550. Its 1986 expenditures were $8,972,769; it had 289 employees and 4,382 students. Tuition and fees for in-district residents were $900.

SOUTH SUBURBAN COLLEGE
15800 S. State Street, South Holland 60473; *phone 596 2000 phone 596 2000*

Formerly Thornton Community College, Community College District 510 serves an area of 90 square miles, with a 1986 population of 283,679. Its 1986 expenditures were $12,713,542; it had 278 employees and 6,474 students. Tuition and fees for in-district residents were $840.

TRITON COLLEGE
2000 5th Avenue, River Grove 60171; *phone 456 0300*

Community College District 504 serves an area of 63 square miles, with a 1986 population of 329,583. Its 1986 expenditures were $31,279,781; it had 1,208 employees and 17,871 students. Tuition and fees for in-district residents were $772.50.

SUBURBAN PUBLIC SCHOOLS

The state agency which supervises public secondary education in Illinois is the State Board of Education, a 17-member unpaid board appointed by the governor for staggered, six-year terms; 4 are from Chicago and 4 from suburban Cook County.

The Superintendent of the Educational Service Region of Cook County is an elected official who has responsibility for disbursement of state funds to school districts in the county and certain oversight and service responsibilities, particularly for suburban schools (see chapter 7 for a description of the office).

Suburban Cook County voters elect 1,086 of their fellow citizens to govern their public schools, at three levels: the Regional Board of School Trustees, which serves all of suburban Cook County; School Township Trustees; and members of school boards within the school townships. All serve without compensation.

Regional Board of School Trustees. In 1951 the state legislature provided for the election of a board of county school trustees in each county. In Cook County, Chicago voters do not participate in the election of this board, which has jurisdiction over school boundary changes and over petitions to form new school districts. Elsewhere in Illinois, the board of trustees holds title to school buildings and sites, but the school township trustees in Cook County continue to hold title to all property. By statute, the board must meet quarterly but may also hold special meetings.

A school trustee must be a registered voter, must reside in Cook County outside of Chicago, and cannot be a school board member or employee or hold any other county office. The seven members of the board serve six-year staggered terms without compensation. Two or three are elected every two years on a separate nonpartisan ballot.

School Township Trustees. There are 26 school townships in Cook County. They are distinct from the congressional or civil townships discussed above. The finances for suburban Cook County school districts originate in a system set up 150 years ago and are handled in a manner different from that of any other area in the nation. In 1819 the Illinois legislature created the Township School System as a way to finance the common schools. In each township, a section of land was set aside for the benefit of free public schools. A three-person board was elected in each township to handle the business of renting out the section to tenant farmers, collecting the profits, and paying for the teachers, buildings, and supplies necessary for educating the children of the township. Over the years the land was sold off and tax levies became the way to finance education. By 1961 the 101 other counties in the state had abandoned the Township School System. Chicago was also exempt. Today suburban Cook County is the only place where this system still exists.

In each school township voters elect three school trustees who serve unpaid staggered six-year terms. Each board of township school trustees receives money from property tax revenues and state and federal claims, designates depositaries for the funds of the school districts in its township, invests the funds, and holds the money for its member districts. The township school trustees hold legal title to school district land and buildings in the township. Township school trustees are required to meet quarterly, on the first Monday of January, April, July, and October, and they may also call special meetings.

Township School Treasurer. The school trustees hire a township school treasurer to run the business of the office. The Illinois School Code requires the treasurer to be a resident of the township, not to be a school board member, and to meet qualifications in financial matters. The treasurer pays out funds for the member school districts at the direction of the school districts. The cost of the office is paid by the school districts in the township; each pays a percentage based on the amount of money handled. The size of the treasurers' offices vary widely: in 1987 the Bloom Fractional School Township handled money for no districts, those of Jefferson and Palatine handled finances for one district each, and the Worth Township treasurer served 12 districts.

Suburban School Districts. There are 143 suburban school districts in Cook County serving 318,016 students in 1986-87. They are independent of the civil townships and the municipalities and do not necessarily conform to village or city boundaries. Each suburban school township is divided into school districts, which may be elementary (K-8), high school (9-12), or unit (K-12). As of 1987, Chicago and Elmwood Park were the only unit districts in the county. Under the dual system, in which elementary and high schools are administered by separate boards, each school board levies a tax for the maintenance of the grades under its jurisdiction.

Suburban School Boards. Each of the 143 school districts in suburban Cook County is governed by a seven-member unpaid board elected for four-year terms on a nonpartisan basis. Some school districts are subdivided into single-member election districts; in others candidates run at large. A candidate must be at least 18 years old, be a registered voter, and have lived in the district for at least a year.

SCHOOL FINANCING. Public schools are financed by local property taxes, state aid, and federal aid. In 1986-87 the local share of school financing in Illinois was 50.39%, state aid provided 42.25%, and federal aid 7.36%. These percentages have varied over the years; the highest proportion borne locally was 67.84% in 1967-68 and the lowest was 45.16% in 1975-76. The percentages of support from the state for school districts vary widely, since the amount depends on a complex formula which in general provides more support to poor districts than wealthy ones. In 1985-86, when state aid provided 41.04% of local school support in Illinois, the percentage of state aid provided to individual school districts in Cook County varied from 3% to 70% of their total school funds for the year.

State Aid. School districts that meet state standards (number of attendance days, certification of teachers, safety of buildings, etc.) are funded by the legislature from the state Common School Fund. The formula for distribution of the state aid is called the Resource-Equalizer Formula; it is based on weighted average daily attendance (WADA) and the equalized assessed valuation (EAV) of the school district.

Average daily attendance (ADA) is computed by taking the average of the district school attendance for each month, and state aid claims are computed by using the best three monthly averages. The WADA figure is computed by weighting the number of students according to grade level and eligibility for Title I programs of the federal Elementary and Secondary Education Act (educationally deprived children). An exceptional three- or four-year-old or kindergarten student in a half-day program is weighted as 0.50, kindergarten students in full-day programs and students in grades 1-6 are weighted as 1.0, students in grades 7 and 8 as 1.05, and students in grades 9-12 as 1.25. Title I students are weighted differently, but they add to the total allotment. The amount of state aid a district can receive is calculated by using the WADA, the EAV of the district, and the district's tax rate. State aid entitlements of districts vary greatly depending on these three amounts.

School Funds. State law requires that local school boards prepare a budget, publicize its availability for inspection, and hold a public hearing before it is adopted. The budget must be divided into separate funds which receive revenue and pay expenses for specific purposes. Most school budgets have six funds: Education; Operations, Building and Maintenance; Transportation; Municipal Retirement; Building Bond and Interest; and Tort Immunity. Under specific conditions, the budgets may have other funds. State law allows borrowing from one fund to meet the obligations of another fund, but interfund loans must be repaid within one calendar year.

TABLE 2.1. SCHOOL DISTRICT TAX RATE LIMITATIONS
For Taxes Collected during 1987
(Chicago District Number 289 not included)

Levy (Fund)	District	Without Referendum %	With Referendum %
Educational	Elem.	0.920	3.50
Educational	H.Sch.	0.920	3.50
Educational	Unit	1.680	4.00
Operations, Building & Maintenance	Elem.	0.250	0.55
Operations, Building & Maintenance	H.Sch.	0.250	0.55
Operations, Building & Maintenance	Unit	0.375	0.75
Capital Improvements	All	—	0.06
Transportation	Elem.	0.120	A.N.*
Transportation	H.Sch.	0.120	A.N.*
Transportation	Unit	0.160	A.N.*
Summer School	All	—	0.15
Bond & Interest	All	N/A	A.N.*
Municipal Retirement	All	A.N.*	N/A
Tort Immunity	All	A.N.*	N/A
Working Cash	All	0.050	N/A
Fire Prevention, Safety, Environmental & Energy	All	0.050	0.10
Special Education	Elem.	0.020	N/A
Special Education	H.Sch.	0.020	N/A
Special Education	Unit	0.040	N/A
Area Vocational Education	H.Sch.	—	0.05
Area Vocational Education	Unit	—	0.05
Tort Judgment Bonds	All	A.N.*	N/A
Pollution Bonds	Eligible	A.N.*	N/A
Pollution Control Facilities Replacement	Eligible	A.N.*	N/A
Facility Leasing	All	0.050	N/A
Temporary Relocation	Eligible	0.050	0.05
Community College Tuition	Eligible	A.N.*	N/A

*As Needed

N/A: Not Applicable   Source: State, Local and Federal Financing for Illinois Public Schools, 1986-87.

Property Taxes. State law sets limits, varying by fund and by district type, on property taxes which may be levied without referendum, and it sets higher limits which may be levied if approved by referendum. The Educational Fund is subject to "Backdoor Referendum" (Illinois Revised Statutes, Chapter 122, 17-2-2): whenever a school district first levies a tax in excess of the maximum permissible levy on June 30, 1965, any taxpayer may file with the board of education a petition signed by 10% of the voters of the school district or 1,500 of them (whichever is less) to put to referendum the question of whether the district may levy the increased tax.

The district must file its anticipated tax levy with the county clerk before the last Tuesday in September. The county clerk divides the total levy of each district by the total equalized assessed valuation of the district to determine the tax rate that will produce the amount of the district tax levy and extends the tax at this rate, or at the maximum rate allowed by law, whichever is lower. Property taxes are received by the school districts a year after they are assessed. (The second payment on 1988 property taxes, adjusted for changes in assessed valuation, is made in August 1989.) Moreover, the fiscal year for most school districts is July 1 through June 30, and the property tax levy year is a calendar year, so the school districts usually receive property tax revenues for a school year from two different tax levies.

The value of property (equalized assessed valuation, or EAV), the number of students in attendance (ADA), and the property tax rates for schools vary widely among districts. All of these affect the amount of money available per pupil and the amount of state aid granted (see table 2.2).

TABLE 2.2. COOK COUNTY SCHOOL TAX RATES (1986)

	Highest	Lowest
District EAV	$2,806,826,201	$9,550,279
A.D.A.	12,303	156
EAV per pupil	$228,141	$60,869
Operating Tax Rate	2.0706	1.97

Most school districts pay current expenses by borrowing through tax anticipation warrants or by using the Working Cash Fund. Districts with populations of under 150,000 are permitted to tax to establish this fund.

Bonds. The legislature has set limits of bonded indebtedness of 6% of total assessed valuation for elementary and high school districts and of 12% for unit districts.

Budgets. State law requires that local school boards prepare a budget, publicize its availability for inspection, and hold a public hearing before it is adopted. An audit of district books must be prepared by a qualified public accountant at the close of each fiscal year, in the form provided by the Illinois Office of Education, and it must be on file at the local district office, the office of the county Educational Service Region, and the Illinois Office of Education.

PUBLIC LIBRARIES

Public libraries are defined by the U.S. Code Service as "libraries which serve free of charge all residents of a community, district or region, receive financial support in whole or in part from public funds and which are not an integral part of an institution of higher education." Illinois law provides for a variety of types of public libraries, including county, municipal, township, and district libraries. As of 1988, there are over 100 public libraries in Cook County, all of which are either municipal or district libraries.

Library Districts. Libraries may be established as "units of local government," which means as special taxing districts within other local governmental bodies or as independent bodies. In 1988 there were 49 independent library districts in suburban Cook County. Special library districts may be established or dissolved by petition and referendum; if a tax-supported municipal library already lies within the proposed district, votes for that municipality are counted separately and a dissenting municipality is excluded from the district.

District Library Boards. District library boards have the power to enact ordinances, levy taxes, issue bonds for capital improvements, buy and sell property, impose user charges, and hire a librarian. The seven-member boards are elected by the voters of the district to serve unpaid staggered six-year terms. The board elects a president, treasurer, and secretary from its membership.

Municipal Libraries. Libraries may be established by a municipality, in which case their boundaries are those of the municipality, and the tax levy is passed by the municipal council or board. The Chicago Public Library and (as of 1988) 52 suburban city and village libraries fall into this category. Municipal library boards have no bonding power of their own and are limited to the bonding power of the municipality for capital expenses. Additional taxes can be levied by passage of a referendum.

Municipal Library Boards. City library board members are appointed for three-year terms by the mayor with the approval of the city council. In a commission village, a six-member library board is appointed by the commissioners to serve six-year terms (unless the commissioners have passed a resolution providing for four-year terms). Other village libraries have an independently elected seven-member board, serving six-year terms (or, by ordinance, four-year terms).

Library Systems. The Library System Act of 1965 established a state network of library systems which is financed and administered by the state. A library system may be (1) a cooperative system consisting of ten or more public libraries, (2) a single public library serving a city with a population of over 500,000 (Chicago), or (3) a multitype library system which includes a city or a 10-member library group and other types of libraries such as academic, school, and special libraries. In Cook County the library systems are the Chicago Public Library (see chapter 6); the North Suburban Library System, with 304 member-libraries, 191 of which are in Cook County; and the Suburban Library System, with 179 member-libraries, 150 in Cook County. All residents of Cook County have access to all resources of the system and, through interlibrary loans, have access to materials in all kinds of libraries, not only in the state but throughout the country. Those who live in a district or municipality with an affiliated library use their library cards and there is no fee. Those who do not live in a district or municipality that is a system member may be required to pay a nonresident fee in order to receive library cards.

Each system has a 5- to 15-member unpaid board of directors chosen from the boards of the participating libraries. Each board elects its own officers. State funds are allocated according to an equalized formula, area grants, and per capita grants.

Centers for Research and Reference. The Library System Act also designated four libraries in the state as centers for research and reference for patrons of the library system network. The Chicago Public Library is one; it receives state support for its interlibrary loan and reference services. Libraries with special collections may also be designated as special resource centers: in Cook County these include the University of Chicago Library, the John Crerar Library (on the University of Chicago campus), the Health Sciences Library at the University of Illinois in Chicago, and the Northwestern University Library in Evanston.

MOSQUITO ABATEMENT DISTRICTS

Enabling legislation passed in 1927 led to the establishment of four mosquito abatement districts within Cook County. These are special taxing bodies formed by referendum, to control mosquitoes in their larval stage in standing water and to spray areas to control the adult mosquito population.

Each district is governed by an unpaid five-member Board of Trustees, appointed to four-year terms by the president of the Cook County Board of Commissioners. Their meetings are open to the public.

NORTHWEST MOSQUITO ABATEMENT DISTRICT
147 Hintz Road, Wheeling 60090; *phone 537 2306*

The Northwest Mosquito Abatement District serves 240 square miles, including all or parts of 23 municipalities in the townships of Barrington, Palatine, Wheeling, Northfield, Hanover, Schaumburg, Elk Grove Village, and Maine. Its 1986 tax rate was $.012 per $100 of assessed valuation, and its budget was $875,476. The district has about 60 full-time employees and additional part-time workers during the summer.

SOUTH COOK COUNTY MOSQUITO ABATEMENT DISTRICT
155th and Dixie Highway, Harvey 60426; *phone 333 4120*

The South Cook County Mosquito Abatement District serves 340 square miles in the townships of Bloom, Bremen, Lemont, Orland, Palos, Rich, Thornton, and Worth in suburban Cook County and parts of Calumet and Hyde Park townships in Chicago. This district had a 1987 tax rate of $.017 per $100 of assessed valuation and a 1987 budget of $1,658,200; it employs 30 persons fulltime and about 28 seasonally. It maintains facilities in Riverdale, Orland Park, Harvey, and South Chicago.

NORTH SHORE MOSQUITO ABATEMENT DISTRICT
117 Northfield Road, Northfield 60093; *phone 446 9434*

The North Shore Mosquito Abatement District serves all or part of 13 villages in New Trier, Evanston, Niles, Maine, and Northfield townships. Its 1986 tax rate was $.010 per $100 of assessed valuation, and its 1987 budget was $569,750. Its 7 full-time employees are augmented by about 22 part-time summer employees.

DES PLAINES VALLEY MOSQUITO ABATEMENT DISTRICT
8130 Ogden Ave., Lyons 60534; *phone 447 1765*

The Des Plaines Valley Mosquito Abatement District serves 31 villages in the townships of Lyons, Proviso, Riverside, River Forest, and Oak Park. With a tax rate of $.006 per $100 of assessed valuation, its 1988 budget of $403,877 provided for 6 full-time employees and 20 - 22 summer employees.

OTHER SPECIAL PURPOSE DISTRICTS

The 1982 U.S. census of local governments of Cook County lists 184 other special districts: 90 park and recreation districts, 41 fire protection districts, 31 sewerage districts, 8 water supply districts, 6 drainage districts, 4 health districts, 2 cemetery districts, 1 irrigation and water conservation district, and 1 soil conservation district. Each is created under state legislation defining its powers and structure.

Special purpose districts are formed as the need for services arises, particularly if funds are not available through a municipality. The process includes a petition to put the question of formation of the district on the ballot and an affirmative vote by those living in the proposed district. Most, but not all, of the districts levy property taxes. Most, but not all, of the districts are governed by elected officials; whether the governing body is elected or not may depend on when the district was created and what state law governing the formation of such a district was in force at the time.

Tax-levying districts as of 1988 include 98 park districts. The Chicago Park District is a tax-levying body and is described in chapter 6. Suburban park districts have a state-imposed tax limit of $.10 per $100 equalized assessed valuation (EAV) for their corporate funds and $.075 for their recreation funds. These limits can be exceeded by referendum. It should be noted that many suburban municipalities have park and recreation departments which are not separate districts.

As of 1988, there were 42 suburban fire protection districts; their tax rate limit was $.125 per $100 EAV, which could be increased to $.30 by referendum. They could also have an ambulance fund, limited to $.30 per $100 EAV. Many suburban municipalities have their own fire departments. Residents of unincorporated areas not served by a municipal fire department or by a fire protection district must pay a fee for obtaining fire protection from a neighboring municipality or district.

Sewerage districts listed by the census are described in the statutes as sanitary districts. They are not the same as the two sanitary districts described in chapter 8 but are set up to provide local sewers feeding into the major sanitary districts. The tax extension division of the county clerk's office in 1988 listed 28 of these smaller sanitary districts supported by property taxes; their tax rate limitations are either $.20 per $100 EAV, or $.083, depending on when they were created. The trustees of such districts are appointed by the county board.

The clerk's office lists two streetlighting districts, with tax rate limits of $.125 per $100 EAV, and one river conservancy district with a tax rate limit of $.083 per $100 EAV.

The cemetery districts listed by the census are cemetery maintenance districts and are supported by fees, as are other special districts which are not tax-levying.

3   Your Rights to Choose: Elections

Elections are the occasion for you to have a share in deciding about candidates, parties, and referendum questions. Voter participation in elections is also used by elected officials to measure the amount of interest and involvement in governmental issues. Thus, a community with a heavy voter turnout may get more attention than one with little apparent interest. Further, the size of the vote individual candidates get often determines their influence and their political futures. Within the parties this is particularly clear, as a party committeeman's vote in slatemaking (choosing candidates the party will support) is determined by the number of votes that party received in the committeeman's ward or township in the preceding primary election. Your vote really does count.

VOTER REGISTRATION

As a resident of Cook County, you may vote if you are a U.S. citizen, are 18 years old as of election day, have lived in your voting precinct for the 30 days immediately preceding the election, and are registered to vote from the place where you are living. Registration is closed for 28 days before and on the day of a primary or general election (however, it is best to wait before registering for a few days after an election). There usually is a precinct registration day when citizens can register to vote in their neighborhood polling places; this is 28 days before the election, and registration at other sites (see below, Where to Register) is closed 35 days before the election.

A member of the armed forces who is otherwise qualified and who has been discharged within 60 days of the election may vote, even though not registered. Federal employees, members of the armed forces on active duty and their spouses, and members of the merchant marine temporarily outside the territorial limits of the United States may register by mail, and in some cases they may vote by absentee ballot without being registered (see

Absentee Voting, below). Physically disabled persons may file affidavits with their election authority certifying that they are unable to appear in person, in which case they are registered at home.

If you have moved to Illinois less than 30 days before a presidential election and you were a qualified voter in another state or in the District of Columbia,.you may vote for president and vice-president in your former state by absentee ballot, or by mail or in person at the office of your new election authority.

Identification. To register to vote, you must present two pieces of identification from different sources. Both must contain your name, and one must have your current address, the one from which you are registering. Pieces of identification which are acceptable include driver's license; social security card; birth certificate; employer, student, or public assistance identification card; credit card; utility bill or letter from a government agency, employer, school, union, or professional association delivered to you at your registration address. Naturalized citizens must supply naturalization information.

Where to Register: Chicago. Chicago citizens may register during regular office hours at the Chicago Board of Elections at City Hall, at any library or library branch, at firehouses, or through volunteer deputy registrars. They must do so at least 35 days before the election. Or they may register, on one day only, in their precinct polling place 28 days before the election. The location of precinct polling places is published before elections and is available by calling the Board of Elections, *269 7900*, or Citizens Information Service, *939 INFO*.

Where to Register: Suburban Cook County. Suburban Cook County residents may register during regular office hours at the county clerk's office in the County Building in Chicago, or with the clerks of municipalities or townships, or at special locations announced in the press. They must register at least 35 days before the election. Or they may register, on one day only, in their precinct polling place 28 days before the election. The location of suburban polling places is available by calling the election department of the county clerk, *443 5150*, township or municipal offices, or Citizens Information Service, *939 INFO*.

Permanent Registration. Illinois has permanent registration, which means that your name remains on the polling list without reregistration at each election. If you fail to vote for four years, however, your name can be removed from the polling lists. If you move or change your name, you must reregister. After each registration, election judges canvass the precinct to be sure the voter registration lists are accurate. If they believe that you no longer live at the address from which you were registered, they leave a notice warning that your name may be removed from the polling list. You must then follow the instructions on the notice in order to remain registered.

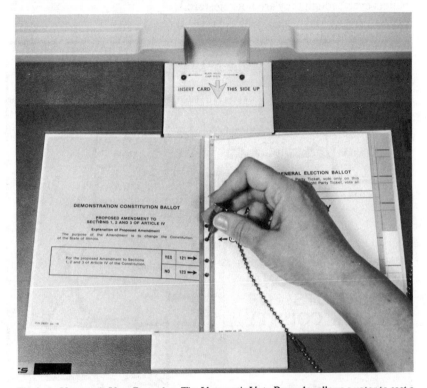

Fig. 3. 1. Votomatic Vote Recorder. The Votomatic Vote Recorder allows a voter to cast a ballot by punching holes in a data-processing card. The names of the candidates are printed on the pages of the booklet. The voter inserts the ballot card and indicates a vote by inserting a stylus into a small hole opposite the name of a candidate. The stylus strikes the perforated area of the ballot card and makes a hole. Each hole has the candidate's ballot number opposite it, so the voter can check the ballot card. The ballots later are counted by computer, and the results are printed.

Source: Chicago Board of Elections

ABSENTEE VOTING

A qualified voter who expects to be out of the county on election day, or who cannot appear at the polling place because of religious prohibitions or because of physical incapacity, may obtain an absentee ballot by applying by mail not more than 40 days or less than 5 days before the election; if applying in person at the office of the appropriate election authority, a voter may vote absentee up to the day before the election. Members of the armed forces, the merchant marine, religious or welfare agencies attached to the armed forces, civilian government employees serving outside the United States, and spouses and dependents of those persons may obtain absentee ballots even though they are not registered.

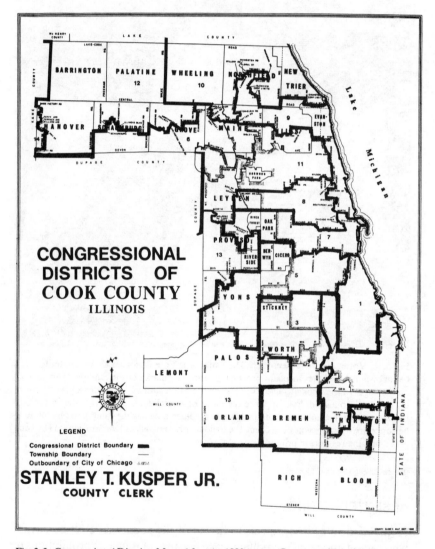

Fig. 3. 2. Congressional Districts Map. After the 1990 census, Congress will decide how many Congressional Districts each state should have, according to its population. The state legislature will then reapportion the districts. There should be new Congressional District boundary lines for the 1992 elections.

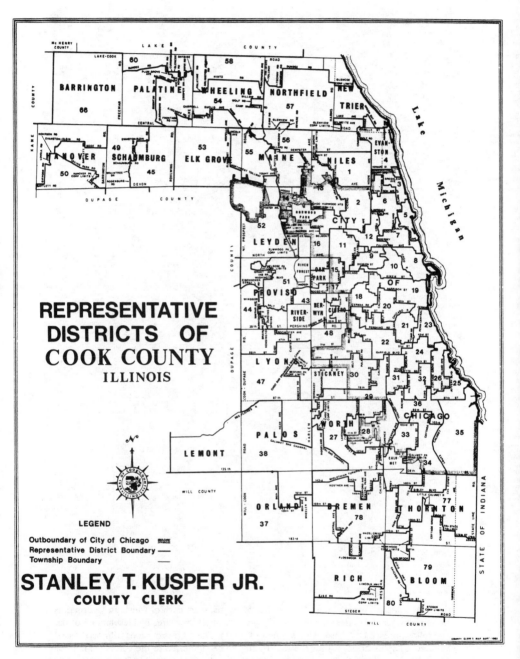

Fig. 3. 3. State Legislative Districts Map. Illinois has 118 state representative districts and
59 state senatorial districts. They must be reapportioned by the state legislature after the 1990
census. Legislative districts must be "compact, contiguous, and substantially equal in population," according to the state constitution. A state senate district is made up of two state representative districts: state senate district 1 is made up of state representative districts 1 and
2, state senate district 2 is made up of representative districts 3 and 4, and so forth.

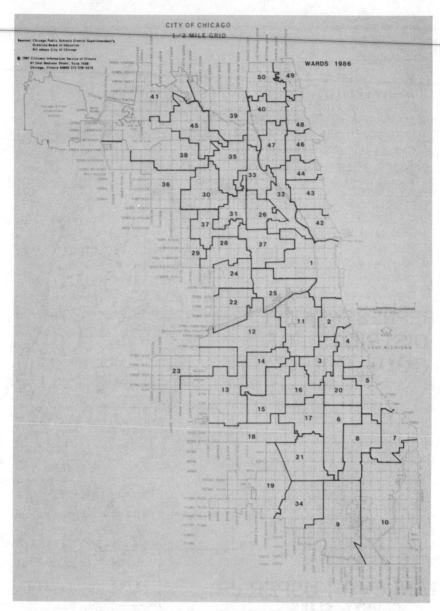

Fig. 3. 4. Chicago Wards Map. Chicago has 50 wards, from each of which an alderman is elected. State law requires that the City Council redistrict the wards by December 1 of the year following each U.S. census (by December 1, 1991). There are provisions (Illinois Revised Statutes, Chapter 21, 39-43) for the redistricting to be submitted to the voters (1) if 10 or more aldermen object to the districting ordinance, or (2) if the council fails to act and 10 or more aldermen submit an ordinance to the city clerk.

PRIMARY ELECTIONS

Political parties have performed their function of nominating candidates for office in various ways: by caucus, by private meeting of party workers, or by convention of representatives from local districts. The caucus and convention are still used, but around 1900 a movement was begun to open party elections to all voters, using the regular election machinery. Such a party election was called a direct primary.

Thus, a primary is an election held within the party. In Illinois on primary day, there are actually two or more elections, one for each party which is nominating candidates through a contested election. The ballot for each party is a separate ballot, and Illinois voters must indicate which party's ballot they intend to vote. Party committeemen and convention delegates are elected at the primary election, and the party's candidates for public office are nominated.

Since the inception of the primary, there has been debate as to whether voting in the primary should be restricted to bona fide members of the party, or to those who are willing at least to declare their adherence to it. Practice varies from state to state. In states with open primaries, voters do not declare their party preference; usually they are given both ballots and mark the one they want in the privacy of the voting booth. At the extreme, crossover voting is permitted; that is, the voter may pick candidates on more than one party ballot.

Closed Primary. Illinois has what is called a closed primary, meaning that voters must declare to the election officials at the polling place the party whose ballot they want. Unlike some states, Illinois does not require voters to declare a party preference at the time of registration. Voters may change their party preference at any primary. Party preference declared in the primary election has no effect on how a voter can vote in the general election, where party choice is secret.

It should be noted that in Illinois the terms open and closed primary, and independent and party candidate, are used, especially in the press, to mean something different from the description above. In this Illinois sense, a "closed primary" is one in which the regular party organization chooses and supports a slate of prospective candidates. An "independent candidate" in this Illinois sense is one who is not endorsed by the party organization but is running in a party primary against the endorsed candidates. (Independent candidates, as defined by statute, can run in the general election, without party label or by forming a new political party, if they obtain enough petition signatures.)

Candidate Petitions. The names of party candidates are placed on the primary ballot by petition, as are the names of candidates running as new party or independent (no party affiliation) candidates in the general election and the names of candidates running in nonpartisan elections. (The only exception is candidacy for election as trustee of the University of Illinois; candidates for this office from an established party are nominated by state party conventions.) These petitions must be signed by a specified number of qualified voters, that is, registered voters residing within the district from which the candidate is running. The time of filing, the form of the petition, and the number of valid signatures required are specified by law and vary according to the office sought. A voter may sign the petition of only one candidate for any office (except where there is more than one position to be filled for that office, as on a board elected at large). A voter may not sign a petition for a candidate running in the general election as an independent if the voter has already voted in the primary election.

Objections to Nominations. A registered voter from the appropriate district can file an objection to the nominating petitions of a candidate or to referendum petitions. These must be filed within five business days of the last day for filing candidate petitions; in the case of statewide public policy referenda, objections may be filed within 35 business days. The State Board of Elections rules on objections to nominations for statewide office and for office in electoral districts that include more than one county. In Cook County, the Cook County Officers Electoral Board rules on objections to nominations for county office. This board is composed of the county clerk, as chair, the state's attorney, and the clerk of the circuit court. The law (Illinois Revised Statutes, 46, 10, 8-11) provides for similar boards for municipalities, townships, and school and college districts. It provides that if there is a Board of Election Commissioners (as in Chicago), that board rules on petitions within its jurisdiction.

Primary Nominations. All candidates are nominated at primary elections, to run for election at general elections, except for the following:
* Presidential electors and trustees of the University of Illinois, who are nominated at state conventions
* Chicago aldermen, who are nominated by petition
* Boards of school directors and certain townships having populations of 5,000 or more, who are nominated by caucus
* Elected boards of education, including non-high-school boards, who are nominated by petition
* Officers in some municipalities or townships that do not use established political parties in their elections but, at each election, form new parties which nominate by petition

The state constitution provides that state circuit, appellate, and supreme court judges can be nominated by primary election or by petition. However, both major parties usually nominate a slate of judges.

Presidential Preference Primary Vote. Candidates for president may have their names placed on the primary ballot, but this vote is to show preference only and is not binding on the party delegation.

Party Elections. Party officials elected at the primary elections are state central committeemen, ward and township committeemen, and the majority of delegates to the party's national convention (others may be chosen by the state central committee). Candidates for the post of delegate may choose, at the time of filing the petition, to declare whom they support for president; if a candidate does so, this preference is indicated on the ballot. Delegates are not obliged to make such a statement and are not permanently bound by their stated choice.

Since the primary is an election within the party, you must vote separately for each candidate you wish to support, but you must not vote for any more candidates than are to be nominated or elected for any given office. To do so would invalidate your ballot. You are not obliged to vote for every office.

ELECTION CALENDAR FOR CHICAGO AND COOK COUNTY UNDER THE CONSOLIDATION OF ELECTIONS ACT

The Consolidation of Elections Act combines all elections held in Illinois into five elections in each two-year period, two to be held in even-numbered years, and three in odd-numbered years. Chicago voters usually have six elections every four years, since city officials have four-year terms, and Chicago does not elect township and special district officials; suburban voters have ten elections in a four-year period. In case of a vacancy, state election law provides that the office shall be filled at the next municipal election under the consolidated election act; in June 1988 the Chicago Board of Elections was under court order to conduct a mayoral election in 1989 to fill the vacancy caused by the death of Mayor Harold Washington.

EVEN-NUMBERED YEARS

MARCH. General Primary Election: Third Tuesday.
Note: You must declare your party to vote in a party primary; since you are choosing among nominees for your party, each office must be voted on individually. You do not have to declare a party if you wish to vote only on a referendum question.

1. Presidential preference (advisory), fourth years from 1988

2. Party nominees for election the following November, except presidential electors and University of Illinois trustees

3. Election of political party officers:
    National convention delegates, fourth years from 1988
    National convention alternates, fourth years from 1988
    State central committeemen, fourth years from 1986
    Cook County township committeemen, fourth years from 1986
    Chicago ward committeemen, fourth years from 1988

4. Referenda

NOVEMBER. General Election: First Tuesday after First Monday.

Note: A straight party vote will cast your vote for all candidates running in that party. It will not cast a vote for retention of judges or for referenda, which must be voted separately.

1. Electors for president and vice-president, fourth years from 1988 (The names of the candidates for president and vice-president are listed on the ballot and not the names of the electors.)

2. U.S. Senators, one every six years from 1986, one every six years from 1990

3. Representatives in Congress, one from each Congressional district

4. State officers: governor, lieutenant governor, secretary of state, comptroller, attorney general, treasurer; fourth years from 1986

5. State senators: one from each legislative district is elected three times in ten years (one two-year term and two four-year terms; there are three groups, 4-4-2, 4-2-4, 2-4-4)

6. State representatives, one from each representative district

7. Trustees of the University of Illinois, three for six-year terms (nominated at the state party conventions)

8. Courts: judges of the supreme, appellate, and circuit courts, running for the first time, to fill vacancies or newly-created judgeships

9. Courts: special retention ballot for judges wishing to be retained in office, every ten years for supreme and appellate judges, every six years for circuit judges

10. County officers: Cook County Board president, commissioners, clerk, sheriff, treasurer, assessor, board of appeals, superintendent of educational service region; fourth years from 1986. State's attorney, recorder of deeds, circuit court clerk, fourth years from 1988

11. Metropolitan Sanitary District, three for six-year term

12. Municipalities which elect annually

13. Referenda

ODD-NUMBERED YEARS

FEBRUARY. Consolidated Primary Election: Last Tuesday.
Note: For Chicago voters, this election is both a party primary and a non-partisan election of aldermen. You must declare your party to vote in the primary election, but you do not have to declare your party to vote in the aldermanic election or on referenda.

1. Party nominees for election in April

2. Chicago aldermen, fourth years from 1987 (If no candidate in the ward receives a majority of votes cast, a runoff election between the two highest candidates is held in the April election.)

3. Referenda

APRIL. Consolidated Election: First Tuesday.

1. Chicago mayor, city clerk, city treasurer, and runoff elections for aldermen; fourth years from 1987 (However, a mayoral election is scheduled for 1989, because of a vacancy in the office 28 months before the election.)

2. Suburban municipal officers (Terms may be two or four years.)

3. Suburban Cook County township, road district, park district, library district officers, fourth years from 1985

4. Referenda

NOVEMBER. Nonpartisan Elections, Suburban Cook County: First Tuesday after First Monday.

1. School officers and boards of education

2. Fire protection, tuberculosis sanitarium trustees, and special districts not otherwise designated

3. Referenda

REFERENDA

A referendum submits a question to the voters for approval or rejection. A referendum may submit a measure already passed by a governmental body and may be required for increasing certain taxes or issuing certain bonds (see chapters 2 and 4); or it may be advisory only. A referendum is required if a home rule county or municipality decides not to be a home rule unit. Municipal and county forms of government, selection of officers, and terms of office may be changed by referendum.

If the referendum is not submitted by a governmental body, it may be put before the voters by petition, usually requiring signatures of at least 10% of the number of voters who voted in the last general election. No more than three public questions, other than "back door referenda" (see chapter 2), and state constitutional amendments may be submitted at the same election.

Amendments to the Illinois Constitution appear on a separate ballot, traditionally blue. Such amendments, except for amendments to the legislative article, must first be passed by the Illinois legislature. Amendments limited to structure and procedures of the General Assembly may also be proposed by petition; the number of signers required is 8% of the votes cast for governor at the last election. To become effective, a proposed amendment must be approved by either three-fifths of those voting on the question or a majority of those voting in the election. Thus failure to vote on a constitutional amendment can amount to a vote against the amendment.

LOCAL OPTION REFERENDA

In a city of over 200,000 population (i.e., Chicago) the voters in any precinct may decide whether to curtail or prohibit the retail sale of alcoholic beverages within the precinct. To place the question on the ballot, a petition must be submitted at least 90 days before the election; it must have the signatures of at least 25% of the voters whose names appeared on the poll list for the precinct as of the last election of county or state officers.

The question is submitted to the voters at the next election. (For detailed procedures, see "Local Option Law," published by Citizens Information Service of Illinois.)

VACANCIES IN OFFICE

State laws (Chapter 46, Article 25) provide for most elective offices that they shall become vacant if the incumbent is convicted of any offense involving a violation of the oath of office or of an infamous crime. Disqualification of U.S. senators and congressional representatives is governed by rules of the Senate and House of Representatives and not by state election laws, but state law provides for their replacement. In home rule counties (Cook) the law provides that vacancies in elective county offices (other than the chief executive) are filled by the county board, but that the county board may provide for other procedures. There are special procedures in state law for filling vacancies in other elective offices.

POLITICAL PARTY ORGANIZATION

For most voters, party membership (or nonmembership) is largely a matter of how they wish to label themselves. However, every party has its core of "professionals" - officeholders, prospective officeholders, patronage workers (generally considered to be those whose jobs depend on their political activity), active supporters, and paid staff - who raise the money, manage the campaign, get out the votes, and make the day-to-day decisions. The two major parties are highly organized, with committees corresponding to the various levels of government.

State Primary Election Law. State law defines the managing committees of each political party, including their composition, selection of chairmen, voting strength within committees, the filling of vacancies, and the powers and duties of the committees. These laws do not necessarily cover all of the political duties which are generally considered to exist regardless of law.

Precinct Captain. The precinct worker with official party status is called a precinct captain and in Cook County is appointed by the ward or township committeeman. (In all other Illinois counties, precinct committeemen are elected.) A precinct captain has no legal status, no official governmental responsibilities because of being a precinct captain, and is responsible to the committeeman. It is the business of a good precinct captain to know the people in the precinct: the party regulars who can be counted on to vote, those who need reminding to get them to the polls, the independent voters who may be swayed by particular issues or candidates, and the confirmed opposition on whom it would be wasteful to spend much effort. Political novices often enter the party system as precinct captains.

Ward and Township Committeemen. Illinois laws governing election of ward and township committeemen in Chicago and Cook County are written to apply to cities with a population of 200,000 or more and counties with a population of two million or more. Chicago is the only city and Cook County the only county to which these numbers apply. Chicago ward committeemen are elected for four-year terms in the March primaries of presidential years. Suburban Cook County township committeemen are elected for four-year terms in the March primaries of nonpresidential years. A party committeeman's voting power is determined by the number of votes the party received in the ward or township in the preceding primary. A party committeeman has no official governmental responsibilities.

Municipal Committee. Ward or township committeemen residing in a municipality are members of the Municipal Committee, which may endorse party candidates to run for municipal office. The chair is chosen by the committee membership.

Cook County Central Committee. The county central committee is made up of the 50 ward committeemen from Chicago and the 30 township committeemen from suburban Cook County. Following the primary, a county convention is held to organize and elect officers. One of the duties of the convention is to select delegates to the state convention, each township or ward committeeman being entitled to one vote for each 500 votes cast by party members in the preceding primary election. The committee may endorse candidates to run for county offices. It also submits names for election judges in suburban Cook County to the county board.

State Central Committee. The Republican State Central Committee is composed of one member elected from each of the state's Congressional districts, the Democratic State Central Committee of one male and one female member from each district. They are elected for four-year terms in the March primary of non-presidential years. This committee calls the state convention, chooses methods for selection of national convention delegates, fills vacancies in the office of national committeeman, and may endorse candidates to run for statewide office.

Legislative Committee. The committee for legislative districts is made up of ward and/or township committeemen of any wards and/or townships lying wholly or in part within the district. It may endorse candidates for state senate and house districts, and it fills any vacancy that arises between the primary and general elections for its party in its legislative district. Each member has one vote for each ballot cast in the party primary in that portion of the ward or township lying within the legislative district.

Congressional Committee. The congressional committee is made up of ward and township committeemen whose ward or township lies wholly or in part within the congressional district. The function of the committee is to fill vacancies on the state central committee, and if a vacancy occurs after a candidate has been nominated in the primary election but before the general election, to nominate a congressional candidate to fill the vacancy.

Third Parties. Although for more than a hundred years the Democrats and Republicans have been the only major political parties in the United States, numerous "third parties" have been formed. Some have proved to be long-lasting; others have disappeared after one or two elections. Many states discriminate to some extent against third parties, but Illinois is particularly rigid in this regard. To enter an election, a new party must run candidates for all the offices to be filled in the political subdivision it wishes to contest. A certificate must be filed with the office receiving petitions for the election of officers of that particular subdivision; the certificate must report the name of the party and its officers, giving names of the officers authorized to fill vacancies in nomination. The number of signatures required on a petition for a new party candidate depends on the size of the political subdivision, but in general it is high. Once on the ballot, the new party must win 5% of the total vote in order to become an established party. Otherwise, at the next election, it must go through the same new party procedure.

Judges of Election. The election laws governing selection of polling place judges of election assume a two-party system, as they provide for five judges in each polling place, two from one party and three from the other. In suburban Cook County, three judges are from the party polling the most votes for governor in the precinct in the last three gubernatorial elections, and two are from the party polling the second highest number of votes. In Chicago, the party with three judges in even-numbered precincts has two in odd-numbered precincts.

Independent Candidates. A candidate who is not affiliated with a political party may run in the general election by filing petitions, signed by registered voters from the district, with the appropriate election authority. The number of signatures required is set by law. The number varies, but is much larger than the number required for candidates who run in a party primary; for instance, for state office a petition for a candidate to run in a party primary requires 5,000 signatures, and a petition to run as an independent requires 25,000. (See Candidates' Calendar for Filing Petitions, below, for signature requirements.)

REQUIREMENTS FOR CANDIDATES AND ELECTED OFFICIALS

A candidate for office must be a registered voter in the district from which he or she hopes to be elected. In addition, there are often requirements about length of residency in the district and, for some offices, professional qualifications. A convicted felon is not permitted to run for office, and "no person shall be eligible to any office who is a defaulter to the municipality" (Illinois Revised Statutes, Chapter 24).

Statement of Economic Interests. The Illinois constitution requires that all candidates for offices created by the constitution must file a statement of economic interests. The legislature has by law extended this requirement to all candidates for office, including those in units of local government and school districts. All elected officials and candidates for public office must file statements of their economic interests and those of their spouses. (This requirement does not apply to candidates for political party office.) Candidates must file with the appropriate election authority (see Candidates' Calendar, below) at the time they file for election.

Disclosure of Campaign Contributions and Expenditures. A Statement of Organization Report is required for political committes. The following are defined as political committees: a candidate for public office, a person or group spending $1,000 or more on behalf of or in opposition to a candidate, or a person or group accepting contributions on behalf of or in opposition to a candidate. The committee has 30 days to file once it reaches the $1,000 figure; if it never raises or spends $1,000 it is not required to file. Any person or group spending more than $1,000 in support of or opposition to a question of public policy must report; if the question is to be submitted to voters of more than one county, the reporting threshold is $3,000. A political committeee must designate a chairman and treasurer and must report immediately a vacancy in those offices, since the oficers must keep complete records. While a vacancy exists, no funds may be accepted or spent.

A local political committee files with the county clerk, and a state political committee with the State Board of Elections. (If a committee acts as both a state and a local committee, it must file with both.) Reports must include an exact account of the total of all contributions, the name and address of everyone who contributes more than $150 within a 12-month period, the total of expenditures, the name and address of anyone paid more than $20, and proof of payment of all expenditures of more than $20. The treasurer must keep all records for two years.

Contributions that must be reported include gifts, loans, subscriptions, dues, purchase of tickets for fund-raising events, transfer of funds from another committee, services of an employee donated by an employer, or anything of value. A report covering up to 30 days before the election is due by 15 days before the election. A report is due 90 days after the election, covering the 30 days before the election and the 60 days after it. Any contribution of $500 or more must be reported within two business days. Reports of expenditures are filed with the annual report of the committee.

Committees must include on the front page of their literature and solicitations of funds a statement that they have filed (or will file) their reports and that the reports are available for purchase from the appropriate election authority. If a committee seeks funds or spends money on behalf of a candidate without written authorization from the candidate, it must state this on its literature or in its commercials. Illinois law forbids publication or distribution of anonymous literature relating to the candidacy of an individual seeking office. Literature must be signed by the organization or person(s) who publish it or distribute it, and addresses must be given. Also forbidden are buying votes or bribing candidates or voters.

Complaints. Citizens may file complaints with the State Board of Elections. Violation of the law is a misdemeanor, punishable by a fine of up to $500 and/or imprisonment of up to six months. The same penalties apply for willfully filing a false complaint.

CANDIDATES' CALENDAR FOR FILING PETITIONS

The form of the petition is specified in the statutes. Signers of petitions must be registered to vote in Illinois. The appropriate election authority publishes the exact number of signatures required for each office in each district. Candidates must attach a statement of candidacy and a receipt for having filed a statement of economic interest. A loyalty oath is optional.

CANDIDATES FOR NATIONAL AND STATE OFFICES
Candidates file with the State Board of Elections

ESTABLISHED PARTY CANDIDATES
Candidates file 92-99 days before the Primary Election, with exceptions noted below. The percentages of the party vote listed are those for the last election.

OFFICE SOUGHT	SIGNATURES REQUIRED
President	3,000-5,000 (78-85 days before Primary)
U.S. Senator	5,000-10,000
U.S. Congressman	0.5% electors in district
State Senator	1% of party vote, minimum 600
State Representative	1% of party vote, minimum 300
Univ. of IL Trustee	none; nominated by party convention
Other State Offices	5,000-10,000
Judges	500
Judges, retention	none (file 6 months before election)

CANDIDATES OF NEW PARTIES
AND INDEPENDENT CANDIDATES

Candidates file 92-99 days before the General Election. The petition signatures required are percentages of votes cast in the last election in the state or the contested district. A statewide new party must run candidates for all state offices. For the petitions of independent candidates, a maximum as well as a minimum number of signatures is set by law for state office: 5-8% for all offices except the General Assembly, where the requirement is 10-16%.

OFFICE SOUGHT	SIGNATURES REQUIRED
President	25,000
U.S. Senator	1%, maximum 25,000
U.S. Congressman	5%
State Senator	5%
State Representative	5%
Other State Offices	1%, maximum 25,000
Judges	5%, maximum 25,000

CANDIDATES FOR COUNTY OFFICE
Candidates file with Cook County Clerk.

ESTABLISHED PARTY CANDIDATES

Candidates file 92-99 days before the Primary Election. The petition signatures required are percentages of the vote for the party candidate who received the highest number of votes in the contested district's last election.

OFFICE SOUGHT	SIGNATURES REQUIRED
Cook County Offices	0.5%
MSD Trustees	0.5%

CANDIDATES OF NEW PARTIES
AND INDEPENDENT CANDIDATES

Candidates file 92-99 days before the General Election. The petition signatures required are percentages of votes cast in the last regular election for that district. A petition to form a new party for county-wide offices must have candidates listed for all offices. For independent candidates, a maximum as well as a minimum number of signatures is set by law: 5-8%.

OFFICE SOUGHT	SIGNATURES REQUIRED
Cook County Offices	5%
MSD Trustees	5%

CANDIDATES FOR MUNICIPAL OFFICE, PARTISAN ELECTION

Chicago candidates (for mayor, clerk, treasurer) file with the Chicago Board of Elections. Suburban candidates file with the appropriate city, village, or town clerk.

ESTABLISHED PARTY CANDIDATES

Candidates file 71-78 days before the Primary Election. The number of signatures required on petitions is 0.5% of the vote cast for the candidate who received the highest number of votes in the last municipal election.

CANDIDATES OF NEW PARTIES
AND INDEPENDENT CANDIDATES

Candidates file 71-78 days before the General Election. The number of signatures required is 5% of the vote cast in the last general election in the district.

CANDIDATES IN NON-PARTISAN ELECTIONS
(NO PARTY IDENTIFICATION)

Chicago candidates for alderman file with the Chicago Board of Elections. Candidates for Regional Board of School Trustees file with the Cook County clerk. Candidates for suburban Boards of Education, Park Districts, and Public Library Districts file with the secretary of the board or district. Candidates for Township School Trustee file with the township school treasurer. Candidates for local Library Boards file with their municipal clerk. All of these file 71-78 days before the election. Candidates for commissioner in municipalities with the commission form of government file with their municipal clerk 42-49 days before the election.

OFFICE SOUGHT	SIGNATURES REQUIRED
Chicago Alderman	2% votes for alderman, last election
Commissioner	1% votes, last election
Regional. School Trustee	50
Township School Trustee	25
Board of Education	10% of voters, maximum 50
Park District	2% of voters, minimum 50
Library District	50
Local Library	50

Source: Illinois Election Code (Illinois Revised Statutes, Chapter 46, Articles 7 and 10).

VOTER INFORMATION

Electioneering is not permitted within 100 feet of the polling place.

Pollwatchers must have credentials; they may represent a party, a candidate, or a civic group. A precinct captain may be a pollwatcher but must have credentials. Pollwatchers may challenge a voter if they think the voter is not qualified to vote.

Sample ballots may be taken into the voting booth but must not be shown to anyone else in the polling place.

Polling Place Procedures: There may be a long line waiting, so be sure to allow enough time.

1. A judge of election will give you an application to vote. Sign your name and give your address.

2. The judge will call out your name and address so pollwatchers can check off who has voted. Pollwatchers do this so they can remind people who have not voted to do so.

3. A judge will compare your signature with your card in the binder.

4. A judge will hand you your ballot in an envelope. The ballot and ballot envelope must be initialled by the judge.

5. A judge will assign you to a voting booth. It should be arranged so no one can see how you vote.

6. After you have voted, hand in your ballot, in the envelope, to a judge, who will put it in the ballot box. The judge will give you the stub from your ballot to show you have voted.

To vote a straight party ticket, punch the hole by the party name. This casts a vote for all the candidates of that party. It does not cast a vote on referenda or on judges running for retention.

To vote a split ticket, vote individually for each candidate.

To write in a candidate not on the ballot, don't punch the hole by the party name and don't punch vote for another candidate for that office. On the inside flap of the ballot envelope is a space marked "THIS SPACE PROVIDED FOR WRITE IN VOTES." Write the title of the office. Draw a box under the title and place an X in the box. Write the candidate's name next to the box.

Time off for voting. Under Illinois law an employer must give an employee time off for voting but is not obliged to pay for the time. The employee must arrange a convenient time in advance.

Physically handicapped voters who can get to the polls may be assisted by a friend or relative, or by two election judges (one from each party). The judges must fill out forms, and the voter must take an oath. Voters who cannot get to the polls can vote absentee by mail but must fill out forms and get medical affidavits. Nursing home residents may vote absentee at their nursing homes.

Source: Excerpts from voter information published by Citizens Information Service of Illinois

4   What You Pay: Financing Local Government

Local government finances are subject to the state constitution and laws. Among the sources of revenue the state permits for local governments are property taxes, sales taxes, utility taxes, user fees, fines, licenses, permits, franchises, sales and leases of property, state and federal grants, and interest on short-term investment of cash. Money can also be borrowed, through the sale of bonds; these may be general obligation bonds (interest and principal to be paid by taxes), revenue bonds (interest and principal to be paid by income from the facility built or bought with the bond funds), or tax anticipation warrants (see below).

PROPERTY TAXES

Property taxes have traditionally been the chief support of local governments, and for some local governmental bodies they are the only source of revenue. Because real estate taxes are paid in lump sums twice a year, they are often the most painful and controversial.

The amount of property tax paid by an owner of real estate depends on the equalized assessment of the property and the tax rates for the various local governments within which the property is located.

Truth In Taxation Act. State legislation requires that a public hearing must be held if a local government appropriation requires an increase of 5% or more in its property tax levy, exclusive of debt service levies, election fund costs, and the permanent road fund levy of road districts. Public notice must be given, and public testimony may be given.

ASSESSMENT

The value of a piece of property for tax purposes is called its "assessed valuation." The assessed valuation is not the actual market value, the amount for which that property or ones similar to it might be sold, but an amount set by law as a proportion of its market value. Fair market value for a piece of property is established by using information on the prices paid for similar properties sold in the area. The amount of income the property can be expected to produce and the cost of replacement are also taken into consideration. State law sets one-third of the fair market value as the ratio for assessed valuation, except for the classification system used in Cook County.

Property values change, of course, and state law requires that each property be reassessed every four years. Cook County is divided into four sections, so that property in one of the four sections is reassessed each year, but any one property is routinely reassessed only once in four years. Since 1986 Chicago has had two sections: the west and south parts of the city were reassessed in 1987; the north and northwest will be reassessed in 1988. Suburban north and northwest sections will be reassessed in 1989, and south and southwest sections in 1990. The change in assessment districts is being evaluated, and further changes may be made, possibly leading to reassessments every two years.

HOW TO APPEAL PROPERTY TAX ASSESSMENTS. When you receive your property reassessment notice, you may want to appeal it if you feel your property has been assessed too high, or if it has been placed in the wrong classification (see below). Taxpayer assistance is available from the assessor's office, the Board of (Tax) Appeals, suburban township assessors, and the Chicago Taxpayer Advocate Program.

1. Within 20 days of the mailing date of the notice, you may file an appeal with the assessor on forms provided at that office. Guidelines and timetables for filing complaints are available through the Assessor's Taxpayer's Assistance Department at the County Building *(443 7550)* or at any of three suburban branch offices. You will receive the assessor's decision by mail, and if you are not satisfied with the result, you may file an appeal with the Board of (Tax) Appeals.

2. After the period for filing an appeal with the assessor has passed, you can file a complaint with the Board of (Tax) Appeals. To do so, you must file a complaint before the deadline set by that board; forms, guidelines, and timetables are available at its office (118 N. Clark St., Chicago, *phone 443 5542*). The Board will notify you of a hearing date when you can present evidence to explain why you think your property is overassessed. The Board's decision will be returned by mail.

3. You may make a further appeal to the Circuit Court. You must, however, pay the taxes in full and file a standard letter of protest with the second installment for the year you are protesting.

Tax Bills. Total real estate tax revenues for a taxing district rise as a result of increased levies (the dollar amounts of property tax revenue passed by governmental ordinance and submitted to the county clerk). The tax bill of an individual property owner depends on the assessed valuation of the property (increases may be due to inflation or to increased property values in the neighborhood), the classification of the property, the multiplier, or an increase in tax rates.

Classification. Unlike all other Illinois counties, which use a one-third assessment ratio for all properties, the following assessment ratios (percentages of fair market values) are in effect in Cook County:

1.	Unimproved land	22%
2.	Single-family homes, co-ops, condominiums, 6-unit or less apartment buildings	16%
3.	Over-6-unit apartment buildings	33%
4.	Not-for-profit	30%
5a.	Commercial, 1987	39%
	1988	38.5%
	1989	38%
5b.	Industrial, 1987	38%
	1988	37%
	1989	36%
6.	Industrial, with tax incentive, 8 years	16%
	next 4 years	30%
7.	Commercial, with tax incentive, 8 years	16%
	next 4 years	30%
8.	Commercial and Industrial in special incentive area	16%
9.	Multi-family building rehabilitation incentive	16%

Equalization. The total assessed valuation of real estate in each county must be one-third of the total market value of all property. Where taxing bodies (such as municipal, school, library, and park districts) cross county lines, variations in assessment levels may lead to inequities for taxpayers who live within the same taxing jurisdiction but within different counties. In addition, bonded indebtedness limitations set by the state are formulated as percentages of assessed valuation, and state aid to school districts is based on the equalized assessed valuation (EAV) of the district. For these reasons, equalization is by law part of the process of arriving at the final valuation for property taxes.

On a real estate tax bill, the assessed valuation (the assessment made by the county assessor) is listed. This is followed by the state equalization factor, commonly called the "multiplier," an amount determined annually by the state Department of Revenue. The multiplier for Cook County for 1987 taxes (paid in 1988), was 1.8916; this means that the department judged that the assessed valuation of real estate in Cook County should be 1.8916 times the total assessments made by the Cook County assessor in order to bring the aggregate county assessed value up to the legally required one-third. On the tax bill the state equalization factor is followed by the equalized valuation.

Tax rates. Next, the tax rates are figured. Each separate taxing body (as many as 8 or 9 in Chicago, and as many as 15 in some suburbs) determines the amount of money it requires from property taxes. State law sets tax rate limitations for some local government funds, as for school districts (see chapter 2). The tax levy ordinance passed by each governing body is submitted to the county clerk, who calculates (extends) the tax rates per $100 of equalized assessed valuation that will provide the amount of money to meet each body's tax levy. The tax rate for each body is then multiplied by the equalized assessed valuation of the property (minus any exemptions) of each taxpayer, to show the amount of taxes due to each governmental body. All of these are added to arrive at the total amount of real estate property tax the taxpayer owes. Exemptions reduce property taxes for certain categories of taxpayers.

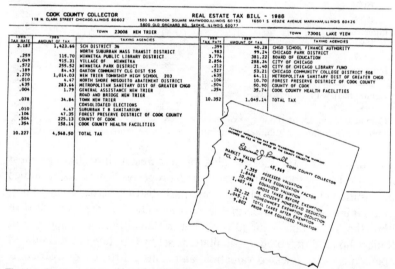

Fig. 4. 1. Portions of suburban and Chicago tax bills, showing tax rates, taxing agencies, and amount of tax for each agency and fund.

Source: Cook County Collector

RESIDENTIAL EXEMPTIONS. There are exemptions for homeowners and for certain property improvements, and an additional reimbursement made by the state to low-income property taxpayers:

The Homeowner Exemption applies to owner-occupied residences which are single-family homes, co-ops, condominiums, or apartment buildings. This exemption is provided by state law and was intended to protect against inflation; it eliminates from taxation any increase of up to

$3,500 in equalized assessed valuation (EAV) over what the EAV was for that property in 1977. The assessor's office sends an application every year to the tax bill mailing address of each of these properties, but not to senior citizens who are registered for the senior citizen homestead exemption (they automatically qualify for the Homestead Exemption).

The Senior Citizen Exemption applies to senior citizens (65 years old during the tax year) who own the property and use it as a principal residence, or who have a lease of a single-family residence if the lease makes them responsible for the taxes. This exemption is also provided for in state law and eliminates from taxation $2,000 of the EAV. To apply, a senior citizen must submit to the assessor's office proof of age and of property ownership and a copy of a recent tax bill.

The Circuit Breaker is a direct state payment of up to $700 a year. It applies to homeowners and renters who are senior citizens or disabled, with household incomes under $14,000 a year. The amount of the grant depends on the household income and the amount of property tax paid. For example, an applicant with a $10,000 household income and a $650 tax bill would receive a grant of $250. Renters are eligible; the real estate tax is considered to be 30% of the rent paid. Tables for figuring the amounts payable and application forms are available from the office of the county treasurer and are filed with the state Department of Revenue.

The Circuit Breaker II is an additional flat grant of $80 for those who qualify for the Circuit Breaker; no further application is required. Also eligible for this grant are persons who live in tax-free housing or pay no property taxes directly or indirectly and are therefore not entitled to the Circuit Breaker. Applications may be filed at any time and are also available from the county treasurer's office.

The Pharmaceutical Assistance Program permits Circuit Breaker II recipients to exchange the $80 grant for a card entitling them to receive free heart, blood pressure, arthritis, or diabetes medication.

The Senior Citizen Real Estate Tax Deferral Program allows senior citizens who are qualified for the Circuit Breaker to defer all or part of their property taxes on their personal residence. It is a form of loan with a 6% interest rate; the loan need not be repaid until the property is sold or the taxpayer dies. It may be extended for the life of the surviving spouse. Applications are available from the office of the county treasurer.

The Home Improvement Exemption provides tax relief to homeowners who spend up to $30,000 for home improvements. When the homeowner applies for a building permit to make improvements, a building inspection is made. A homeowner who meets the standards qualifies for deferral of increased assessment due to the improvement for four years. This exemption is applied automatically by the county assessor.

Homeowners Exemptions for Disabled Veterans are available to veterans who have successfully applied through the Illinois Department of Veterans' Affairs for federally funded purchase or construction of specially adapted housing. This exemption can reduce assessed valuation by as much as $30,000. Application is made to the state Department of Veterans Affairs.

Rehabilitation of Registered Historic Structures entitles the property owner to an eight-year property assessment freeze, provided that the building is a single-family, owner-occupied residence and at least 25% of the property's market value is spent on rehabilitation. Application for this tax reduction is made to the state Historic Preservation Agency.

Rehabilitation of Multifamily Units is a tax-incentive program which applies to buildings with seven or more units of rental housing, provided they are in census tracts where at least 51% of the residents have low or moderate incomes and provided that the owner invests at least $5.00 per square foot toward rehabilitation. The program entitles the owner to an assessment of 16% of market value for eight years; at least half of the rentals for the eight-year-period must not exceed 80% of the fair market rent set by the U.S. Department of Housing and Urban Development.

NONPROFIT GROUPS AND GOVERNMENTAL BODIES. Property owned by charitable, educational, and religious groups is exempt from property taxation, if the property is used for the tax-exempt purposes of the owner. Property owned by federal, state, and some local governmental bodies is exempt; for other local governments, both ownership and use for a governmental purpose is required.

COMMERCIAL AND INDUSTRIAL TAX REDUCTIONS. Cook County has created classifications through which property taxes on new commercial or industrial construction or substantial rehabilitation can be abated for up to 12 years (see 6, 7, 8 and 9 in Classification, above). Applications for these abatements are made to the county assessor and may also require approval by municipal ordinance.

Tax Increment Financing. Bonds are sold to finance the costs of public improvements made in order to bring developers into blighted commercial and industrial areas. The funds may also be used to provide financial assistance to such developers. When the land is developed, the increase in property taxes due to the development is set aside to pay for the public improvements. Until the bonds are paid off, only the taxes based on the original assessed valuation are paid to the taxing bodies. Additional sales taxes attributable to the development may also be used to retire the bonds.

SPECIAL SERVICE AREAS. Counties and municipalities may establish special service areas and levy additional property taxes within such areas to provide additional services. Before a special service area is established, persons whose property is to be taxed must be notified, and a public hearing must be held. The proposal may be rejected by a petition signed by 51% of the registered voters and 51% of the property owners within the proposed district. If the proposal is accepted, improvements are funded by a bond issue repaid by taxes paid by property owners in the district. In the case of the Home Equity Program in Chicago (see chapter 5), taxes on residential property support the Guarantee Fund which provides for payment of any difference between fair market value and sale price of residences of program members. Taxes for these purposes are income-tax deductible to the owner, since they are part of the property tax bill.

SPECIAL ASSESSMENTS. Many local improvements such as streets, sewers, street lighting, and sidewalks may be financed through special assessments. These are paid for by the property owners of the area served, but not by property taxes and are not tax deductible; they are considered an addition to capital.

DELINQUENT TAXES

Tax bills not paid by the penalty date accrue interest at 1.5% per month. A listing of properties on which taxes are delinquent must be published (listed by permanent real estate index number).

Tax Sales. Taxes (not the property) that remain delinquent are sold at an annual auction. Purchasers of the delinquent taxes pay the taxes to the county treasurer. The law gives most property owners two years to redeem their taxes. (For residential structures of six units or less, at least one of which is owner-occupied, the redemption period is two and a half years. For certain property sold at a scavenger sale, the redemption period is six months.)

A series of notices must be sent to the delinquent taxpayer. When the court determines that all procedures have been complied with and redemption has not been made, the real property is transferred to the purchaser of the taxes. If there has been no purchase of the taxes, and the property remains delinquent after five years, these delinquent properties are offered for sale. Under the Scavenger Act, bids may be accepted for less than all taxes due, in order to bring the property back onto the tax rolls.

The 1970 constitution prescribes that the right of redemption from all sales of real estate for nonpayment of taxes shall exist in favor of the owners and that real property shall not be sold without judicial proceedings.

TAXES COLLECTED FOR LOCAL GOVERNMENTS BY THE STATE

The state Department of Revenue collects nine taxes which are distributed to local governments, less collection fees charged by the state. Collection by the state permits the taxes to be collected at a lower cost per dollar collected than would be incurred by local collection.

Corporate Personal Property Replacement Tax (CPPRT). Under the 1870 Illinois constitution a personal property tax was assessed as a part of a general property tax. A 1969 referendum and subsequent court decisions abolished all personal property taxes on individuals and unincorporated businesses except for those held in partnership or trust. The 1970 constitution required that by January 1, 1979 the personal property tax on corporations had to be abolished and replaced by other statewide taxes.

Under court order, the state legislature enacted a law effective in July 1979 for statewide taxes to replace the tax which had been levied on corporate personal property. The tax was replaced at the rate at which it had previously been actually collected, which in Cook County was at about 40% of the taxes billed. The tax is added to the income tax as an additional tax of 2.5% of taxable income of corporations, 1.5% of the income of partnerships, trusts, and subchapter S corporations, and 0.8% of the invested capital of public utilities.

The proceeds from the tax go into the personal property replacement tax fund of the state and are paid eight times a year to local taxing districts. In 1987 the state distributed $335,260,000 to Cook County. The Cook County share was then distributed to the taxing districts in the county on the basis of the share each received of personal property tax collection for the 1976 tax year. (Distributions within other counties are based on the 1977 tax year.) By state law, money from this source must first be used for bond redemption and pension funds.

Sales Tax. On many purchases in Cook County, you pay seven or eight cents in sales tax on each dollar; if your purchase is food or drugs you pay two cents. Sales taxes support the state, the municipality or county, and the Regional Transportation Authority.

The sales tax in Illinois is called the Retailers' Occupation Tax (ROT). It is a tax on the gross receipts of sales of tangible personal property (whatever things you buy), a tax on tangible property involved in the sale of services (i.e., you should be charged a sales tax for the paint applied to your wall but not for the work of applying it), and a use tax on tangible personal property titled or registered in the metropolitan region but purchased outside the state (for instance, the car you bought in another state). In September, 1990 a use tax will be imposed on the purchaser of any tangible personal property (registered or not) used in Illinois but purchased outside of the state.

Of the sales tax you pay on each dollar, five cents goes to support the state itself; this tax is not imposed on food and drugs. One cent is collected by the state and returned to municipalities (Municipal Retailers Occupation Tax, MROT); this tax includes food and drugs. If you make a purchase in an unincorporated area, instead of the municipal tax you pay one cent for the County Retailers' Occupation Tax, which goes to the county government.

Another cent of your sales tax goes to support the Regional Transportation Authority; this Mass Transit District Tax also includes food and drugs. In 1990 this tax will be reduced to 0.75%. (The sales tax for residents of the area served by the RTA outside of Cook County is 0.25%. This tax also includes food and drugs.)

Home rule municipalities may charge an additional sales tax (MROT); the city of Chicago imposes an additional one cent. This tax is collected by the city until 1990, when the city council will decide whether to turn over collection to the state. It is not charged on food and drugs.

The Municipal Hotel Tax. A tax is collected by the state for the city of Chicago, at the rate of 1% on gross hotel receipts; it is earmarked for promoting tourism. The state charges a 4% collection fee. The city itself charges and collects an additional 3% tax, which goes into the corporate fund. Since March 1988 a further 2% tax has been levied by the Illinois Sports Facilities Authority.

Automobile Rental Tax. Counties and municipalities impose a 1% tax on the rental of automobiles; it is a tax collected by the state on the occupation of leasing automobiles. Taxes collected within Chicago go to the city, and taxes collected in unincorporated areas of Cook County go to the county. (The state itself imposes an additional 5% tax.)

Motor Fuel Tax. The state imposes a 13 cents per gallon motor fuel tax which is divided among state and local governments according to a complex formula set by law. The tax is levied on the privilege of operating motor vehicles on public highways and recreational watercraft on public waterways. An additional tax of 2.5 cents per gallon on diesel fuel is also collected. These taxes are paid by distributors and suppliers, who collect the tax from their customers. The state refunds taxes on fuel used for operation of farm machinery and other off-highway uses. The tax is collected by the state Department of Revenue but distributed by the

Department of Transportation to Cook County and municipalities in the
county. Part of the county receipts are redistributed to road districts.
(Cook County collects an additional 4 cents per gallon, Chicago 5 cents per
gallon, and Oak Park, Rosemont, and Stone Park 1 cent. A tax on leaded
gas imposed by the city of Chicago was repealed in 1987.)

State Income Tax. Illinois has a flat-rate income tax based on federal
adjusted gross taxable income of individuals and taxable income of
corporations. It is 2.5% for individuals and 4% for corporations.
One-twelfth of the amount collected is distributed by the state to
municipalities and counties on the basis of population.

FEDERAL INHERITANCE TAX

An Inheritance Tax Distributive Fund was set up as part of the federal
Estate Tax, and 6% of this is distributed to the county of residence of the
decedent. In 1987 Cook County received $2,778,734 from this source.

TAXES COLLECTED BY COOK COUNTY

Tax on Retail Sale of New Motor Vehicles. A flat tax on the retail sale of
categories of new motor vehicles is collected by the county, as follows:
two-wheeled vehicles, $7.50; three-wheeled, $11.25; four-wheeled, $15.00;
special mobile equipment, $18.75; truck, truck tractor, trailer, $22.50.

Cook County Wheel Tax (Unincorporated Areas). In unincorporated areas
the county collects a wheel tax, a license fee which corresponds to the
vehicle tax funds collected by municipalities through the sale of city vehicle
stickers or plates. The fee is waived for the physically handicapped,
disabled veterans, church and school buses, and municipally owned
vehicles. As of May 1988, the fees are as follows: senior citizens $1; privately
owned school buses, motor bicycles, or motor tricycles, $5; passenger autos,
recreational vehicles, ambulances, and hearses, $10; commercial trailers,
$50; and trucks and buses, $25 to $95, depending on weight.

Cook County Gasoline Tax. The Cook County tax on the retail sale of
gasoline is a tax of four cents per gallon paid throughout the county.
Gasoline distributors or suppliers must register with the county and make
monthly reports of sales and remittances of the tax.

Alcoholic Beverage Tax. The Cook County tax on the retail sale of alcoholic
beverages is to be paid by the purchaser and is not considered a tax on the
occupation of beverage dealer (thus separating the tax from the Retailers
Occupation Tax). The tax is 6 cents per gallon on beer, 16 cents per gallon
on wines containing 14% or less alcohol, 30 cents per gallon on wines
containing more than 14% alcohol, and $1.00 per gallon for alcohol and
spirits. (Chicago also collects a liquor tax; see below.)

Cigarette Tax. A tax on the retail sale of cigarettes at the rate of 4 mills per cigarette (8 cents per pack of 20 cigarettes) is collected throughout the county. The tax is paid through purchase of tax stamps, except in the city of Chicago, where the city collects the county tax along with its own cigarette tax and remits the county tax to the county.

MUNICIPAL TAXES

Utility tax. Municipalities may tax up to 5% of the gross receipts from electric, natural gas, telephone, and water businesses. This tax generally appears as a separate item on utility bills. A home rule unit is bound by these limits unless it enacted higher rates before October 1, 1981. State law provides that cities with populations of over 500,000 (Chicago) may impose a tax of up to 8% of the gross receipts from natural gas distribution businesses, and Chicago does so.

Motor Vehicle License Tax. Municipalities may charge an annual motor vehicle license tax in addition to the state charge for license plates. A city sticker indicates payment; the charge in Chicago is $50 per car.

Liquor and Cigarette Taxes. Municipalities may tax liquor and cigarettes. In Chicago the tax rate on liquor is 12 cents per gallon on beer, 15 cents per gallon on wine, and 50 cents per gallon on alcohol and spirits. The Chicago municipal cigarette tax is imposed on wholesalers at the rate of 15 cents a pack.

Amusement Tax. A license tax is imposed at the rate of 4% on the gross receipts from admission fees to all amusements within Chicago except automatic amusement machines.

Employer's Expense Tax (Head Tax). Chicago imposes a tax, often called the Head Tax, on employers of 15 or more persons, at the rate of $5.00 per employee per month.

Vehicle Fuel Tax. In 1986 Chicago imposed a 5 cents per gallon tax on gas, including aircraft fuel; the tax was contested in the courts but was upheld by the state Supreme Court in 1987.

Other Taxes. Other municipal taxes imposed by Chicago include a real estate transaction tax ($7.50 per $1,000) and a parking tax applicable to parking lots and garages. A boat mooring tax applicable to pleasure boats moored in Chicago Park District harbors was repealed in 1988.

OTHER LOCAL SOURCES OF REVENUE

Counties and municipalities have other sources of revenue in addition to taxes; these include fines, permit fees, licenses, and special assessments.

Fines. Municipalities within incorporated areas and counties within their unincorporated areas may impose fines for violating local ordinances. These fines are collected by the appropriate court clerk and transmitted to the municipalities. In addition, if violators of state traffic laws are arrested and prosecuted by local enforcement authorities, the fines that are imposed go to the local jurisdiction.

Earned Income. Income comes to local governments through the sale of goods and services. This category includes transportation fares, hospital charges, sale of water and charges for use of sewers, rentals of property by the Board of Education and the Sanitary District, landing fees, space rental concessions at airports and in parks, tuition fees, and parking fees for municipal garages and lots. It also includes interest on investments and sales of salvage materials.

Municipalities may charge permit fees, including building permit and inspection fees, or fees for special uses of public streets. Counties may charge fees for their services (for birth and death certificates, for instance). By law, fees must bear a relation to the cost of the government service.

Enterprise Fund Projects. Activities which generate revenues and are expected to be self-supporting from fees charged to users are called enterprise fund projects. Examples are water and sewer services, airports, and tollways. Revenue bonds usually paid the original costs.

Licenses. License fees must be commensurate with the cost of regulation and may not be imposed as a revenue source. Municipalities may license for regulation activities such as ambulance services, amusements, animal care, bakeries, barber shops, dry cleaning establishments, liquor stores, restaurants where liquor is served, and so forth, and may impose a license fee. In unincorporated areas counties may license house trailers, house cars or tents, lodgings for transients, garbage disposal, ambulances, dogs, the sale of liquor, and businesses that provide recreation or entertainment.

Federal and State Grants. Local governments receive grants from the federal and state governments for general purposes (block grants) and for specific purposes (categorical grants). Federal grants to local governments, generally referred to by their initials, include Community Development Block Grants (CDBG), Urban Development Action Grants (UDAG), Housing Development Action Grants (HODAG, eliminated in 1987-88)), Social Services Block Grants (SSBG), and Community Services

Block Grants (CSBG). Most categorical grants are spent on health and human services, education, urban development, and infrastructure improvements such as roads, bridges, transportation improvements, and sewers.

Tax Anticipation Warrants. During the depression, property taxes were deferred for a year. This is why real estate property tax bills paid in 1988 are for the calendar year 1987. Because every local government which depends on property taxes is always a year behind in collections, tax anticipation warrants (or daily tender notes) may be issued by any unit of local government or school district for up to 85% of the taxes levied for a specific purpose for the year during which the notes are issued. The interest costs for the city of Chicago for tax anticipation warrants in 1986 was $9,392,831.

Revenue Bonds. Bonds whose principal and interest are paid from revenues earned by the facility purchased or built with the bonds are called revenue bonds. State law specifies what facilities may be financed by revenue bonds. In some cases a referendum is required before they may be issued; in others, a referendum must be held if a certain percentage of the voters in a district petition for a referendum.

Revenue bonds carry a higher rate of interest than general obligation bonds because they are backed by the earning power of the facility rather than by the taxes of an issuing governmental body. Revenue bonds do not create a local government debt limited by Illinois law, so there is no fixed limit on the amount of revenue bond debt a local government may incur. Their issuance is limited by the willingness of investors to buy them.

General Obligation Bonds. General Obligation (GO) bonds are usually issued to pay for major capital improvements and are secured by the full faith and credit of the issuing body. Usually this means levying additional property taxes to pay principal and interest. The amount of interest that must be paid is affected by the bond rating made by agencies such as Standard and Poor and Moody's Investment Service; the higher the rating, the better the investment is considered and the lower the interest required to persuade investors to buy the bonds.

Home rule municipalities and counties may issue general obligation bonds without referendum. Non-home-rule governmental bodies must submit the issue to a referendum, the ballot for which must indicate the purpose for which the bonds are being issued. A majority vote is needed for approval.

BUDGETS

Local governments supported by local taxes must pass annual budgets, must make them public at least 30 days before their adoption, and must hold public hearings on them. Budget procedures, fiscal years, budget timetables, and opportunities for public review vary; they are described in this book under the description of the local government. However, the fiscal years and procedures for some sources of funds, such as bond funds and federal and state grants, may not coincide with the development of local annual budgets, and these funds may not be included in those budgets. In order to find out whether a particular service is planned and how it will be paid for, it may be necessary to review funding applications and Capital Improvement Programs as well as annual budgets.

The municipal and county budgets which attract most attention are the Corporate Fund budgets, but other funds may support services and capital improvements. In addition to its Corporate Fund budget, Chicago has 20 funds with separate budgets (all published in the same budget document). The Cook County annual appropriation ordinance lists 15 funds in addition to its Corporate Fund; one of the largest is that which supports the hospitals and health services. There are two kinds of budget documents providing the same information broken down in different ways for different purposes:

Line-Item Budgets. Line-item budgets are required by state law. They are detailed item-by-item listings of every expenditure in such categories as personal services (a complete listing of positions and salaries), contractual services, travel, commodities (supplies, etc.), equipment, and permanent improvements. From a line-item budget, for instance, one can find out how many foresters the city plans to employ at what levels of pay.

Program Performance Budgets. Program performance budgets are not required by state law and are not issued by all governmental bodies. The city of Chicago and the Chicago Board of Education are among those bodies who do issue performance budgets listing expenditures by programs each department is to accomplish. Output is measured by work performed, services provided, or improvements made. From its program budget, one can find out how many trees the city expects to plant during the year.

FISCAL ORDINANCES

Budgets are passed and property taxes levied through the passage of ordinances. Municipalities must prepare three documents: the appropriation ordinance, the tax levy ordinance, and the expenditure or voucher ordinance. State law requires that the appropriation and expenditure ordinances be published in local newspapers.

Appropriation Ordinance. The appropriation ordinance outlines the expenditures from all funds for the current fiscal year and must be adopted by the governing body before the close of the first quarter of the fiscal year. The governing body may set an earlier date for itself.

Tax Levy Ordinance. The ordinance which specifies those items in the appropriations ordinance which are to be financed by the property tax is the tax levy ordinance. It must be adopted and filed with the county clerk before the second Tuesday in September.

Audit. Within six months after the end of the fiscal year, the municipality must provide for an annual audit of all funds. The audit is performed by an auditor of the municipality's choice, is filed with the state comptroller, and is on file for public inspection at the office of the county clerk.

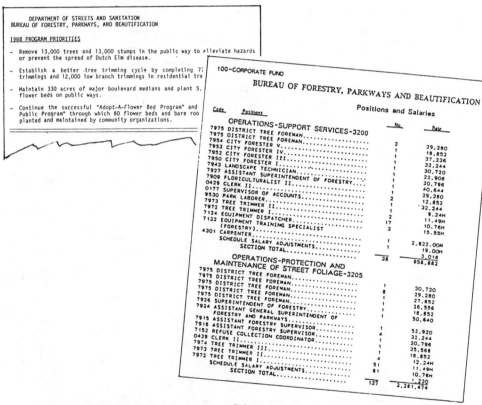

Fig. 4. 2. Example of Budget Documents: Chicago
Chicago issues a program performance budget as well as the line-item budget required by state law. At the top is an excerpt from the 1988 Program and Budget Summary for the section on the Bureau of Forestry, showing activities planned for 1988. Below is an excerpt from the 1988 Annual Appropriation Ordinance showing part of the personnel section of the Forestry Department's line-item budget, the people needed to carry out the program.

Source: City of Chicago Office of Managment and Budget

COOK COUNTY 1988 BUDGET

PROGRAM - PROTECTION OF HEALTH   NO. 11

FUND - HOSPITAL   NO. 0003   PROGRAM - COOK COUNTY HOSPITAL
ELEMENT   NO. 897

897-16 Emergency Services

This activity provides the general administration of emergency treatment to the ill and injured on an unscheduled basis.

The Sub-Activities within this activity are:

01 On Duty Administrators

02 Main

WORK UNIT MEASUREMENT: NUMBER OF PATIENTS VISITS

DESCRIPTION OF WORK UNIT: Each Patient Visit is counted as one work unit.

COOK COUNTY 1988 BUDGET   PERFORMANCE INDICATORS

PROGRAM - PROTECTION OF HEALTH   NO. 11

FUND - HOSPITAL   NO. 0003   PROGRAM - COOK COUNTY HOSPITAL
ELEMENT   NO. 897

ACTIVITY SUB-ACTIVITY	WORK UNITS			TOTAL OPERATING COSTS			COST PER UNIT		
	1988 EST	1987 BUDGET	1987 ACTUAL	1988 EST	1987 BUDGET	1987 ACTUAL	1988 EST	1987 BUDGET	1987 ACTUAL
897-16 EMERGENCY SERVICES									
• 02 MAIN									
NUMBER OF PATIENT VISITS	124,350	124,700	124,324	795,277	965,964	1456,047	6.39	7.74	11.71
NUMBER OF POSITIONS	46	51	51						
• 03 PEDIATRICS									
NUMBER OF PATIENT VISITS	68,277	70,700	68,177	196,411	184,955	247,960	2.87	2.61	3.63
NUMBER OF POSITIONS	10	10	10						
• 04 AMBULATORY SCREENING CLINIC									
NUMBER OF PATIENT VISITS	68,277	75,000	68,183	100,813	101,486	132,646	1.47	1.35	1.94
NUMBER OF POSITIONS	7	7	7						

COOK COUNTY 1988 BUDGET   PERSONAL SERVICES-   SUMMARY OF POSITIONS

PROGRAM - PROTECTION OF HEALTH   NO. 11

FUND - HOSPITAL   NO. 0003   PROGRAM - COOK COUNTY HOSPITAL
ELEMENT   NO. 897

JOB CODE	TITLE	GRADE	RANGE	1987 APPROPRIATION		1988 REQUEST		PRESIDENT'S RECOMMENDATION	
				AUTH POS.	TOTAL SALARIES	POS. REQ.	TOTAL SALARIES	POS.	TOTAL SALARIES
	16 EMERGENCY SERVICES								
	01 ON DUTY ADMINISTRATORS								
0050	ADMINISTRATIVE ASSISTANT IV	18	$ 2095- 2678		$	5	$ 150,012	5	$ 150,012
	02 MAIN								
0050	ADMINISTRATIVE ASSISTANT IV	18	$ 2095- 2678	5	$ 154,020		$		$
0912	ADMINISTRATIVE AIDE	CC	1178- 1282	1	15,384	1	15,384	1	15,384
0907	CLERK V	11	1272- 1633	3	57,660	3	58,596	3	58,596
0905	CLERK III	7	1000- 1297	12	181,872	12	178,608	12	178,608
0910	CLERK (5 MONTHS)	5	908- 1177	1	4,800	1	5,505	1	5,505
0910	CLERK	5	908- 1177	23	250,608	23	269,892	23	269,892
1688	PATIENT SERVICE DIRECTOR	20	2525- 3212	1	38,364	1	38,544	1	38,544
0911	SENIOR CLERK	9	1101- 1426	2	34,224	2	34,224	2	34,224
0273	STATISTICIAN AND INFORMATION TECHNICIAN II	13	1465- 1880	1	22,560	1	22,560	1	22,560
0935	STENOGRAPHER IV	11	1272- 1633	1	17,580	1	18,468	1	18,468
0910	CLERK	5	908- 1177	1	10,188	1	10,896	1	10,896
	TOTAL			51	$ 787,260	46	$ 652,677	46	$ 652,677

Fig. 4. 3. Example of Budget Documents: Cook County
The county budgets include performance measure and line-item listings in the same document, though in different sections. For instance, in the 1988 Health Program budget for emergency services in Cook County Hospital, Work Unit Measurements (number of patient visits) are defined in the section shown at top. Performance Indicators show the number of patient visits, the number of positions needed to serve the patients, the costs to serve those patients, and the cost per patient visit; the 1987 budget estimates and actual numbers are also given. In a third section, shown at the bottom, are the line-item appropriations for each position.

Source: Cook County Department of Budget and Managment Services.

5   Chicago Governments: The City

The city government of Chicago provides many of the local government services that Chicago residents receive, but not all of them. Within the city independent agencies are responsible for schools, libraries, parks, transportation, public housing, elections, and a number of other special services. This chapter will describe the government of the city itself, and chapter 6 will describe the independent agencies.

CITY OF CHICAGO

The government of the city of Chicago is divided into executive and legislative branches. Unlike the federal and state governments, it has no judicial branch; the Municipal Court is part of the state court system. The mayor is the chief executive officer, and the city council, elected from 50 wards, is the legislative body. Chicago voters also elect the city clerk and city treasurer.

The city's powers to govern are derived from the state constitution and the state Cities and Villages Act. Under the 1970 constitution, the city has home rule powers. The state, however, limits the city's bonding power and forbids it to enact a tax based on income, or to license for revenue, or to provide for punishment of a felony. The state can preempt the city's power to license occupations and has done so, notably in licensing of real estate activities.

The city has approximately 40,000 employees (as opposed to budgeted positions, since there are always vacancies) and spends more than 2.6 billion dollars a year.

MAYOR
City Hall, 121 N. La Salle St., Chicago 60602; *phone 744 4000*

The mayor is the chief executive officer of the city, responsible for directing the city's departments and for appointing the heads of the departments with the advice and consent of the city council, as well as most members of the

24 boards and commissions funded by the city's corporate budget. The city's *Municipal Handbook* states that there are more than 100 city boards, commissions, and advisory groups; some are temporary, and some do not require funding beyond staff assistance from the agencies they advise. Most (but not all) of the members of these boards and commissions are appointed with the advice and consent of the city council. The mayor, with the approval of the council, has the power to appoint the members of the boards of a number of otherwise independent agencies, including the Board of Education, the City Colleges, the Chicago Housing Authority, the Park District, the Public Library, four members of the Chicago Transit Authority, six members of the Chicago Public Building Commission, and four members of the International Port District.

The mayor presides at city council meetings and can vote in the event of a tie. The mayor must approve or veto all ordinances passed by the city council and has the power to veto whole ordinances or parts of appropriation bills. The veto may be overridden by a two-thirds vote of the council.

Election. The mayor is elected for a four-year term. Regular mayoral elections are held on the first Tuesday in April of years preceding a presidential election (1991, 1995). Candidates for mayor run on party ballots and are nominated at primary elections held on the last Tuesday in February. In the event of a vacancy in the office, or in the event the council determines by a three-fifths vote that the mayor is unable to serve, the vice-mayor (elected from among its members by the city council) serves as mayor until the council elects one of its members acting mayor. State law states that if a vacancy occurs with 28 months or more remaining in the term, and at a time 130 days or more before the next general municipal election scheduled under the consolidated election law, the office is filled at that election. As of June 1988, the Chicago Board of Elections was under court order to hold a primary election in February 1989 and a general election in April 1989. The salary of the mayor is $80,000 a year.

Office of the Mayor. The office of the mayor is budgeted for 59 positions in addition to that of the mayor. The executive office of the mayor includes two administrative assistants and three secretaries. The Administrative Section includes the chief operating officer, who is paid $85,000 a year ($5,000 more than the mayor), and 29 other positions. The Office of the Press Secretary has 14 positions, and the Office of Intergovernmental Affairs has 11. (Additional personnel are assigned from time to time from other city departments.) The total 1988 budget for the Office of the Mayor is $3,441,420.

CITY CLERK

121 N. LaSalle St., Chicago 60602; phone 744 6873
Business licenses, *744 6875*
Dog licenses, *744 6875*
Hunting and fishing licenses, *744 3206*
Vehicle sticker license information, *744 6877*

The city clerk is nominated and elected on a party ballot at the same elections as the mayor. If a vacancy occurs in the office of the city clerk, the mayor fills the vacancy with the advice and consent of the city council.

The clerk is record keeper for the city council and supervises the issuing of general and vehicle licenses. The clerk's office also distributes state hunting and fishing licenses. The clerk transmits claims against the city to the city council and publishes proposed ordinances, orders, and resolutions to be presented at each council meeting. The *Journal of Proceedings of the City Council* is published by the clerk's office, and certified copies of official city documents may be obtained from this office. The clerk is official parliamentarian for the council. (As of 1988 the mayor also had a parliamentarian.)

In 1988 the city clerk's office was budgeted for 55 employees for record keeping, research, and general licensing at a cost of $1,776,905 from the corporate fund and for 78 employees for vehicle licensing at a cost of $3,056,289 from the vehicle tax fund. The salary of the clerk in 1988 was $60,000 per year.

CITY TREASURER

City Hall, 121 N. LaSalle St., Chicago 60602; *phone 744 3356*

Like the city clerk, the city treasurer is elected on a party ballot at the same time as the mayor. If a vacancy occurs in the office of treasurer, it is filled by the mayor with the advice and consent of the city council.

The treasurer is a part of the Department of Finance, which is headed by the city comptroller appointed by the mayor. The treasurer acts as bank depositor and custodian of the city funds, serves as ex officio treasurer for the Board of Education, and is a member of four of the five city employees' pension fund boards.

This office receives, pays out, and accounts for all city of Chicago and Board of Education funds. It prepares monthly statements for the city comptroller, Board of Education, and city pension funds by fund or by appropriation; it prepares annual reports for the city council and the Board of Education; and it is responsible for custodial care of securities held by the city, the Board of Education, and city pension and trust funds. It also handles short-term investments for those agencies; such investments earned the city over $110,000,000 in 1987.

In 1988 the treasurer's office was budgeted for 29 employees. The salary of the treasurer was $60,000 per year, and the appropriation for the treasurer's office was $933,717 from the corporate fund.

CITY COUNCIL
City Hall, 121 N. LaSalle St., Chicago 60602; *phone 744 6800*
Aldermen's offices, *744 3081*

The Chicago City Council is composed of 50 aldermen, 1 from each of the city's 50 wards. It is the legislative branch of city government. (The Illinois law creating the office uses only the term "alderman," and a woman member of the city council is addressed as "alderman.")

Each alderman represents about 60,000 people and serves a four-year term. Aldermanic elections are nonpartisan in the sense that the ballots have no party designation, and there is no primary election. Candidates for the office are nominated by petition of the voters in each ward. The regular aldermanic elections take place on the last Tuesday in February in the year preceding a presidential election (1991, 1995), at the same time as the mayoral primary but on a separate ballot. If no candidate receives a majority of the votes cast in the February election, a runoff election between the two highest candidates is held on the first Tuesday in April of the same year, at the time of the mayoral election.

An aldermanic candidate must be a registered voter in the ward in which the candidate seeks election and must have lived in the city for at least one year before the election. No person is eligible for public office who is delinquent in taxes or other debts to the city, or who has been convicted in the Illinois state courts of bribery or misconduct in office. In case of a vacancy in office, if there are fewer than 28 months remaining in the term, the vacancy is filled by the mayor with the advice and consent of the city council. If there are more than 28 months remaining in the term and at least 130 days before the next municipal election scheduled under the consolidated election law, the vacancy is filled at that election. (The decision as to whether this means 1989, when other municipal elections are scheduled, or 1991, the next scheduled Chicago municipal election, may be made by the courts.)

After the mayoral election, the council elects one of its members vice-mayor, to serve as interim mayor in the event of a vacancy in the office of mayor, until the council elects one of its members acting mayor. One alderman is elected president pro tempore by the council and serves as presiding officer in the mayor's absence.

An alderman is sometimes also the ward committeeman, the Democratic or Republican party representative in the ward. This is a separate, unpaid, elective party office.

Powers. The council may exercise municipal legislative powers based on state law and the home rule powers granted by the 1970 Illinois constitution. It enacts the ordinances which govern the city and also has some administrative responsibilities. The council has the power to amend and pass an annual appropriation ordinance which has been prepared by the mayor, to appropriate funds, to authorize borrowing funds, to approve bond issues, to levy taxes (real estate taxes, however, are assessed, collected, and distributed by county officials), to pass building and zoning codes, and to approve mayoral appointees. The council may investigate all matters relating to its legislative powers, such as violations of city ordinances, misuse of city funds, and misconduct of city officers and employees.

Committees. Much of the council's work is done through committees which recommend legislation to the full council. In 1988 there were 28 standing council committees, the largest of which were the finance and budget committees. The council may also create special committees. The chairman, vice-chairman, and membership of the committees are selected by the council as part of adopting rules at the beginning of each four-year term; these selections may be altered during the term. Committees generally have 13 or 14 members, except for the budget committee, which has 36, and the finance committee, which has 35. Council standing committees are the following:

Aging and Disabled
Aviation
Beautification and Recreation
Budget and Government Operations
Buildings
Claims and Liabilities
Committees, Rules, and Ethics
Capital Development
Historical Landmark Preservation
Economic Development
Education
Energy, Environmental Protection, and Public Utilities
Finance
Health
Housing
Human Rights and Consumer Protection
Intergovernmental Relations
Land Acquisition, Disposition and Leases
License
Local Transportation
Municipal Code Revision
Police, Fire, and Municipal Institutions
Ports, Wharves, and Bridges
Special Events and Cultural Affairs
Streets and Alleys
Traffic Control and Safety
Veterans' Affairs
Zoning

Meetings. Committees meet on call of the chairman or on written request of a majority of the committee members. Committee meetings must, by law, be open to the public. Anyone may request permission to testify before a committee, but the decision whether to grant the request is up to the committee, usually acting through the chairman. Notice of all committee meetings is posted on the bulletin board in the anteroom of the council chambers, and written notice is sent to civic groups on request.

The council meets on the second and fourth Wednesdays of each month unless it decides otherwise at the previous meeting; at the end of each meeting the council usually sets the date for the next meeting. The mayor or any three aldermen may call a special meeting. A quorum consists of a majority of council members and the mayor (26 persons). Meetings are usually held at 10 A.M. in the council chambers, on the second floor of City Hall. Meeting dates, which may be any day of the week, may be obtained by calling *744 6800*.

Anyone may visit the council while it is in session, but no one other than an alderman has the right to address the council when it is meeting unless the rules are suspended. There are 244 seats available in a section at the rear of the chamber and a balcony. There is a section of seats for cabinet members and staff on the left and a section for the press on the right. Schools and groups desiring reserved seats for a council meeting should call the Mayor's Office of Inquiry and Information, *744 5000*.

Records. A summary of substantive matters acted upon by the council is prepared after each meeting by the Legislative Reference Bureau and is available at Room 306, City Hall. A copy of an ordinance or a proposed ordinance may be obtained at the city clerk's office, Room 107, City Hall, or from the committee to which it was referred. All action taken by the council is listed in the *Journal of Proceedings of the City Council*. Single copies of the journal are free and available at the city clerk's office.

Finances. An alderman's salary is $40,000 a year, and each alderman is entitled to a secretary with a salary of $25,272, two assistant secretaries with salaries of $21,828 each, a transportation and expense allowance of $5,280, and a contingency fund of $18,000 (often used for expenses of an office in the alderman's ward). The 1988 appropriation for the council was $8,589,899. In addition, each council committee can hire staff as authorized by its appropriation. The budget for council committees in 1988 was a total of $5,632,603 from the corporate, vehicle tax, and special events funds.

Legislative Reference Bureau. The Legislative Reference Bureau is the research staff of the council. Its function is to prepare ordinances and orders on request of aldermen and to publish the *Digest of New Legislation*. In 1988 it had eight employees and a budget of $329,000 from the corporate fund.

CITY DEPARTMENTS

DEPARTMENT ON AGING AND DISABILITY
510 N. Peshtigo Court, Chicago 60611; *phone 744 4016*

In 1956 Chicago established the first municipal agency in the United States related to aging, the Commission for Senior Citizens. In 1974 responsibility for disabled adults (18 and older) was added, and in 1984 the Mayor's Office for Senior Citizens and Handicapped became the Department on Aging and Disability (DAD). It is an Area Agency on Aging for the Illinois Planning Service Area 12 (Chicago) under the federal Older Americans Act of 1965 The department is charged with coordinating city departments' training and technical assistance to ensure the city's compliance with regulations forbidding discrimination against the disabled. It is also in charge of facilities for the elderly and for the disabled. Its programs, open to persons over 60 and disabled persons over 18, include the following:

Information and Referral Center locates services and provides short-term counseling and assistance in filling out forms. *Phone 744 4016; TDD 744 6777.*

Employment Service provides training in job seeking and job placement. *Phone 744 4407.*

Foster Grandparents provides part-time employment working with children with special needs. *Phone 744 3221.*

Golden Diners Club provides low-cost meals. Reservations are required. *Phone 744 4016* for nearest location.

Home-delivered Meals are provided for those unable to prepare their own food; a donation is required.

In-home Services provide help with shopping, cleaning, and meal preparation.

Legal Services offers counseling and legal assistance. *Phone 744 4016.*

Message Relay Service is a service to hearing-impaired residents of all ages; they can dial *744 6777 (TDD)* to relay a message to hearing persons. Hearing persons may also use the service to deliver messages to the hearing impaired.

Nursing Home Ombudsman provides help to nursing home residents or others who have problems with nursing home care. *Phone 744 5957.*

Protective Services include Ombudsman/Elder Abuse Programs to handle complaints of abuse of the elderly, counseling for family care givers, and monitoring of federal, state, and local laws, regulations, and policies affecting the elderly in long-term care facilities. *Phone 744 5957.*

Sewer Charge Exemption assistance is given to seniors over 65 who own their homes and may be entitled to a reduction of the sewer charge included in the city water bill or other city discount programs. *Phone 744 4016.*

Five regional centers provide programs and services, including meals, RTA passes, city college courses, and social activities:

Central/West, 2102 W. Ogden Ave., Chicago 60612; *phone 226 2525; TDD phone 744 0319.*

Northeast (Levy Center), 2019 W. Lawrence Ave., Chicago 60625; *phone 878 3564; TDD phone 744 0320.*

Northwest (Copernicus Center), 3160 N. Milwaukee Ave., Chicago 60618; *phone 744 6681; TDD phone 744 0321.*

Southeast (Atlas Center), 1767 E. 79th St., Chicago 60649; *phone 731 5523; TDD phone 744 0322.*

Southwest, 6117 S. Kedzie Ave., Chicago 60629; *phone 476 8700; TDD phone 744 0323.*

The department is headed by a commissioner appointed by the mayor with the advice and consent of the city council, at an annual salary of $60,000. The 1988 budget showed 205 full-time and 498 part-time employees, and a total budget of $2,203,398 from the city's corporate fund and $20,796,655 from federal and state funds.

COMMISSION ON ANIMAL CARE AND CONTROL
2741 S. Western Ave., Chicago 60608; *phone 650 1400.* Open noon to 7.30 P.M. for adoption or lost pets.

The Commission on Animal Care and Control investigates complaints of animal bites, and it inspects all animal-related businesses in the city. It cooperates with private humane agencies to protect domestic animals from cruel treatment, protects the public from dangerous and stray animals by impoundment, and confines or disposes of stray animals. It operates a housing facility for lost pets and a pet adoption program which includes a fee. It inoculates and neuters all dogs and cats adopted from the agency.

It sells dog licenses issued by the city clerk. Cats are not required to have licenses.

The commission provides publications in English and Spanish on care of pets and a publication listing dog trainers and obedience clubs. For law enforcement personnel, it provides a pamphlet on illegal animal fighting.

The commission consists of 9 unpaid members appointed by the mayor for two-year terms. The staff of 90 employees, all but 2 career service, is headed by an executive director appointed by the mayor with the advice and consent of the city council. The director's salary in 1988 was $46,368 a year. The 1988 budget was $1,817,419 from corporate funds.

DEPARTMENT OF AVIATION

20 N. Clark. St., Chicago 60602; *phone 744 6892*
Aircraft noise complaints (24-hour hotline), *686 2377*
Parking hotline, *686 7525*
O'Hare information, *686 2200*
Midway information, *785 0500*
Meigs Field information, *744 4787*
Visitor tour information, *686 2300*
Travelers Aid, *686 7562*

The Department of Aviation is responsible for planning, design, construction, operation, management, and maintenance of the three airports located in Chicago: Chicago O'Hare International Airport, on the northwest side of Chicago at Wolf Road and Bryn Mawr Avenue; Chicago Midway Airport, on the southwest side at 63rd Street and Cicero Avenue; and Merrill C. Meigs Field, on land leased from the Park District on the lakefront at 15th Street. It provides for maintenance and operation of the airfields, terminal complexes, parking facilities, and access and service roads, and it provides for safety and security.

More than 50 airlines carry 58 million passengers and over 994,000 tons of freight, mail, and express in and out of Chicago's airports each year. O'Hare International Airport ranks as the busiest in the world; it handled more than 57 million passengers in 1987. Meigs Field serves mainly private and corporate general aviation and has a commuter service to the state capital in Springfield.

The department includes six major divisions: Commissioner's Office, Airport Operations and Management, Property Management, Security and Safety, Finance and Administration, and Public Relations. A Noise Abatement Office, located in Terminal 3 at O'Hare Airport, issues an annual report.

The Commissioner of Aviation is appointed by the mayor with the advice and consent of the city council, at a salary in 1988 of $77,000 a year. There are 1,750 employees, hired through the city Department of Personnel. Meigs Field in 1987 was funded by $600,000 from federal funds, and its 1988 corporate fund appropriation was $435,807. O'Hare and Midway Airports are supported entirely by the carriers using the facilities, concessions that have businesses there, and parking fees. Services such as police and fire protection, refuse removal, and road repair are supported by charges paid by airport tenants. The department reported 1985 revenues from the airports of $144,040,000 from O'Hare, $1,345,397 from Midway, and $173,347 from Meigs Field. As of 1987, a development program of $1.6 billion was being carried out at O'Hare, funded by the airline industry.

OFFICE OF BUDGET AND MANAGEMENT
City Hall, 121 N. LaSalle St., Chicago 60602; *phone 744 3340*

The Office of Budget and Management prepares the mayor's annual executive budget for submission to the city council and administers the annual appropriation ordinance. It also prepares an annual capital budget. It reviews city requests for federal and state funds and coordinates allocation of federal Community Development Block Grants (CDBGs) by monitoring and reporting. It also provides an estimate for each department receiving state and federal funds as to what amounts are expected to be spent in the fiscal year. It coordinates public forums on the corporate fund budgets and the CDBG budgets. The office conducts studies and surveys, including ones on management, on salaries and wages, on municipal finance, and on taxation. The Data Center, formerly under this office, became the Department of Management Information Systems in 1988.

The office is headed by the Budget Director, appointed by the mayor at an annual salary of $77,000. The 1988 budget of $1,634,102 provided for 44 employees.

OFFICE OF CABLE COMMUNICATIONS ADMINISTRATION
510 N. Peshtigo Court, Chicago 60611; *phone 744 4052*

The Office of Cable Communications Administration administers the Chicago television cable ordinance, monitors private cable companies' compliance with franchising agreements, and initiates enforcement action. It distributes information about cable television and handles citizen complaints. It also administers two municipal cable television channels.

In 1988 the corporate budget for the office was $783,114. The office had 21 employees. It is headed by the cable administrator, appointed by the mayor, at a salary of $65,000. The administrator also serves as chair of the Chicago Cable Commission.

THE CHICAGO CABLE COMMISSION is responsible for regulation of cable television in the city, upon initiation of enforcement action by the Office of Cable Communications. The cable administrator serves as chair, and four additional members are appointed by the mayor for five-year staggered terms. They receive a stipend of $20,000 a year. Members must live in the city, and at least two of the members must not hold public office.

The commission meets in the Cable Communications Administration office at 9:30 A.M. on the second Tuesday of the month (unless this date falls before the 9th of the month, in which case the meeting is held the following Tuesday). Meetings are open to the public.

CHICAGO ACCESS CORPORATION (Chicago's Community Access Television Network)
322 S. Green St., Chicago 60607; *phone 738 1400*

When the city enacted a cable television ordinance in 1982, the Chicago Access Corporation was designated as an independent, not-for-profit agency to promote community use of cable television for cultural, educational, health, social service, civic, and community purposes. Under their franchise agreement with the city, cable operators provided the corporation with six cable channels and start-up funding for operating costs and equipment. The corporation administers the use of the access channels, and it provides hands-on training to individuals and not-for-profit groups to plan and produce television programs, It also provides use of equipment, including a studio and mobile production van. With a 1988 operating budget of $1,503,830, the corporation is funded by the cable companies, by grants, contributions, and fund-raising activities, and by some fees and membership dues of the Chicago Access Network (CAN). CAN is open to individuals, organizations, and institutions, at fees beginning at $10 for an individual. CAN members elect 15 of the 50-member Board of Directors.

The Board of Directors governs and oversees the work of the corporation; members serve three-year staggered terms and are unpaid. The board itself nominates and elects 35 board members and its own officers, and chooses the chief executive. There are 22 full-time and 7 part-time employees, with additional volunteer staffing.

COMMUNITY DEVELOPMENT ADVISORY COMMITTEE
Department of Planning, City Hall, 121 N. La Salle St., Chicago 60602;
phone 744 3025

Regulations of the U.S. Department of Housing and Urban Development (HUD) require that citizens participate in decisions on the city's Community Development Block Grant program, funded by HUD. The Community Development Advisory Committee (CDAC) reviews and advises on all initial and final proposals for CDBG funding. The CDAC has 45 members, who serve without pay. Requests for nominations are sent to community and citywide organizations each year. The mayor appoints the members for two-year terms which begin at the start of the Community Development Program Year. Appointments do not require city council approval. Vacancies are filled by alternates selected at the time appointments are made. The Department of Planning provides staff for the

CDAC. Meetings are open to the public and are held at the Department of Planning on third Tuesdays of each month at 3:30 P.M. (This date is subject to change when a new committee is appointed.) Much of the CDAC's work is done through subcommittees, usually meeting twice a month; information on times and places is available from the Department of Planning.

CITY COMPTROLLER, DEPARTMENT OF FINANCE
City Hall, 121 N. La Salle St., Chicago 60602; *phone 744 7100*

According to the Municipal Code of Chicago, the city comptroller is the director of the Department of Finance. The comptroller is the city's fiscal agent, supervising all fiscal matters except those under the jurisdiction of the Department of Revenue. The comptroller decides whether expenditures are authorized by an appropriation ordinance, keeps the city's financial records, and is responsible for preparing and publishing a detailed annual audited financial report. Other duties include management of city-owned and city-leased real estate, management of the city's debt, participation in investment of city funds, and adjustment of claims against the city. The comptroller's office authorizes payment of wages and salaries after payrolls are certified by the Department of Personnel. Together with the mayor, the Law Department, and the purchasing agent, the comptroller must approve requisitions involving purchases of more than $10,000. The comptroller authorizes payment of bills on all purchases after deliveries have been checked and approved.

The comptroller is appointed by the mayor with the advice and consent of the city council, at an annual salary of $77,000. In 1988 there were 284 employees budgeted for this office under the corporate fund, at an appropriation of $8,980,383; an additional $2,750,518 was to be reimbursed from federal funds.

DEPARTMENT OF CONSUMER SERVICES
City Hall, 121 N. LaSalle St., Chicago 60602; *phone 744 5092*
  Business complaints, *744 9400*
  Business license assistance, *744 9090, 744 9086, 744 9085.*
  Condominium regulations, *744 8595*
  Energy and environmental protection complaints, *744 7734.*
  Motor vehicle repair complaints, *744 9400*

1000 E. Ohio St., Chicago 60611
  Consumer protection, *744 8538*

510 N. Peshtigo Court, Chicago 60611
  Credit counseling, *744 6426*
  Farmers Market, *744 5092*
  Public Vehicle Operations, *744 6227*

The Department of Consumer Services enforces city ordinances protecting consumers against fraudulent practices in business and advertising, regulates weights and measures, enforces regulations on food and dairy products, and investigates businesses for proper licensure. It licenses and regulates State Street Mall vendors and outdoor restaurants. It enforces the city's condominium ordinances. It tests and licenses (in addition to the required state licenses) public chauffeurs and public passenger vehicles, including taxis, ambulances, liveries, and horse-drawn carriages. It enforces the environmental protection codes for air, water, noise, solid waste, and hazardous materials and distributes air quality information and pollution data.

The Department of Consumer Services also provides services: it sponsors the summer Chicago Farmers Markets at the Daley Center Plaza and in several neighborhoods, and it provides individual and group credit counseling and advisory assistance to those seeking business licenses. It provides workshops on request on any of its services and distributes literature on home improvements, winterization, energy use, and prescription drugs.

The department is headed by a commissioner appointed by the mayor with the advice and consent of the city council at an annual salary of $62,000. There were 163 employees in 1988, and the 1988 budget, from the corporate fund, was $4,411,130.

DEPARTMENT OF CULTURAL AFFAIRS
Executive Offices, 174 W. Randolph St., Chicago 60601; *phone 744 8923*

The Department of Cultural Affairs was created in 1984 to encourage, support, and further the professional and economic development of the arts, entertainment, and culture. The department contains five divisions: the Chicago Office of Fine Arts, the Mayor's Office of Special Events, Cultural Development and Tourism, Finance and Administration, and Communications.

The department is headed by a commissioner, appointed by the mayor, with a salary of $60,000. It has a total of 93 employees, and its funding in 1988 came from four sources: (1) a corporate fund budget of $1,438,927; (2) the Municipal Hotel Operators Occupational Tax fund (which is earmarked for promoting tourism), $5,186,899; (3) Year XIV (1988) Community Development Block Grant funds, $992,290; and (4) miscellaneous support such as foundation grants, special events revenue, and corporate sponsorships. The three programmatic divisions conduct a variety of projects.

The Cultural Development and Tourism Division has responsibility for programs that link the economy of the city and development of the arts. The division gives grants to convention and tourism agencies and promotes tourism. The Office of Film and Entertainment Industries *(744 6415)* provides services to film production, including scouting for locations and obtaining clearances for public and private locations.

The other two program divisions are at different locations:

CHICAGO OFFICE OF FINE ARTS
78 E. Washington, Chicago 60602; *phone 744 6630*
Events Hotline, *346 3278 (F-I-N-E-A-R-T)*

The Chicago Office of Fine Arts offers programs and services designed to increase opportunities for artists and and arts organizations and to increase public involvement in the arts. It cosponsors with the Public Library free programs and exhibits at the Cultural Center. It also presents free exhibits and performances "Under the Picasso" at the Daley Civic Center. "CityArts" is a series of grant programs funding art organizations. The Neighborhood Arts Program provides grants to artists and organizations for workshops, performances, and works of art that benefit the elderly, youth, and the disabled. The Community Arts Assistance Program provides funds for artists and nonprofit arts organizations for projects that promote professional, artistic, and organizational development and that reflect the multicultural communities of the city. Percent for Art is a program, administered in cooperation with the city architect, which commissions or buys public art works. The "Dial-a-Poem" program *(744 3315)* provides recorded readings by local writers.

MAYOR'S OFFICE OF SPECIAL EVENTS
City Hall, Room 703., 121 N. LaSalle St., Chicago 60602; *phone 744 3315.*
Events Hotline, *744 3370*

The Mayor's Office of Special Events promotes tourism in the city by presenting special events. It is responsible for neighborhood festivals and major festivals on the lakefront such as Taste of Chicago and blues, gospel, and jazz festivals. It also handles protocol for the city and manages the "Sharing It" campaign during the holiday season to raise contributions for the needy.

DEPARTMENT OF ECONOMIC DEVELOPMENT
20 N. Clark St., Chicago 60602; commissioner's office, *744 3882*
International business, *744 3883*
Financial assistance, *744 3911*
Research and development, *744 0796*
Capital improvements, *744 1600*
Technical assistance and business service, *744 4163*
Field operations (new businesses), *744 1604*

The Department of Economic Development was established in 1982 by consolidating existing community and economic development programs into one agency. It is charged with promoting commerce and industry in the city by developing programs and policies which will retain existing businesses and help them to expand and which will attract new business to the city.

The department administers federal and state funds (chiefly federal Community Development Block Grants). It provides services for neighborhood economic development, such as technical assistance for federal Small Business Administration loan programs, market studies, parking improvement plans, and a program providing matching funds for facade improvements of neighborhood stores and for streetscape beautification. It has an International Business Program intended to develop export opportunities and attract overseas investment.

It publishes brochures describing its programs and booklets designed to attract business and industry to the city.

The department is headed by a commissioner appointed by the mayor with city council approval at an annual salary of $71,000. In 1987 it administered $20,655,000 in federal funds and $1,889,000 in state funds. Its 1988 corporate fund budget was $977,289, which paid for 10 employees. An additional 102 employees were paid with grant funds.

ECONOMIC DEVELOPMENT COMMISSION.
W. Merchandise Mart Plaza, Chicago 60654; phone 744 9550

The Economic Development Commission is charged with advising the Department of Economic Development, developing a long-range economic plan for the city, and providing assistance to businesses in relation to city government. It recommends to the city council the issuance of industrial revenue bonds and reviews revolving loan funds and land write-down applications. The commission has 17 members: the chairs of the City Council Finance and Economic Development Committees, 3 city department heads, and 12 private citizens appointed by the mayor for four-year unpaid terms. In 1987 it had a staff of 2, from the Department of Economic Development budget. Its meetings, which are open to the public, are held the second Thursday of each month, usually at the offices of Helene Curtis Industries, 325 N. Wells.

COMMERCIAL DISTRICT DEVELOPMENT COMMISSION
Department of Planning, City Hall, 121 N. La Salle St., Chicago 60602; phone 744 4186

The Commercial District Development Commission is responsible for recommending to the city council the designation of Commercial Development Districts and for the acquisition and disposition of land and buildings within those districts (under Chapter 15.1 of the Municipal Code). The commission has powers of eminent domain. It has seven members: two city department heads and five private citizens appointed by the mayor for five-year unpaid terms. It has no separate budget and is staffed by the Department of Economic Development and the Department of Planning. Its meetings are held on the third Tuesday of each month and are open to the public. Locations and times may vary.

MAYOR'S OFFICE OF EMPLOYMENT AND TRAINING
510 N. Peshtigo Court, Chicago 60611; *phone 744 8787*

The Mayor's Office of Employment and Training was established by executive order of the mayor in 1980 to administer federally funded job training, retraining, and placement programs for Chicago. Programs are designed to provide employment and training to youths and adults who are economically disadvantaged or long-term unemployed, or to workers dislocated because of industrial relocation. The Chicago First Program, administered by this office, refers and places unemployed Chicago residents in jobs created through city-assisted projects. The following programs are offered by the office:

* Academic skills training
* Classroom vocational training
* Career counseling
* Job placement
* On-the-job training
* Summer youth employment
* Student job opportunities

The office is headed by the assistant to the mayor for employment and training, who is appointed by the mayor at an annual salary of $71,000. The 1988 budget shows an appropriation of $138,140 from the city's corporate fund and funds from two federal grants: $2,152,846 from Year XIV Community Development Block Grant (CDBG) funds and $46,029,896 from the Job Training Partnership Act. The office had 186 employees.

PRIVATE INDUSTRY COUNCIL (PIC). The federal Job Training Partnership Act requires that a council, a majority of whose members must be local business leaders, share responsibility and oversight with chief elected officials for programs under the act. The Private Industry Council (PIC) is a 45-member policy advisory council appointed by the mayor to serve unpaid terms of one, two, or three years. Half of the business membership represents minority or small businesses; other members represent education, labor, rehabilitation agencies, community-based organizations, economic development agencies, the state employment service, and the Illinois Department of Public Aid.

BOARD OF ETHICS
Suite 1320, 205 W. Randolph St., Chicago 60606; *phone 744 8822*

In 1987 the city council passed a governmental ethics ordinance setting standards for officials and employees of the city concerning the reporting of economic interests, the employment of relatives, the influencing of the granting of contracts, and the lobbying of city agencies. The ordinance and the board's powers and procedures are described in the section Your Rights to Know in the Preface.

The Board of Ethics is made up of seven members appointed by the mayor with the consent of the city council for four-year staggered terms. The mayor designates the chair. Members serve without compensation but may be reimbursed for expenses. The mayor has the power to remove a member for cause, with the consent of the remaining board members.

The board is empowered to hire staff, subject to city council appropriation of funds. In 1988 it had eight employees and a budget of $342,668.

FIRE DEPARTMENT

City Hall, 121 N. LaSalle St., Chicago 60602; *Emergency phone, 911*
Information, *744 6666*

The Fire Department is responsible for preventing fires as well as fighting them: fire prevention includes public education on fire hazards and building inspection (including monthly inspections of hotels and nursing homes and annual inspection of schools and day care centers). The Fire Department is the city agency which regulates attendance capacity in public buildings. The department does not conduct arson investigations; those are the responsibility of the Police Department.

The Fire Department is responsible for rescuing people in emergencies, for airport disaster protection, and for emergency preparedness and disaster services, including civil defense.

Fire fighting. Six fire-fighting divisions are located throughout the city. There are 104 fire stations, which are placed according to population density. Each division is supervised by a district chief who works five days a week, from 9 A.M. to 5 P.M. Under the chief are three or four deputy district chiefs; their work schedule is 24 hours on and 48 hours off, the hours of all field personnel. In each district there are four battalion chiefs who are responsible for personnel and for engine, truck, and special function apparatus.

The 104 fire stations contain the engine companies, truck companies, and flying squads (rescue trucks and trained personnel who cover accidents as well as fires). A fire company includes its apparatus, such as a fire truck, and the personnel who operate it. A fire station may have several companies in it. Fire station structures are owned by the Public Building Commission and are transferred to the use of other city departments or sold when they are no longer used by the Fire Department.

In addition to engines, trucks, and ambulances, the department has such special equipment as snorkels, smoke ejectors, trucks equipped with floodlights, air compressor units, foam units, dry chemical units, and heavy appliance or deluge units which can direct heavy streams of water up to ten stories high. Helicopters above major fires coordinate the placing of equipment.

Marine rescue. The Fire Department has three helicopters which operate from Meigs Field, flying regular patrols to provide port and harbor protection. Marine rescue boats equipped with fire-fighting equipment, scuba gear, and inhalators patrol Chicago harbors and waterways from early spring until formation of solid ice in winter, when fireboats with ice-breaking equipment take over.

Accident rescue. The helicopters are also often used in rescue work for accidents. Chicago was the first city in the country to initiate a full-time air evacuation program for victims of expressway accidents where heavy traffic prevents effective use of ambulances.

The Emergency Medical Services Bureau of the department provides a fleet of 53 ambulances which provide emergency medical service and transport to hospitals. The fee for ambulance service in 1987 was $125 for transportation to a hospital, and an additional $70 if medical services were required, but no one is refused service because of inability to pay. The Department of Revenue bills users for ambulance services.

Emergency Preparedness. The Office of Emergency Preparedness and Disaster Service reports directly to the fire commissioner. Its responsibility is to prevent, minimize, repair, and alleviate injury and damage resulting from disasters caused by hostile action, or fire, flood, earthquake, or other natural causes. It is responsible for implementing the city's Disaster Plan. It is also responsible for a Hazardous Materials Unit, which is dispatched to hazardous materials incidents. Emergency Preparedness Defense Systems (EPDS) warning sirens are tested each Tuesday at 10:30 A.M. In an actual emergency, a straight tone would be a warning to take shelter immediately. However, the city no longer maintains designated shelters for emergencies.

Administration. The Fire Department is divided into five bureaus: Administration, Fire Suppression and Rescue, Fire Prevention, Emergency Medical Services, and Support Services. The Office of Emergency Preparedness and Disaster Service is separately budgeted and staffed. Fire-fighting candidates have a 90-day training course and fire prevention inspectors a 258-hour course at the Fire Academy.

The Fire Commissioner has the authority, with approval by the mayor, to enter into reciprocal contracts with other municipalities and fire prevention districts for mutual aid. In 1987, the department had such an agreement with the village of Lincolnwood but had given the village notice that the contract would be terminated.

The department is headed by the Fire Commissioner, who is appointed by the mayor with the advice and consent of the city council, at an annual salary of $87,600. In 1988 there were 5,578 employees and an additional 18 in the Office of Emergency Preparedness and Disaster Service. The department's budget was $214,023,787 from the corporate fund, with an additional $690,842 budget for the Emergency Preparedness and Disaster Service.

DEPARTMENT OF GENERAL SERVICES
320 N. Clark St., Chicago 60610. *Phone 744 7711*

The Department of General Services was established in the 1988 budget to be responsible for the operation and maintenance of buildings, fleet, inventory, real estate leasing, and telecommunications services. Its Bureau of Inventory Management replaces the former Warehouse and Stores Division of the Purchasing Department. Its Bureau of Facilities Management manages North Park Village, which is on the site of the former Municipal Tuberculosis Sanitarium on the northwest side of the city; this 155-acre site contains two senior citizen housing developments, a Department of Health clinic, Peterson Park (leased to and managed by the Park District), a 48-acre nature preserve, and a 12-acre nature study area. This bureau maintains Navy Pier and 32 city-owned facilities; it also negotiates city lease agreements. Its Bureau of Fleet Administration is responsible for maintenance of city vehicles and for gasoline and diesel fuel.

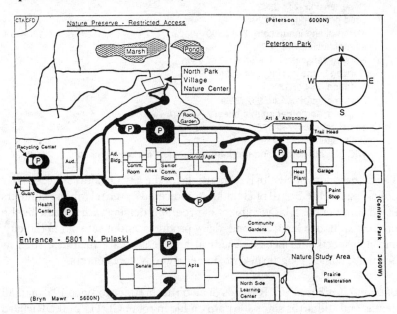

Fig. 5. 1. North Park Village, managed by the Department of General Services
Source: Chicago Department of General Services

The Department of General Services is headed by a commissioner at a salary of $71,000. Its total 1988 budget is $61,005,400; of this $60,300,700 is from the corporate fund, providing for 1,100 positions; $172,000 of its budget comes from the sewer fund, $359,000 from the water fund, and $173,700 from the special events fund.

GRAPHICS AND REPRODUCTION CENTER
City Hall, 121 N. LaSalle St., Chicago 60602

The Graphics and Reproduction Center provides editorial, design, typesetting, printing, and photographic services to city departments. It is headed by a director with a 1988 salary of $48,456. Its 1988 budget provides for 53 positions and a total of $2,134,000, all of which is to be reimbursed by other city agencies.

DEPARTMENT OF HEALTH
Richard J. Daley Center, 50 W. Washington St., 60602; *phone 744 3558*
Public health education and information, *744 8500*
AIDS hotline, *1 800 AID aids*
Chicago's Addiction Center, *254 3680*
Birth and death certificates, *744 3790*
Child abuse hotline, *1 800 25 ABUSE*
Immunizations, *808 3780*
Complaints (environmental, etc.), *744 4395*
Dental, *744 3187*
Hypertension, *744 3842*
Lead poisoning, *254 2294*
Maternal and infant care, *744 8500*
Mental health, *744 8033*
Nursing services and referrals, *744 4346*
Nursing home hotline, *744 4395*
Nutrition, *744 0657*
Poison control center, *942 5969*
Rat, dog, and other animal bites, *744 4340*
Social services, *744 1753*
Utility shut-off, *744 4395*
WIC (supplemental food program for mothers and young children), *744 6517*

The Department of Health is responsible for the city's health services under policies set by the Board of Health. As indicated by the telephone numbers listed above, it has a large number of programs dealing with specific health problems. It also inspects food, dairy products, and meat sold in the city, and it inspects and licenses medical and health care facilities, such as hospitals, clinics, long-term-care homes and day-care centers.

Birth and death records. Records of all births in Chicago since 1955 and all deaths and stillbirths since 1961 are on file in room CL 111 of the Richard J. Daley Center, 50 W. Washington St. The city charges $5 for a birth certificate, $10 for a death certificate, and $2 for additional copies on the same order. Validation of the International Certificate of Vaccination is processed in the same office.

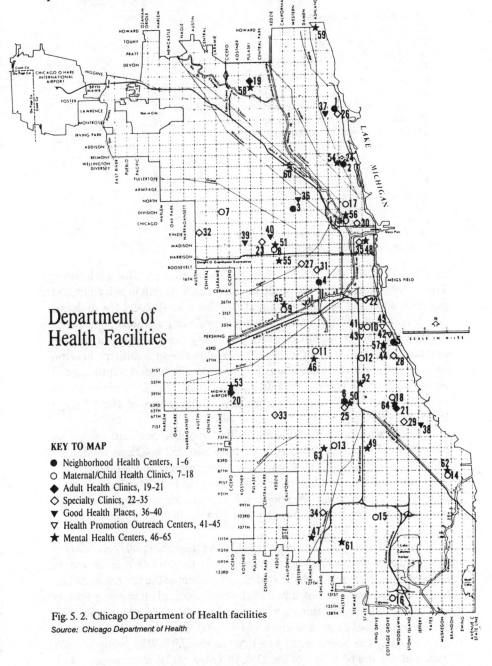

Department of Health Facilities

KEY TO MAP

● Neighborhood Health Centers, 1–6
○ Maternal/Child Health Clinics, 7–18
◆ Adult Health Clinics, 19–21
◇ Specialty Clinics, 22–35
▼ Good Health Places, 36–40
▽ Health Promotion Outreach Centers, 41–45
★ Mental Health Centers, 46–65

Fig. 5. 2. Chicago Department of Health facilities
Source: Chicago Department of Health

Health services. Health services may be provided by the department or in cooperation with other agencies and community organizations and include the following:

Prenatal and postpartum care
Family planning
Infant and pre-school care
School physical examinations
Dental health care
Eye care services
Podiatric services
Immunizations for prevention of childhood diseases (free)
Rheumatic fever registry and prevention program
Teen health services and counseling
Tuberculosis control
Mental health services
Alcoholic treatment
Lead screening and treatment
Sickle cell screening
Cancer screening
Diabetic screening
Hypertension control program
Adult health and aging programs

As of 1987, the department's facilities included the Chicago Alcoholic Treatment Center, 6 neighborhood health centers, 3 adult health clinics, 12 maternal and child health clinics, 3 alternative school clinics for students, and 5 health promotion outreach centers in Chicago Housing Authority apartments. In cooperation with community organizations, it had 19 community mental health centers, 4 neighborhood health promotion centers, and 6 outreach programs for the federally funded Supplemental Food Program for Women, Infants, and Children (WIC). Clinic locations and telephone numbers are listed in the blue pages of the Chicago telephone directory.

The department's 1988 budget provided for 1,048 positions funded by $39,547,456 from the city's corporate fund and 252 positions funded by $10,305,254 from Year XIV Community Development Block funds.

Additional state and federal funding was expected. The department is headed by a commissioner appointed by the mayor with the advice and consent of the city council, at a 1988 salary of $80,000.

BOARD OF HEALTH. The Board of Health establishes policy and directs the programs of the Health Department. It consists of nine members appointed by the mayor with the advice and consent of the city council. The length of their terms is not stated in the ordinance. The mayor appoints one of the nine as president, who must be a licensed physician. The president receives an annual stipend of $25,000; the other board members are not paid. The board meets at 3 P.M. on the third Wednesday of each month in the Board Room of the Daley Center, 50 W. Washington. The board is funded through the corporate fund budget of the Department of Health and has one staff member.

HOME EQUITY GOVERNING COMMISSIONS

Under the Home Equity Assurance Act, passed by the state legislature in 1988, the voters of a contiguous area within the city may create a home equity program. The purpose of the program is to guarantee that the value of the property of each member of the program does not fall below fair market value. The program applies to one-to-six-unit housing occupied by the owner or a family member and to sales made at least five years after the owner joins the program, and it does not apply to any decrease in value due to neglect or natural disasters. It provides that an owner who has applied for the program and who is unable to sell the property for fair market value (as determined by the commission under provisions of the law) may receive from commission funds the difference between the sale price and fair market value.

A home equity area may be created by city council action or by petition. If by petition, each precinct to be included must submit a petition signed by at least 10% of its registered voters. In either case, approval by referendum of the voters in the area is required. The program is to be financed by a property tax (not to exceed 0.12% of equalized assessed valuation) on residential property of six units or less within the area.

Each program is to be administered by a nine-member unpaid governing commission appointed by the mayor with consent of the city council for three-year staggered terms. Seven of the members must be appointed from nominees submitted by community organizations, and at least five must be residents of the area. No commission member may serve more than two terms.

DEPARTMENT OF HOUSING
318 S. Michigan Ave., Chicago 60604; *phone 922 7922*

The Department of Housing was established in 1980 to coordinate city housing services and programs. It helps people buy, repair, or build privately owned housing, with emphasis on low- and moderate-income areas. It administers loan and grant programs directly or through not-for-profit neighborhood organizations. It works with developers to redevelop urban renewal land and to build new housing under federal and state programs. Its Real Estate Section sells city-owned properties, primarily those received through foreclosure of demolition liens.

The department's staff coordinates the Heat Receivership Program (formerly administered by the Mayor's Office of Inquiry and Information), under which a heat receiver is appointed by the Housing Court to supply heat to tenants of multifamily dwellings when the landlord fails to do so.

The department is also responsible for enforcing the Fair Housing Ordinance, the Residential Landlord-Tenant Ordinance, and affirmative action programs for publicly financed housing construction.

Fair Housing Ordinance. The Fair Housing Ordinance forbids discrimination in rental or sale of housing on account of race, color, sex, marital status, national origin or ancestry. Complaints of violation of the ordinance may be made by calling *922 7925.*

Landlord-Tenant Ordinance. The Landlord-Tenant Ordinance became effective in 1987. It provides remedies for tenants in residential rental properties if the landlord fails to keep the property in compliance with the building code or if essential services (gas, electricity, water, heat, hot water, or plumbing) are stopped. Included in the remedies are deductions of the cost of repairs or substitute services from rent, provided proper notice has been given. Remedies are also provided to landlords in the event of nonpayment of rent or tenant damage to the premises. The ordinance does not apply to owner-occupied buildings with six or fewer units, to owner-occupied co-ops and condominiums, to dormitories or shelters, or to hotels unless rental is for more than a month. A summary of the ordinance must be given to tenants by the landlord; copies may be obtained from the department.

LOAN AND GRANT PROGRAMS *(all have eligibility requirements):*

Senior/Handicapped Home Maintenance Program provides minor rehabilitation funding of up to $750 in costs of materials per unit. This program is available to low- and moderate-income renters as well as home owners. Proof of income is required. The program is implemented by not-for-profit delegate agencies which have contracts with the department.

Weatherization Program provides grants to low-income persons for caulking, weather-stripping, storm windows and doors, and other weatherization improvements. The program is available for single-family and multifamily rental buildings and for owner-occupied housing.

Chicago Energy Savers Fund provides low-interest loans to property owners for energy conservation improvements. It is jointly sponsored and funded with the Peoples Gas Light and Coke Company. The multifamily program is administered by the Community Investment Corporation *(phone 341 0700),* and the single-family program is administered by Neighborhood Housing Services *(phone 738 3311).*

Neighborhood Home Improvement Program provides low- interest loans to owners of one-to-four-unit properties in Chicago for all types of home improvement projects. It is jointly sponsored and funded by Continental Illinois National Bank and Trust Company and the Illinois Housing Development Authority (IHDA). Applications are taken by Neighborhood Lending Services, a not-for-profit subsidiary of Neighborhood Housing Services of Chicago, at 17 neighborhood offices.

Chicago Assistance Program (CAP) provides loans to low-income owners of one-to-four-unit buildings for repairing potential building hazards. This program will be available until funds are exhausted.

Section 312 Loan Program is a low-interest loan program to assist owners of single-family or multifamily housing in target areas to bring their buildings into compliance with the building code.

Supplemental Rehabilitation Program provides low-interest rehabilitation loans to low- and moderate-income owner-occupants of one-to-four-unit properties in Chicago, to augment other Department of Housing rehabilitation loans in which funding limits are insufficient to correct building code violations.

Emergency Housing Assistance Program provides financial assistance for emergency repairs of heating units to owner-occupied one-to-four-unit buildings.

Homeless Shelter provides rehabilitation grants, loans, and technical assistance to shelter facilities operated by experienced not-for-profit organizations.

Multi-Family Rehabilitation Loan Program is a rehabilitation loan program for owners or purchasers of multifamily rental properties of five or more units located in specified target areas.

Urban Homestead Program is a program under which the department sells vacant, repossessed HUD properties to low- and moderate-income residents who can afford to rehabilitate the property to compliance with the building code within three years. (Properties are available through a lottery only when properties and financing are available.)

Chicago Housing Partnership provides loans and financial and technical assistance to neighborhood not-for-profit developers to finance the rehabilitation of low- and moderate-income housing units. This program was undertaken in cooperation with the Local Initiatives Support Corporation, an affiliate of the Ford Foundation. It is a partnership of the city, local corporations and lenders, and neighborhood housing developers. In the two-year period of 1985-87 the program generated $50,000,000.

Urban Development Action Grant (UDAG) provides low-interest loans to developers of residential, commercial, and industrial projects which could not be developed without this assistance. Funding is received from the U.S. Department of Housing and Urban Development (HUD).

142(d) Multi-Family Bond Program, formerly 103(b), provides construction and mortgage financing for developers to build or rehabilitate rental housing with 100 or more units. The developer must rent an agreed-on percentage to low-income tenants (rents must not exceed 30% of tenants' income); 20% of the units must be made available to tenants whose income is no more than 50% of the median income of the Chicago area, or 40% of the units must be made available to tenants with no more than 60% of the median income. Revenue bonds (within limits set by federal law) are sold by the city to finance this program.

Low Income Housing Tax Credits is a tax-incentive program for developing low-income housing; it was part of the federal 1986 tax reform act. An amount of tax credit is allocated to the city by the federal government. By city ordinance, the commissioner of the Department of Housing can allocate this credit to eligible building owners, investors, or developers who meet criteria set by the department under the federal law.

Adjacent Neighbors Land Acquisition Program provides for property owners to purchase adjacent city-owned vacant lots at reasonable costs.

Technical Assistance to Organizations. The Department of Housing contracts with more than 50 community-based organizations to extend their programs and provide housing-related services. Under its Housing Abandonment Program, the department has contracted with 10 community-based organizations to identify troubled buildings and attempt to save them from abandonment and to develop a system to deter abandonment of buildings. The department also operates a computerized property information program (called the Harris File) and provides informational services to the public.

Assistance to Individuals. The department's Neighborhood Housing Support Program counsels persons in default on their mortgages, seeking forbearance agreements and providing money-management counseling. Its Relocation Program provides assistance and benefits to both residential and nonresidential occupants displaced because of government-assisted projects.

URBAN RENEWAL BOARD. The former Department of Urban Renewal is now part of the Department of Housing, except that economic and commercial development aspects of its responsibilities are now part of the Department of Economic Development and the Commercial District Development Commission. The Urban Renewal Board has the power to designate slum and blighted areas, to acquire such land and clear it, and to review proposals for redevelopment, hold public hearings, and recommend final approval on such matters to the city council. The board has powers of eminent domain.

The five members of the board are appointed by the mayor and approved by the city council for staggered four-year terms. They are not paid. State law requires board members to be citizens of broad civic interest, with administrative ability in finance, real estate, or related endeavors. At least three members must be residents and electors of the municipality, and not more than three members may belong to the same political party. One member is designated by the mayor as chairman (currently the commissioner of housing). Funding for urban renewal comes from Community Development Block Grant (CDBG) funds. The board meetings are open to the public and are held at 2 P.M. on the third Tuesday of each month, in the auditorium of the Britannica Center, 310 S. Michigan Avenue, or as otherwise designated by the board.

CONSERVATION COMMUNITY COUNCILS. The Urban Renewal Board has the authority to designate areas of the city as conservation areas; these are basically sound residential neighborhoods with blighted sections. Once an area has been so designated, the mayor must appoint 9-15 residents of the area to serve as a Conservation Community Council. Members serve without pay and hold office until a successor has been appointed. Members may not hold public office or political party office. Their responsibilities include stimulating citizen involvement; consulting, advising, and ultimately approving the conservation plan before it is submitted to the Urban Renewal Board and the city council; and assisting in implementation of the plan.

Funding and Administration. The Department of Housing is headed by a commissioner appointed by the mayor with the consent of the city council, at a salary in 1988 of $71,000. The department had 22 employees paid from the city's corporate fund, with a 1988 budget of $1,292,207. The department's primary funding, however, is from federal grants; these totaled $57,319,000 in fiscal year 1988. It received $27,818,950 in Year XIV (1988) Community Development Block Grant (CDBG) funding, which paid 317 employees, and $11,174,000 for the weatherization program, which paid 83 employees. Other federal funding was primarily for the grant and loan programs (but not for their administrative costs). It included $6,412,000 for the rental rehabilitation program, $2,000,000 for the single-family loan program, $1,100,000 from Urban Development Action Grant (UDAG) funds, and an $8,955,000 Housing Development Action Grant (HODAG). The federal housing bill passed in December 1987 did not provide further HODAG funds for future years.

COMMISSION ON HUMAN RELATIONS
500 N. Peshtigo Court, Chicago 60611; *phone 744 4100*

The Commission on Human Relations was established by city ordinance in 1947; the ordinance was substantially amended in 1979. The commission is responsible for identifying and correcting instances of prejudice or discrimination based on race, color, sex, creed, national origins, or ancestry. In 1980 its fair housing enforcement responsibilities were transferred to the Department of Housing, and its contract compliance responsibilities were transferred to the Department of Purchases. It continues to investigate complaints of discrimination in public accomodations such as hotels and bars.

The commission is empowered to investigate complaints of discrimination, hold public hearings, conduct research, issue publications, and make recommendations to the mayor and city council. In 1987 its programs included crisis intervention, a program to assist neighborhoods which are experiencing integration, an Asian-American liaison program, a veterans' liaison and job services project, a refugee and immigrant liaison program, a project on new immigration laws, a drop-out prevention program, gang prevention workshops, and human relations training assistance to agencies.

The mayor, with city council approval, appoints 15 commissioners, who serve without pay for three-year terms, or until their successors are appointed and qualified. The mayor designates the commission's chair. An executive director is appointed by the mayor (city council approval is not required) with a 1988 salary of $50,640 a year.

The commission holds meetings, which are open to the public, at 12:30 P.M. on the second and fourth Thursdays of each month at its offices.

The 1988 staff of the commission was 20 persons funded from the corporate fund and an additional 7 funded from Community Development Block Grants (CDBG). Its corporate fund budget for 1988 was $686,796; it received an additional $278,213 of CDBG Year XIV funding and $55,128 from the Illinois Department of Public Aid for the refugee liaison program.

THE ASIAN-AMERICAN ADVISORY COMMITTEE is a committee of 17 persons appointed by the mayor to advise on the Asian-American liaison program. The committee's meetings are open to the public and are held monthly or bimonthly on the second Wednesdays of the month at the commission's office.

THE VETERANS LIAISON ADVISORY COMMITTEE is a committee of 30 persons appointed by the mayor to advise the city on matters of concern to veterans. The committee's meetings are open to the public and are held at 11 A.M. the third Saturday of each month in the fourth floor conference room at 500 N. Peshtigo Court.

THE REFUGEE AND IMMIGRANT LIAISON ADVISORY COMMITTEE is a committee of 17 persons appointed by the mayor to advise on concerns of refugees and immigrants. Its meetings are at 6 P.M. the second Wednesday of every other month at the commission's office.

THE MAYOR'S COMMITTEE ON GAY AND LESBIAN ISSUES is also housed in the Commission on Human Relations. In 1987 the committee focused on gaining passage of an ordinance which would protect against discrimination based on sexual orientation and on expanding city programs dealing with AIDS. A 16-member board is appointed by the mayor. Its meetings are open to the public and are held at 7:30 P.M. on the last Wednesday of each month at the Rodde Center, 3225 N. Sheffield.

DEPARTMENT OF HUMAN SERVICES
510 N. Peshtigo Court, Chicago 60611; *phone 744 8111*

The Department of Human Services provides direct services to city residents in emergency and crisis situations. It administers social programs for children, youth, and families through other public and private agencies. It informs the public about human service needs and available services and participates in social policy development. In 1987 the department managed 26 departmental offices, 71 private outstations, 586 delegate agency sites, and 450 summer lunch sites. It provided emergency, information and referral, and special child, youth, and family services to 778,000 Chicago residents.

Emergency Services. Crisis intervention services are provided 24 hours a day (*744 5829* or *TDD 744 6189*) by the department's Communications Center and Mobile Unit teams. The department received 132,000 emergency calls in 1987 and sent mobile teams to make 12,000 crisis interventions. These services are provided in the following categories:

Disasters
Fire victims
Abandoned, neglected, or abused children
Evictions
Attempted or threatened suicide
Alcohol or drug abuse\
Lost senior citizens
Psychological disorientation
Family, neighbor-to-neighbor, snd tenant-landlord disputes

Emergency Food Program. Through its Community Services division, the department provides food packages to persons who lack food because of an emergency. In 1987 the department distributed 272,000 emergency food boxes and maintained 50 food distribution sites.

Emergency Shelter. A toll-free hotline (*1 800 654 8595*) is operated for the homeless needing emergency shelter. Contact cards with this number are distributed to the homeless and to shelters. The department works with overnight and transitional shelters and other service providers to secure emergency assistance. It also operates a shelter clearinghouse to provide information about available shelter beds (*744 5829*). Through its Family-Related Services division (*744 0887*), the department follows up emergency shelter placements and attempts to help individuals and families find independent living situations. In 1987 the department funded 32 shelters with 1,989 beds for the homeless, as well as 12 drop-in shelters and 12 agencies to provide social services.

Sexual Assault Assistance and Prevention Program (Hotline phone, *744 8418*). The Sexual Assault Assistance and Prevention Program provides support, referral, and follow-up services to victims.

CHILD AND FAMILY SERVICES
Child Services, *744 7275*

Youth and Family Services, *744 0887*

The Department of Human Services provides a variety of services to children, youth, and families. Some are offered directly, others through neighborhood organizations. A number of the programs are available only to low-income families.

Direct Family Services. Multi-problem families receive counseling, referral, and follow-up in response to such needs as employment, public assistance, shelter, and food through Direct Family Services. These services are available in nine District Community Service Centers (CSCs) and their subsidiary offices:

1. Broadway CSC, 4554 N. Broadway (*989 2700*)
    Northwest Office, 4810 N. Milwaukee (*283 7831*)

2. Near North CSC, 961 W. Montana (*880 6414*)
    Cabrini-Green Office, 1161 N. Larrabee (*744 5946*)

3. King CSC, 4314 S. Cottage Grove (*548 6700*)
    Robert Taylor Office, 4525 S. Federal (*624 3401*)

4. South Chicago CSC, 8516 S. Commercial (*375 4400*)

5. Mid-South CSC, 10833 S. Halsted (*568 8696*)
   Altgeld Office, 967 E. 132nd Place (*995 8600*)

6. Englewood CSC, 6201 S. Halsted (*962 0236*)

7. Cermak CSC, 3113 W. Cermak (*277 8000*)
   Chinatown Office, 250 W. 22nd St. (*326 3900*)
   Southwest Office, 6254 S. Kedzie (*471 2711*)

8. Garfield CSC, 10 S. Kedzie (*265 5400*)
   Austin Office, 5900 W. Chicago (*287 3069*)

9. Trina Davila CSC, 1437 N. California (*772 9135*)

Infant Mortality Reduction Initiative. A program to help new mothers in 10 communities with high rates of infant mortality is provided through the Infant Mortality Reduction Initiative. It operates through day-care centers and offers social services and counseling on parenting, nutrition, and health.

Delegated Family Services. The department funds and provides technical assistance to neighborhood-based organizations with programs to help families in cases of sexual assault and domestic violence and to provide counseling in parenting and budgeting.

Child Care Programs. All child care programs have income eligibility requirements. In 1987 the department provided child care for 19,600 children at 379 sites and provided 828,000 summer lunches. Parent-Child Centers provide preschool programs for children up to 5 years old, emphasizing parental involvement. Head Start/Home Start programs provide early childhood education for children 3 to 5 years old, through neighborhood organizations. Also through neighborhood organizations, the department supports Pre-School and School Age Day Care Programs for children from ages 3 to 13. Its Child Care Food Program provides meals for children in the department's child care programs. The Summer Nutrition Program provides free lunches for participants in organized children's programs. District numbers and addresses where Parent Child Centers (PCCs) are located are as follows:

3. Near South PCC, 4210 S. Berkeley (*538 4010*)
4. Brooks PCC, 6921 S. Stony Island (*752 3433*)
5. Gautreaux PCC, 975 E. 132nd St. (*785 1510*)
8. Garfield PCC, 7 N. Homan (*744 6185*)
   Fletcher PCC, 3140 W. Ogden (*277 4664*)

Youth Services. Direct services to youth, available in most of the nine Community Service Centers, attempt to deal with poor school performance, lack of work, pregnancy, and gang intimidation. The department funds and provides technical assistance to neighborhood-based organizations with programs to help with problems of education, truancy, school dropouts, and teen pregnancy. The 1988 budget provided for a Summer Youth Showcase to recognize academic and athletic accomplishments through competition for prizes at neighborhood, regional, and citywide levels.

The Youth Development Coordinating Council. The department provides a forum for community and professional input on programs and advocacy for young people through the Youth Development Coordinating Council..

Chicago Intervention Network (CIN), *744 1815.* The Chicago Intervention Network is a city-wide program designed to involve neighborhood groups in prevention of youth crime. It funds private agencies to provide services to youth, families, and victims and to operate neighborhood watch programs. In 1987 department staff provided services to 7,000 young people, and more than 25,000 were served by delegate agencies.

Workshops and Resource Centers. The department provides workshops, referral, and technical assistance to parents, teachers, and social work professionals to prevent child abuse. It operates a Head Start Resource Center in cooperation with the Chicago Public Library.

Information, Assistance, Referral. The department offers assistance to individuals with immigration problems and to those applying for housing, tax relief, or public transit reduced fare cards. It provides information and assistance in obtaining benefits.

Illinois Home Energy Assistance Program, 744 6717. Financial assistance in paying heating and utility bills is provided to persons meeting income eligibility requirements. In 1987 the department processed more than 81,000 such applications.

Neighborhood Farm Program. A garden program provides starter sets and seeds for maintaining gardens (often on vacant city-owned lots).

Technical Assistance to Community Groups. Many of the department's programs are conducted in cooperation with citywide agencies or neighborhood groups. The department offers support services, including preparation of program proposals, establishment of linkages with other organizations, and program implementation. The department funds and provides technical assistance to neighborhood organizations in developing programs to strengthen families and counteract youth gangs.

Administration and Funding. The department is headed by a commissioner, appointed by the mayor with the consent of the city council, at a salary of $77,000. In addition to administrative and planning divisions, it has sections on Community and Family Services, Children and Youth Services, and the Chicago Intervention Network.

The 1988 corporate budget of $11,362,904 included 163 employees. Most of the department's services, however, depend on the availability of federal and state funds for the programs it administers. Funds for its day care and Headstart services and its community service centers depend in large part on federal grants from the U.S. Department of Health and Human Services (granted to the state and allocated by it), and federal Social Services Block Grants. The Chicago Intervention Network, the crisis hotlines, and most of the emergency services are supported by Community Development Block Grant (CDBG) funds as well as by the corporate fund. The Home Energy Assistance program is supported by state and federal grants. The department received $21,136,190 in Year XIV CDBG funds and expected to receive an additional $82,406,000 in other state and federal funds.

MAYOR'S OFFICE OF INQUIRY AND INFORMATION
City Hall, 121 N. LaSalle St., Chicago 60602; *complaint phone 744 5000*

The Mayor's Office of Inquiry and Information was first established in 1955, was changed to the Department of Neighborhoods from 1980 to 1984, and was reestablished in 1984. It is the general information center for the city government, and it assists in adjusting complaints about city services. It staffs the City Hall Information Booth located near the LaSalle Street entrance to City Hall, at which tourist information and brochures on city departments are available. It provides speakers from city departments to community meetings.

The office publishes the *City of Chicago Municipal Handbook* (a guide to departments and services of the city of Chicago), the *Citizens' Information Catalogue* (a list of the city's brochures), the *Winter Protection Program,* and *Welcome to City Hall.* It also publishes the *Neighborhood Bulletin,* which provides information about city programs, services, appointments, and meetings; the *Bulletin* is available at Chicago Public Library branches and city department neighborhood offices.

The office manages a citywide computerized service request system which refers complaints and requests for services to the responsible city departments. A project called Action Line--Inside Track helps citizens resolve problems with city services through the Inside Track column appearing in selected community newspapers.

The office is headed by a director, with an annual salary of $58,000. Its 1988 corporate fund budget was $2,259,500; it had 87 employees.

DEPARTMENT OF INSPECTIONAL SERVICES
City Hall, 121 N. La Salle St., Chicago 60602; *phone 744 3402*

The Department of Inspectional Services, formerly the Building Department, issues building permits and is responsible for enforcement of the building code of the city. The code provides for building, electrical, heating and ventilating, housing, and plumbing inspections. The department insures that plans for new construction and rehabilitation comply with the code and that work is performed according to the approved plans. It receives and investigates complaints about violations of the code, and it is responsible for demolition of hazardous buildings. It also examines applications and issues licenses and certificates of registration for plumbers, plumbing and mason contractors, stationary engineers, supervising electricians, and motion picture operators.

The department is headed by a commissioner appointed by the mayor with the consent of the city council, with an annual salary of $65,000. In 1988, 459 positions were funded under a corporate fund appropriation of $17,554,984, and an additional 26 under an appropriation from the water fund of $1,084,000.

BUILDING BOARD OF APPEALS
320 N. Clark St., Chicago 60610; *phone 744 4466*

The Building Board of Appeals hears appeals of decisions on building permits made by the Department of Inspectional Services and may grant exceptions to the building code provided safety standards are maintained. It is made up of seven voting members appointed by the mayor with the consent of the city council for staggered two-year terms, and nonvoting members from the Department of Inspectional Services and the Fire Department. Membership must include an architect, an engineer, a representative of building contractors, and a building trade union representative. The chairman is paid $18,000 a year, the vice-chairman $15,000, and one member is paid $12,000. There is a staff of four and a 1988 corporate fund appropriation of $137,623.

COMMISSION ON CHICAGO LANDMARKS
320 N. Clark St., Room 516, Chicago 60610; *phone 744 3200*

The present Commission on Chicago Landmarks was created in 1968 by city ordinance. It recommends to the city council adoption of ordinances designating Chicago Landmarks, which may be areas, places, buildings, structures, works of art, and other objects having special historic, community, or aesthetic interest or value. Chicago is world-renowned for its historically significant architecture, and many of the designated landmark buildings are part of this heritage.

Designation as a landmark requires that the property be preserved, enhanced, rehabilitated, and protected. Any alteration of a landmark must have the commission's approval. There may be property tax advantages in having landmark status, depending on the zoning: for instance, a house with landmark status in an industrial area would be taxed on a residential basis rather than on the potential sale value of the land.

The commission, or any group or individual, may recommend that an area be included in the National Register of Historic Places. Recommendations are reviewed by the Illinois Historic Sites Advisory Council, part of the state Department of Conservation. Such a listing provides eligibility for grants and tax benefits for rehabilitation. Information on this program is available from the commission.

The public may make suggestions to the commission on designating landmarks. The commission itself identifies potential landmarks through a citywide Historic Resources Survey. Documentation is prepared, the Commissioner of Planning is consulted, and the consent of the property owner is requested. If the property owner does not consent, a public hearing is held. The commission's recommendations for landmark designation are forwarded to the city council, and its Committee on Historical Landmark Preservation conducts additional public hearings. Landmarks are finally designated by vote of the city council.

Commission staff are available for speaking engagements, and the commission provides publications on landmarks and procedures for designation. Proceeds from publication sales go into the Rincker Fund, which is used for preservation.

The Commissioner of Planning is an ex officio member of the commission, and the mayor appoints eight additional members who serve without pay for four-year terms. The mayor selects the commission's chair. The commission meets the first Wednesday of every month at its offices.

The mayor appoints the director, at a salary of $42,444. In 1988 there were 10 employees, and the budget was $342,179 from the corporate fund.

MAYOR'S ADVISORY COMMISSION ON LATINO AFFAIRS
Room 703, City Hall, 121 N. LaSalle St., Chicago 60602; phone 744 4404

The Mayor's Advisory Commission on Latino Affairs was established by executive order in October 1983 for a two-year period and was renewed in 1985 and 1987. Its function is to advise the mayor on matters of concern to the Hispanic community and make policy recommendations. It functions through community-based monitoring committees on economic development, housing, health, public safety, human services, education, and culture.

The mayor appoints 15 members, who serve without pay. The chair is elected by the members and confirmed by the mayor. An executive director is appointed by the mayor, at a salary in 1988 of $42,444 a year. In 1988 the commission had six employees and a corporate fund budget of $263,651.

Meetings are open to the public and are held at 6 P.M. on the last Tuesday of each month in room 703, City Hall. The commission publishes a quarterly newsletter.

DEPARTMENT OF LAW

City Hall, 121 N. LaSalle St., Chicago 60602; *phone 744 6900*

The Department of Law is headed by the Corporation Counsel, who superintends the law business of the city. It is responsible for providing legal advice to the mayor, the city council, and city boards, commissions, and departments. On request, it drafts ordinances and prepares legal documents such as deeds, leases, and contracts.

The department appears in legal proceedings for the city or any municipal officer, board, or department, and for city employees sued on account of actions taken in the performance of their duties. When a judgment is entered against the city, the Corporation Counsel decides whether to appeal the decision. All settlement decisions on lawsuits and claims against the city are made in this department and are reported in writing to the city council at the first regular meeting after the settlement has been made.

The department is responsible for collecting money overdue to the city. It also provides legal services to complete transactions involving acquisition, use, or disposition of city property. In city labor negotiations, it is responsible for collective bargaining, arbitration hearings, and contract administration.

The Corporation Counsel is appointed by the mayor with the advice and consent of the city council. The 1988 salary for this position was $85,000. In 1988 there were 372 budgeted employees, 328 of them funded by an appropriation of $13,953,786 from the corporate fund, and 44 traffic enforcement employees funded by $1,153,908 from vehicle tax funds.

MAYOR'S LICENSE COMMISSION AND LIQUOR CONTROL

City Hall, 121 N. LaSalle St., Chicago 60602; *phone 744 0071*

Under the Illinois Liquor Control Act, the mayor is the city's liquor control commissioner but has the authority to appoint an assistant. The Mayor's License Commission and Liquor Control acts in that capacity; it grants and revokes liquor licenses and publishes a handbook for retail liquor license applicants. (The License Appeal Commission acts as an appeal court for liquor license decisions.)

The commission also approves new amusement devices for licensing and approves arcade and raffle licenses. In addition it has jurisdiction over violations of all other city licenses, such as those issued by the Revenue Section of the Department of Finance. Hearings on revocation of licenses are open to the public. Decisions on licenses other than liquor licenses may be appealed to the Cook County Circuit Court.

The mayor appoints the director of the commission, who has a salary of $52,920. In 1988 there were six employees, and the budget, from the corporate fund, was $278,280.

LICENSE APPEAL COMMISSION
510 N. Peshtigo Court, Chicago 60611; *phone 744 4095*

The License Appeal Commission receives appeals on any order of the liquor control commissioner (the mayor) granting or revoking a liquor license or refusing to do so, or refusing to hear a complaint. It tries such appeals and enters orders on them.

The commission consists of three members: a city resident appointed by the mayor, who acts as the commission's chair; the chair of the Illinois Liquor Control Commission; and an additional member of that commission. The two Illinois commission members must be from different political parties. The commission's chair is appointed for four years and is paid $90 a day, with 100 days allocated in the budget. There were two budgeted positions in 1988 and a budget of $73,426 from the corporate fund.

DEPARTMENT OF MANAGEMENT INFORMATION SYSTEMS
Daley Center, 50 W. Washington, Chicago 60602; *phone 744 5844*

The Department of Management Information Systems was formerly the Data Center of the Office of Management and Budget. It operates the city's central computer facility, maintains and develops the city's computer systems, and provides assistance in preparing statistics and management reports. It is headed by the director of data processing, who is appointed by the mayor at an annual salary of $71,000; its 1988 budget provides for 231 employees and total expenditures of $11,010,696 from the corporate fund.

OFFICE OF MUNICIPAL INVESTIGATION
510 Peshtigo Court, Chicago 60611; *phone 661 0310*

The Office of Municipal Investigation is responsible for detection and elimination of misconduct on the part of city employees (with the exception of the Police Department, whose employees are under the jurisdiction of the Police Department's Office of Professional Standards and Internal Affairs Division). The office investigates citizens' complaints of wrongdoing, waste, or corrupt practices in city government. Complaints may be made by phone or letter and are held in confidence. Investigations are confidential, but the office reports the number of investigations to the city's chief operating officer; it does not issue a public report. The Office of Municipal Investigation is headed by an executive director, with an annual salary of $56,052. In 1988, 20 employees were budgeted under a corporate fund appropriation of $740,346, and 4 employees were budgeted for a total of $110,831 from the Chicago-O'Hare International Airport Revenue fund.

OVERSIGHT COMMITTEE. The actions of the Office of Municipal Investigation are monitored by a five-member select civilian oversight committee appointed by the mayor with the approval of the city council. Members serve, without pay, for three-year terms. Also serving on the committee, but without votes, are the budget director, the director of personnel, and the corporation counsel (or their designees). Meetings are held at 9 A.M. the second Friday of each month and are open to the public.

MUNICIPAL REFERENCE LIBRARY
City Hall, 121 N. LaSalle St., Chicago 60602; *phone 744 4992.* Open Monday - Friday, 8.30 A.M. to 5 P.M.

The Municipal Reference Library is primarily an information center for city officials and agencies, but it is also open to the public for reference use. The collection includes codes of law, annual reports, and special reports of the city of Chicago and other municipalities. There is also a small collection of historical material about Chicago. The library distributes free copies of *Facts about Chicago* and *Checklist of Publications Issued by the City of Chicago.* It sells copies of *Mayors of Chicago--A Chronological List.*

The library is headed by the Municipal Librarian, who is appointed by the mayor with the advice and consent of the city council, at a salary in 1988 of $52,920 a year. The 1988 budget, from the corporate fund, was $849,558. There were 20 full-time and 2 part-time employees.

DEPARTMENT OF PERSONNEL
City Hall, 121 N. LaSalle St., Chicago 60602; *phone: 744 4966*
   Job information, 744 4890

Employees of city departments, except for exempt personnel, are hired by the departments from lists of candidates submitted by the Department of Personnel. The Department of Personnel examines applicants and verifies that candidates are qualified for jobs according to specific job requirements. After a probationary service of a year, employees achieve Career Service status and are entitled to a hearing if discharged or disciplined. Employees hired under exempt categories are not eligible for Career Service status.

The Department of Personnel issues the city's Personnel Rules. Public notice must be given when rules are to be changed. A ten-day period for public comment must be provided before a proposed rule or amendment takes effect. The department administers job-related examinations and selection procedures and establishes eligibility lists for jobs. It provides help in personnel administration to city departments. It operates recruitment centers where job announcements are available in seven community centers (see Department of Human Services).

The department is headed by the Commissioner of Personnel, who is appointed by the mayor with the advice and consent of the city council, at a salary in 1988 of $70,000 a year. There were 183 employees budgeted, and the total 1988 budget, from the corporate fund, was $7,699,431.

Exempt Personnel. The Municipal Code provides (Section 25.1-3) that certain positions are exempt from the city Career Service. These include the following:

* Elected officials and a private secretary for each elected official
* Executive heads of city departments
* Administrative assistants to the mayor
* Members of boards and commissions whose appointment is subject to confirmation by the city council
* Employees of the city council (unless included in the Career Service by ordinance)
* Employees of the Law Department, police above the rank of captain, and firefighters above the rank of battalion chief
* Employees whose work is seasonal and not more than 180 days in a year
* Other positions recommended by a department head, reviewed by the director of personnel, and approved by the mayor (These exemptions must involve policy, confidentiality, or be necessary in order to carry out programs to which Career Service requirements would not apply, such as student or trainee programs or public service employment programs.)

PERSONNEL BOARD
City Hall, 121 N. LaSalle St., Chicago 60602; *phone 744 4970*

In 1976 the Personnel Board superseded the Chicago Civil Service Commission, and the term Civil Service was changed to Career Service. The Personnel Board was created by ordinance to provide advice and counsel to the mayor on all aspects of public personnel administration, including training, grievances, and salaries. The board provides hearings on charges against career service employees. It provides published rules for suspensions of 30 days or less. The board, a member, or a hearing officer is empowered to conduct hearings on employee suspensions of more than 10 days and on demotions and discharges. Hearing proceedings are recorded, and the board has the power to subpoena evidence and witnesses and to administer oaths. After the hearing, the full board makes a final determination.

The board consists of three members appointed by the mayor and approved by the city council for five-year staggered terms. One member is designated as chair by the mayor for a one-year term. The board is funded through the budget of the Department of Personnel. In 1988 the chair received a salary of $23,964 and the other members $13,332 each. Hearing officers receive $50 an hour. The board has two employees. It meets on the second and fourth Tuesdays of every month at 3:30 P.M. Meetings are subject to the Open Meetings Act.

DEPARTMENT OF PLANNING
City Hall, 121 N. LaSalle St., Chicago 60602; *phone 744 4160*

The Department of Planning is the planning and coordinating agency for development of the city, including programs for redevelopment of vacant areas and for conservation and physical improvement of neighborhoods and industrial and commercial areas. (See also the Department of Housing and the Department of Economic Development.)

Affirmative Neighborhood Information Program. The Affirmative Neighborhood Information Program provides reports to community organizations on housing violations in their areas, including court dates and information on building owners. *(Phone 744 4455.)*

North Loop/South Loop Development. The Department of Planning is responsible for planning and implementing redevelopment projects in the central area of the city.

Energy Conservation. The department is responsible for developing and administering programs to reduce both city and private energy costs. (See also Department of Housing.)

Grant Application and Administration. The department prepares a long-term Community Development Plan and issues and receives Community Development Block Grant (CDBG) applications; it provides staff assistance to the Community Development Advisory Committee, which makes recommendations on CDBG programs.

Planning Grants. Under the CDBG program, the department provides matching grants to community-based not-for-profit organizations for planning studies.

Information. The department analyzes and publishes census data on the city's population, housing, and economic resources.

The Department of Planning is headed by the commissioner of planning, who is appointed by the mayor with the consent of the city council, at a salary in 1988 of $71,000 a year. The 1988 budget provided for 58 employees and a budget of $2,500,035 from the corporate fund; for up to 26 employees from bond funds for the North Loop project; and for planning grants, technical and professional services, and up to another 26 employees from $1,521,783 in CDBG Year XIV (1988) funds.

CHICAGO PLAN COMMISSION

Department of Planning, City Hall, 121 N. LaSalle St., Chicago 60602; *phone 744 7221*

Chicago was one of the first major cities to have a general plan to guide its development. The 1909 Plan of Chicago was prepared by Daniel Burnham and Edward Bennett and was financed by businessmen. The 1909 plan recommended creation of a commission to study and promote its proposals, and the mayor appointed a 328-member advisory Chicago Plan Commission. This original commission helped to provide Chicago with some of its greatest physical assets: the lakefront park system; the ring of forest preserves around the city; Chicago River improvements; and sites for the Field Museum, the Shedd Aquarium, the Adler Planetarium, the Museum of Science and Industry, the Michigan Avenue bridge, and the Outer Drive.

In 1939 the Chicago Plan Commission was greatly reduced in size and became in effect a part of city government with the statutory responsibility of reviewing city policies and programs. In 1961 the Illinois Inter-Agency Planning Referral Act broadened the scope of the commission, yet retained its advisory nature. The act required that all proposals for any development within Chicago by a public body be reviewed by the plan commission for compliance with the city's long-range planning goals. The commission under this act does not have the authority to enforce its decision, but its vote has an unofficial sanction.

In 1973 the commission's authority was enhanced by passage of the Lake Michigan and Chicago Lakefront Protection Ordinance, which requires a public hearing and commission approval for any public or private construction, landfill, or road building within the lakefront protection district. In 1974 the Planned Development Ordinance was passed, requiring the commission to hold public hearings on planned developments and to recommend to the city council approval or disapproval of the developer's plan.

The commission consists of 17 members: 9 private citizens, appointed by the mayor to serve without pay for five-year terms; and 8 ex officio members, including the mayor, the president of the Board of Local Improvements, the chairman of the Chicago Transit Authority, the commissioner of the Department of Planning, and chairmen of four city council committees (Finance, Housing, Traffic Control, and Zoning). One of the private members chairs the commission, and the Planning Commissioner serves as secretary. Staff support is provided by the Planning Department. The commission meets on the second Thursday of each month in the City Council Chambers at 1 P.M. Minutes of the meetings are kept on file at the Planning Department. All meetings are open to the public, and an agenda is sent to interested persons on request.

POLICE DEPARTMENT
1121 S. State St., Chicago 60605; phone, Emergency, 911
Non-emergency, 744 4000
Complaints against police, 744 5496
Tours of headquarters, 744 5570

The town of Chicago, incorporated in 1833, elected its first constable in 1835. In 1837 the city charter gave the city council power to appoint police constables as needed, not to exceed one from each of the six wards the city had at that time. The force consisted of two men until 1840. On April 10, 1855 the city council established the Chicago Police Department. The department's responsibilities include preserving law and order and enforcing state laws, city ordinances, and the orders of the mayor and city council. The department also is responsible for traffic control and for order at public events, and it provides services in medical and noncriminal emergencies.

The superintendent of police, the highest-ranking employee of the department and its chief administrative officer, is selected by the mayor from a list of three candidates submitted by the Police Board. The central police headquarters contains the office of the superintendent and most administrative department offices, including the crime laboratory, data systems and records, the communications system, and the offices of the Police Board. The communications system is centralized and automated. An emergency call to 911 is routed by computer, which shows the name, address, and telephone number used to make the call. The dispatcher has a map on a zone console which permits identification of the nearest police car to be sent to the scene.

Bureaus. By function, the department is divided into service bureaus: operational, investigative, technical, and community. Each bureau is headed by a deputy superintendent appointed by the superintendent. The first deputy superintendent is next in command after the superintendent and heads the Bureau of Operational Services, which includes the Patrol Division. Each bureau is divided into divisions, and divisions are generally made up of smaller units (e.g., the Gang Investigation Section).

Districts. By geography, the department is divided into 25 districts. The districts are grouped into 6 areas composed of 3 to 5 contiguous districts.

Each area office houses courtrooms, a gang enforcement division, a youth division, and a decentralized detective division. The area detective division is further divided into two main field units, one to handle property crimes and the other to handle violent crimes. The superintendent appoints a deputy chief for each area; their offices are at the central headquarters.

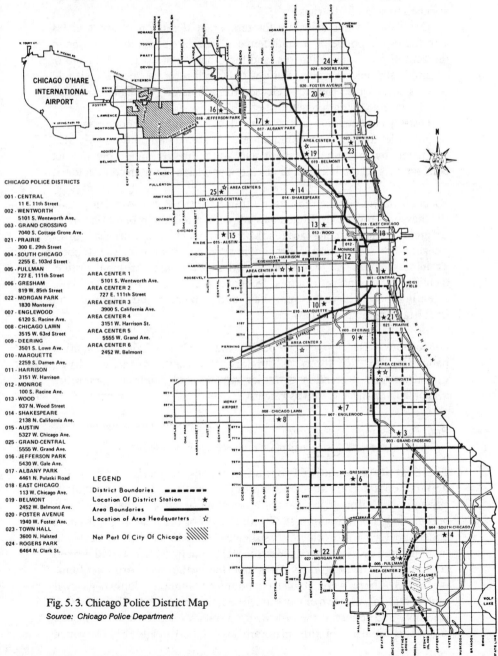

CHICAGO POLICE DISTRICTS

001 - CENTRAL
   11 E. 11th Street
002 - WENTWORTH
   5101 S. Wentworth Ave.
003 - GRAND CROSSING
   7040 S. Cottage Grove Ave.
021 - PRAIRIE
   300 E. 29th Street
004 - SOUTH CHICAGO
   2255 E. 103rd Street
005 - PULLMAN
   727 E. 111th Street
006 - GRESHAM
   819 W. 85th Street
022 - MORGAN PARK
   1830 Monterey
007 - ENGLEWOOD
   6120 S. Racine Ave.
008 - CHICAGO LAWN
   3515 W. 63rd Street
009 - DEERING
   3501 S. Lowe Ave.
010 - MARQUETTE
   2259 S. Damen Ave.
011 - HARRISON
   3151 W. Harrison
012 - MONROE
   100 S. Racine Ave.
013 - WOOD
   937 N. Wood Street
014 - SHAKESPEARE
   2138 N. California Ave.
015 - AUSTIN
   5327 W. Chicago Ave.
025 - GRAND-CENTRAL
   5555 W. Grand Ave.
016 - JEFFERSON PARK
   5430 W. Gale Ave.
017 - ALBANY PARK
   4461 N. Pulaski Road
018 - EAST CHICAGO
   113 W. Chicago Ave.
019 - BELMONT
   2452 W. Belmont Ave.
020 - FOSTER AVENUE
   1940 W. Foster Ave.
023 - TOWN HALL
   3600 N. Halsted
024 - ROGERS PARK
   6464 N. Clark St.

AREA CENTERS

AREA CENTER 1
   5101 S. Wentworth Ave.
AREA CENTER 2
   727 E. 111th Street
AREA CENTER 3
   3900 S. California Ave.
AREA CENTER 4
   3151 W. Harrison St.
AREA CENTER 5
   5555 W. Grand Ave.
AREA CENTER 6
   2452 W. Belmont

LEGEND

District Boundaries   ▬ ▬ ▬ ▬
Location Of District Station   ★
Area Boundaries
Location of Area Headquarters   ☆
Not Part Of City Of Chicago   ▨▨▨

Fig. 5. 3. Chicago Police District Map
Source: Chicago Police Department

Each of the 25 districts has a district station; their names, addresses, and telephone numbers are listed in the blue pages of the Chicago telephone directory. Districts serve to distribute the work load of the Patrol Division, and district boundaries are changed periodically to equalize work loads (the number of calls for services). Most patrol officers and cars are assigned to specific districts.

Every district has a lockup for temporary detention of adult males arrested by the police. For adult females, there are seven lockups, one in the central police headquarters, and the others in areas 1, 2, 4, 5, and 6. Juveniles are held at police stations only until they are seen by juvenile officers, after which they are released to parents or guardians or turned over to juvenile detention authorities.

District commanders are appointed by the superintendent and are responsible to the area commander. Watch commanders are also appointed by the superintendent and work directly under the district commanders. Captains work under the supervision of watch commanders.

Police Academy. Police recruits are trained at the Police Academy, 1300 W. Jackson Boulevard. Illinois law requires a minimum of 144 hours of training; the department exceeds this requirement, with a program of 14 weeks at the academy and 25 weeks of in-service training at district stations. Training includes 124 hours on the administration of criminal justice, including ethics and procedures; 58 hours on the criminal code and laws affecting police arrests, searches, and seizures; and 22 hours on understanding human behavior.

Publications. The department publishes a number of crime prevention pamphlets, on such topics as burglary, auto theft, con artists, drugs, vandalism, and protection of senior citizens and children. Some are available in Spanish as well as English.

Beat Representative Program
Director's office, 2001 S. Michigan, Chicago 60616; *phone 744 7931*

The Beat Representative Program began in the early 1970s in the departments's Bureau of Community Services as a cooperative citizen-police effort to exchange information about criminal activity. It became fully operational in 1977 with the aid of the federal government under the Law Enforcement Assistance Act (LEAA), which provided funds to open district service centers in storefront locations, staffed by paid coordinators. The program is now supported by the city's corporate fund.

In 1987 there were 16,000 community volunteers, known as beat representatives, who live or work in the beat they represent. Their function is to note and report to the police any suspicious activities they observe. Also participating in this program are 50,000 neighborhood watch members, who display blue and white signs in their windows and are trained for the community block watch. Safe sanctuaries for children and senior citizens in need of help are provided by 1,900 safe home program participants, who display orange and black window signs.

Under the program, paid staff and volunteers appear in court to assist victims and witnesses of crime; they also educate communities on victim/witness programs. The program hosts conferences designed to bring together police, clergy, and neighborhood residents to share responsibilities and develop innovative ways to reduce crime. It includes a Community Gang Control program, which attempts to intervene with marginal gang members referred by schools, community groups, or police; this program tries to place such young people in jobs, schools, and community activities.

Office of Professional Standards. The Office of Professional Standards investigates complaints about police use of excessive force. Other types of complaints are referred to the Internal Affairs Division. Complaints are investigated by civilian personnel who have never been employed by the police department. Investigators' reports are reviewed by the administrators of the office, who recommend action to the superintendent.

A complaint may be made in person, by telephone, or by letter to the Office of Professional Standards at 1024 S. Wabash. Complaints may also be made to district police stations. Two Beat Representative offices accept complaints from 11 A.M. to 7 P.M. on Mondays through Fridays; they are District 9, 5005 S. Ashland Ave., and District 13, 2156 W. Chicago Ave.

A complaint should include the time and place of the incident, any other witnesses, and any identification the complainant may have of the officer's name or badge number or the police car's number. A complaint may be made without giving the complainant's name. If this is done, however, the complainant cannot find out the results of the complaint. In other cases the department reports the outcome of the case to the complainant.

When the office was first established there were three administrators, one black, one white, and one Spanish-speaking. In recent years, however, there have been two: one black and one white. The 1988 budget provides for 80 additional employees and a total budget for personnel of $2,600,632.

Police Department Budget. The 1988 corporate fund budget for the Police Department was $543,015,776, and there were 15,864 employees. In 1987 there were 15,822 employees, of whom 12,597 were sworn officers, 1,981 were civilian employees, and 1,244 were school crossing guards. The department is funded by corporate funds; in 1988 it was budgeted for an additional $3,000,000 from federal community development funds to provide patrols in public housing. The 1988 salary of the superintendent was $96,000; salaries of sworn police range from $24,930 a year to $74,592.

POLICE BOARD
1121 S. State St., Chicago 60605; *phone 744 6268*

The Police Board is composed of nine private citizens who serve without compensation; they adopt the governing rules of the Police Department. They submit to the mayor the names of three candidates for the position of superintendent of police when there is a vacancy in that position. The board conducts hearings on serious disciplinary actions (those in which violations could result in discharge or suspensions of more than 30 days) for police officers and civilian employees of the department. The board may discharge, suspend, or reinstate employees. The board also reviews the department's budget. By ordinance, the police superintendent may attend all meetings of the board and take part in the deliberations but has no vote. A majority of members present at a meeting is required to implement any order or resolution.

The nine members are appointed by the mayor to serve five-year staggered terms. The mayor designates a president and vice-president from among the members. An executive director, who also serves as secretary to the board, is paid $42,444 a year; there is a supervising clerk and there are hearing officers who are paid $75 an hour. A hearing officer, who must be a licensed attorney, is present at all disciplinary hearings. The 1988 budget for the board was $214,012 from the corporate fund.

Transcripts, findings, and decisions of all separation cases are available to the public for inspection. The board usually meets on the second Thursday of every month at 10:30 A.M. in the auditorium of the fifth floor annex at 1121 S. State St. Except for executive sessions, meetings are open to the public. Meeting dates may vary, so it is important to call to verify dates and times.

DEPARTMENT OF PUBLIC WORKS
City Hall, 121 N. LaSalle St., Chicago 60602; *phone 744 3600*
Chicago Traffic Hotline, dial STREETS

The Department of Public Works is responsible for design and construction of capital improvements, repair maintenance of city property and buildings, development of transportation system projects, and design and implementation of traffic-related programs. It is responsible for designing and building airport improvements, subways, bridges, highways and streets, off-street parking, sewers, and waterworks. It maintains viaducts and operates movable bridges. It maintains the city's basic map records, and it is the agency which issues house numbers. It also issues permits for parades, carnivals, street openings and closings, and driveways.

The department includes the commissioner's office, an administrative division, and seven bureaus. The bureaus of Transportation Planning and Programming, of Engineering, of Architecture, of Construction Services, and of Construction Management are concerned with planning and carrying out capital improvements. The Bureau of Traffic Engineering and Operations is responsible for design and implementation of traffic-related programs. The Bureau of Maps and Plats prepares ordinances for new subdivisions, the vacation of streets and alleys, street names, and changes in the city boundaries. It also assigns house numbers. The department provides a number of services.

Model Block Improvement Program (744 5900) makes public improvements for blocks where residents have committed themselves to maintaining their properties.

50/50 Sidewalk Program is a program under which the city helps property owners by paying half of the costs of restoring sidewalks. The city pays 75% of the costs for senior citizens who own and occupy single-family residences or apartment buildings of four units or less. Residents apply to the city for this service by calling *744 4537*.

Vaulted Sidewalk Program is a program that deals with dangerous conditions in vaulted sidewalks adjacent to noncommercial property. In certain parts of Chicago, street levels were raised, leaving sidewalks with space underneath (often used for coal storage) and stairs to enter the houses at the old street level. Property owners apply for this service by writing to the Department of Public Works, Bureau of Architecture, 320 N. Clark St, Chicago 60610.

New Alleys Program paves unimproved alleys, on petition of owners of the abutting property. A public hearing is required, and property owners are assessed. Petitions are available from the Board of Local Improvements, *744 7189*.

New Street Construction Program replaces unimproved streets built in the 1930s by the federal Works Progress Administration (WPA). Property owners representing at least 51% of the total frontage of a block must submit a signed and notarized petition. Property owners are assessed $17 per foot of the front lot and $6 per foot on the side of a corner lot; the rate for senior citizens is half of those charges. The Bureau of Engineering (*744 7350*) provides petitions.

Industrial Streets Program is a cooperative program with the Department of Economic Development to upgrade streets within selected industrial areas.

Chicago Utility Alert Network (CUAN), also called "Diggers," is a network operated by the Department of Public Works to collect and transmit information to the various utilities with underground installations when a contractor plans to do digging that might interfere with those installations. It is located in room 802, City Hall, and its phone is *744 7000*. (Also see Board of Underground.)

Permits are issued by the Bureau of Traffic Engineering and Operations for work on or use of streets. Permits are required for overweight or oversize vehicles, street openings and closings, newspaper stands, carnivals, parades, canopies, and driveways. (Some of these require a city council ordinance as well.) To request a permit call *744 4652* or *744 4656*.

Traffic Information regarding street conditions, construction activity, routing and parking for special events, and emergency transportation advisories is offered by the Mayor's Traffic Management Task Force, *787 3387* (dial *STREETS*).

As of 1987, major improvements being undertaken by the department included expansion of terminals, roadways, parking, and transit at O'Hare airport; water purification and pumping station projects; design of the Southwest Rapid Transit line; the Howard/Dan Ryan project to link those two transit lines; and renovation of the Loop elevated system, the Jackson Park elevated branch, and the State and Dearborn street subways.

Administration and Finance. The Department of Public Works is headed by the Commissioner of Public Works, who is appointed by the mayor with the consent of the city council at a 1988 salary of $80,000. The 1988 corporate fund budget provided for 1,207 employees and a total of $43,063,555. Other funds for the department in 1988 were $2,049,000 for Special Service Area No. 1 (the State Street Mall), $6,902,645 from Community Development Block Grant Funds, $975,000 from the water fund, $12,392,635 from the vehicle tax fund, $14,390,000 from the motor fuel tax fund, and $4,392,600 from the Chicago Skyway Toll Bridge revenue fund. The total budget from all funds for 1988 was $83,617,790.

BOARD OF LOCAL IMPROVEMENTS. Under the provisions of the state Local Improvement Act, all ordinances for local improvements which are to be paid for wholly or in part by special assessment or special taxation must originate with the Board of Local Improvements. This board is part of the Department of Public Works and is made up of five members appointed by the mayor with the consent of the city council. Members are appointed for no set terms, serve at the discretion of the mayor, and are paid. A member may hold no other position in city government. The president, vice-president, and assistant secretary are elected by the board. The board meets as needed and meetings are open to the public. A superintendent of special assessments is in charge of making special assessments, subject to board direction, and is the ex officio secretary to the board. The 1988 budget provides for stipends of $13,332 for the president, $11,316 for the vice-president, and $9,588 for the other three board members. The 1988 budget was $461,703 from the Vehicle Tax Fund.

DEPARTMENT OF PURCHASES, CONTRACTS, AND SUPPLIES
City Hall, 121 N. LaSalle St., Chicago 60602; *phone 744 4900*

According to the *Municipal Handbook*, the Department of Purchases, Contracts, and Supplies is responsible for purchasing all materials, equipment, and services (including construction for public works) for city departments and the public library. The purchasing agent is responsible for control of inventories. The department conducts conferences on city purchasing procedures for small minority and female-owned businesses.

The Municipal Purchasing Act (Illinois Revised Statutes, Chapter 24) and Chapter 26 of the municipal code establish the laws governing the department. The act requires competitive bidding after formal advertisement when purchase orders or contracts involve $10,000 or more. Purchase orders or contracts less than $10,000 may be let in the open market without advertising in an informal bidding process. Contracts not adapted to competitive bidding, such as utilities or certain professional services, may be awarded without competitive bidding, but professional service contracts must have the approval of the Sole Source Review Board (see below). In case of an emergency involving public health, safety, or welfare, contracts up to $40,000 may be let without formal advertising.

Contracts over $50,000 are submitted to the Finance Committee of the city council for review. The Finance Committee also reviews all no-bid contracts; if objections are raised, the contract goes back to the department for more information or competitive bidding.

The Division of Contract Monitoring and Compliance certifies the businesses of minority and women owners and small businesses for city work and monitors compliance with orders and ordinances requiring that such businesses be given an opportunity to bid on city purchases. This division publishes a *Directory of Certified Disadvantaged Business Enterprises, Minority Business Enterprises, and Women's Business Enterprises.*

The department is headed by the purchasing agent, who is appointed by the mayor with the consent of the city council for a four-year term at a salary in 1988 of $71,000. In the 1988 budget, there are 143 positions funded by a budget of $4,420,976 from the corporate fund and 4 positions funded by $112,305 from Year XIV (1988) Community Development Block Grant funds.

THE SOLE SOURCE REVIEW BOARD is a six-member board made up of members from various city departments. It reviews requisitions for supplies or materials to be purchased from a sole source without competitive bidding, professional service contracts in excess of $10,000, and any other item the Purchasing Department may request it to review.

THE SOLE SOURCE REVIEW PANEL is a five-member panel which is appointed by the mayor with approval of the city council Finance Committee to make recommendations on disputed no-bid contracts.

DEPARTMENT OF REVENUE
City Hall, 121 N. LaSalle St., Chicago 60602.
License information, new business, 744 1502
Business renewal, 744 3948
Liquor, 744 1519
Sales tax information, 744 8760

The Department of Revenue was created in 1973 to replace the City Collector's office, was absorbed in 1979 by the Comptroller's Office, and was reestablished in 1984.

This department receives payment for all city taxes, licenses, permits, special assessments, inspections, parking tickets, and other fees not specifically provided for. It investigates evasion of payments and facilitates specialized collection efforts. State legislation has passed to permit the shift of parking ticket collections from traffic court (part of the state court system) to administrative judication by the department.

The department is headed by a director appointed by the mayor with the advice and consent of the city council, at a 1988 salary of $67,000. The department was budgeted for 395 employees with an appropriation of $17,948,886 from the corporate fund.

DEPARTMENT OF SEWERS
City Hall, 121 N. La Salle St., Chicago 60602; phone (24-hour service) 744 7050
Senior citizen sewer charge exemption information, 744 7456

The Department of Sewers was formed in 1980 when the Department of Water and Sewers was separated into two departments. This department operates and maintains the Chicago sewer system, which is a part of the drainage system of the Metropolitan Sanitary District of Greater Chicago. The Chicago sewer system collects and transports wastes from local sewers to the intercepting sewers of the Sanitary District, which carry them to the district's plants for treatment and disposal.

The Department of Sewers is responsible for repair and maintenance of sewer mains and their installation, except that the cost of construction may be paid for by special assessment under certain circumstances: that is., when adjoining property owners pay by special assessment for pavement of a street or alley and sewer construction is needed in connection with the paving. The department issues all permits for connection with, repairs to, and extension of the sewage system. It has supervision and control of street grades (slope of streets to provide drainage).

A commissioner is appointed by the mayor with the advice and consent of the city council, at an annual salary of $68,000. The department is funded almost entirely by an 84% surcharge on water bills, initiated in 1980. Senior citizens (65 or older) who live in single-family dwellings or two-flats where the second flat is not rented may apply for an exemption to the sewage charge. In 1988 the department was budgeted for 954 employees, with $56,660,000 from the sewer fund. The Metropolitan Sanitary District is a separate taxing body.

How To Identify Sewer Structures

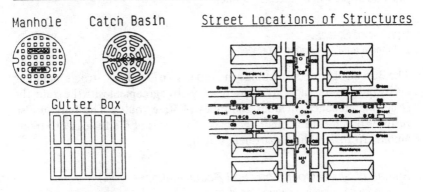

Manhole   Catch Basin   Street Locations of Structures

Gutter Box

Fig. 5. 4. Manhole covers
Source: Chicago Department of Sewers

DEPARTMENT OF STREETS AND SANITATION

City Hall, 121 N. La Salle St., Chicago 60602; phone *(complaints and requests, 8:30 A.M. to 4:30 P.M.)* 744 8020, *(24-hours)* 744 5000. See blue pages of Chicago telephone directory for ward offices, open for complaints 7 A.M. to 3:30 P.M. (summers, 6 A.M. to 2:30 P.M.) and the last Saturday of each month, 10 A.M. to 1 P.M.

The Department of Streets and Sanitation is responsible for improving, maintaining, cleaning, and lighting public ways and removing garbage from residences with up to four units. The department's Bureau of Sanitation has offices, headed by a ward superintendent, in each of the city's 50 wards. There are six bureaus in the department:

Bureau of Sanitation
Information on new garbage carts, *427 2243 (G-A-R-B-A-G-E)*

The Bureau of Sanitation collects and disposes of nearly one and a quarter million tons of household waste and bulk items a year, with about 400 garbage trucks operating each weekday. About one-fourth of the garbage is burned at the city's incinerator, and the remainder is sent to landfills. As of 1988, a new system of refuse collection containers (90-gallon plastic "Chicago Carts") was being phased in, to minimize lifting and reduce injuries to workers.. The department was making plans for a citywide recycling program to reduce dependence on landfills. This bureau uses 42% of the department's budget.

Refuse Disposal Reimbursements. Although apartment buildings over four units in size must pay for private scavenger service, managers of condominium and cooperative apartment buildings may apply annually or semiannually through their aldermen for reimbursement for refuse collection costs. Forms and receipts are required, and each reimbursement must be approved by the city council.

Bureau of Streets
Pothole repair, *744 8020, 744 5000*

The Bureau of Streets maintains and repairs 3,677 miles of streets including curbs and gutters, and 1,906 miles of alleys; by agreement with the state, the street maintenance includes 200 miles of state routes. The bureau also restores pavement for other agencies. Expenses of the Bureau of Streets amount to 10% of the department's budget.

Bureau of Street Operations and Beautification
Tools for community cleanup, *744 8020*
Tree planting, trimming, removal, stump removal, *744 8020* or *744 5000*
Street-sweeping schedule, call ward office (see Chicago telephone directory blue pages)

The Bureau of Street Operations and Beautification salts and plows major streets during snowfalls. It sweeps streets, cleans vacant lots, and loans rakes, brooms, and shovels for community clean-ups. It sets out and empties litter baskets in the Loop, Gold Coast, and New Town areas. It responds to lakefront or river flooding emergencies on a 24-hour basis. Its beautification division (formerly the Bureau of Forestry, Parkways, and Beautification) maintains the 450,000 trees on the city parkways and cares for 300 acres of boulevard systems, including planting, flower beds, and picking up litter. The division plants 5,500 trees, trims 50,000 trees, and removes 15,000 dead, diseased, or damaged trees a year. Its share of the department's budget is 15%.

Bureau of Rodent Control
Rodent complaints and requests for pickup of dead animals, *744 6465*

A Chicago ordinance requires that all new buildings be rat-proofed and kept in that condition and that old buildings be rat-stopped and maintained rat-free. The Bureau of Rodent Control enforces the ordinance and has a baiting program for public areas and empty lots. It also picks up dead animals for proper disposal. Its share of the department's budget is 2%.

Bureau of Electricity
Street and alley light and traffic signal malfunctions, 744 8020, 744 5000

The Bureau of Electricity installs, operates, and maintains the city's street and alley lights, traffic signals, fire alarms, police and fire communications systems, and city employees' radio communications. It services about 194,000 streetlights, 45,000 alley lights, and traffic signals at 3,200 intersections. Costs of this bureau amount to 25% of the department's budget.

Bureau of Labor
To report abandoned cars, 744 8020, 744 5000

A new bureau was established in the 1988 budget, to provide motor truck drivers, steam roller engineers, and security personnel to meet seasonal and annual needs of the other bureaus of the department. The Bureau of Labor is responsible for the city's towing of illegally parked or abandoned cars and for emergency towing. It provides barricades and other services for special events, handles traffic-control programs such as reverse lanes on Lake Shore Drive, and responds to traffic-control emergencies. This bureau was budgeted for 4% of the department's appropriation.

Budget. The total budget for the Department of Streets and Sanitation in 1988 was $242,256,659, with 3,233 budgeted positions, 670,743 additional position-hours (equivalent to 329 full-time positions), and seasonal employees as funding permits. There were four sources of funds for the department: $183,805,929 came from the city's corporate fund; $22,200,405 from the vehicle tax fund; $35,163,325 from the motor fuel tax fund; and $1,087,000 from the State Street Mall tax fund (a special taxing district). The department is headed by a commissioner appointed by the mayor with the advice and consent of the city council, at a 1988 salary of $81,000. The commissioner's administrative staff accounts for 2% of the budget.

BOARD OF UNDERGROUND WORK OF PUBLIC UTILITIES
Room 300 A, 320 N. Clark St., Chicago 60610; *phone 744 7295*

The Board of Underground is a quasi-governmental agency which serves as a clearinghouse to keep track of the location of underground utility installations and utility services for the city government, the Park District, the Metropolitan Sanitary District, private utilities such as gas, electric, and cable TV companies, and the railroads. The board answers requests for information as to whether there are public utilities in existence or being used on a piece of land. A letter of inquiry and a service fee of $50 are required. The board has three employees, headed by the secretary of the board. It is funded 20% by governmental agencies and 80% by private utilities. (See also Chicago Utility Alert Network of the city's Department of Public Works.)

DEPARTMENT OF WATER

James W. Jardine Water Purification Plant, 1000 E. Ohio St., Chicago 60611;
phone 744 7001

Chicago's first water system was a private utility that began operating in 1842, using Lake Michigan water. A new, municipally owned waterworks was built and began operating in 1854. Currently the Chicago water system serves about 4.5 million people, including not only city residents but also residents of 94 suburbs. Charges for water sold to municipalities within the Metropolitan Sanitary District are at the same metered rates as those for users within the city. Some municipalities not adjoining Chicago receive city water through the facilities of other communities that are directly connected to Chicago.

The water system includes the world's two largest water-purification plants (the James W. Jardine Plant north of Navy Pier and the South Plant at 79th Street and the Lake), three active water intake crib complexes and one standby crib, 11 water pumping stations, over 65 miles of water supply tunnels, more than 4,200 miles of water mains, and 47,000 fire hydrants.

Water is obtained either at the intake cribs, two or three miles offshore, or at the shore intakes of the water purification plants. The water flows to the purification plants where it is treated before it enters storage reservoirs. It takes water about eight hours to go through the entire treatment process, during which it is fluoridated to help prevent tooth decay.

The water system is a self-supporting utility deriving moneys for operating expenses from water charges; it does not receive tax funds. The water fund, however, is part of the city budget. In 1988 appropriations for the water department from this fund amounted to $151,415,590; there were 2,329 employees in the water department. The department is headed by a commissioner appointed by the mayor with the consent of the city council, at a salary of $76,000 a year.

MAYOR'S COMMISSION ON WOMEN'S AFFAIRS

Room 6B, 510 N. Peshtigo Court, Chicago 60611; *phone 744 4427*

The Mayor's Commission on Women's Affairs was established by executive order in 1984. Its function is to advise the mayor and city departments on ways to address the needs of women. It has the power to conduct surveys, hold public hearings, undertake research, and make recommendations on public policy. The commission has seven public committees: Health, Economic Opportunities, Human Services, Employment, Safety and the Legal System, Special Projects, and Legislative.

The mayor appoints 33 members, who serve without pay for two-year terms. The chair is appointed by the mayor. An executive director is appointed by the mayor at an annual salary of $42,444. In 1988 the commission had eight employees. Its corporate fund budget for 1988 was $311,848.

Committees meet monthly. The commission meets every other month, at 5:30 P.M. on fourth Thursdays. Information as to where the meeting will be held is available by calling the office. The commission publishes a newsletter.

DEPARTMENT OF ZONING

City Hall, 121 N. LaSalle St., Chicago 60602; *phone 744 3455*

The Department of Zoning, previously a bureau within the Department of Buildings, was made a separate department in 1982. Its responsibility is to enforce compliance with the city's zoning ordinance. The department is headed by the zoning administrator, who is appointed by the mayor with the consent of the city council, at an annual salary in 1988 of $52,920. The department had 19 employees in 1988 and a budget of $560,823 from the corporate fund.

Zoning Ordinance. The Chicago Zoning Ordinance, a chapter of the city's Municipal Code, controls the sizes and uses of buildings within specified areas and related facilities that may be required, such as off-street parking space. It limits the number of homes, apartments, and commercial or industrial buildings that can be built on a specific lot, encourages open space around buildings, and prevents a mixture of conflicting land uses. The ordinance, which was adopted in 1957, has been amended frequently.

The ordinance consists of a map which divides the city into zoning districts and text which contains use and bulk regulations applicable to those districts, as well as procedures regarding zoning. Copies of the ordinance are available for examination at the department or at the Municipal Reference Library. The zoning map may be altered only by amending the zoning ordinance approved by the city council. Exceptions to the zoning map, however, often are sought in the form of either of two types of variation. Proposed construction which involves either of these types of variation must be approved by the Zoning Board of Appeals, regardless of the zoning area.

The first type of variation is an exception to the zoning ordinance granted for an individual piece of property which will not alter the essential character of the locality; for example, a variation may be sought to build a structure which will have a yard smaller than the size required for the zoning district.

The second type of variation is a variation in the nature of a special use. It is applied for and processed in the same manner as other applications for variation, but it is for purposes that might affect property values or public facilities. Variations for special uses are not granted by the Zoning Board of Appeals unless they are found to have the following characteristics. They are necessary for public convenience; they are designed and located and will be operated so that public health, safety, and welfare will be protected; they will not cause substantial injury to the value of other property in the neighborhood; and they conform to the regulations of the zoning district.

Planned developments were redefined in the zoning ordinance in 1974 so that developments (of specified sizes and/or for which certain specified types of structure are proposed) are rezoned as planned developments and are not subject to the requirements of the previous zoning district. The purpose of this redefinition is to provide for unified planning and development, but the intensity of use permitted must be in conformity with zoning regulations presently applicable to the property. Planned developments, if granted, alter the zoning map by changing the zoning to include them. Applications for planned developments must be submitted to the Chicago Plan Commission for review, which must include a public hearing. After the commission makes its recommendations, the application is submitted to the city council; procedures are the same as those for amendments to the zoning ordinance. Amendments to the ordinance alter the zoning map permanently. A zoning amendment must be for a parcel of land which is at least 10,000 square feet, or which has at least 100 feet of frontage, or which adjoins another parcel proposed for amendment.

Applications for amendments to the ordinance may be initiated by any resident or property owner, by the commissioner of planning, or by members of the city council. Applications must be presented to the zoning administrator, except for those filed by city council members. The city clerk presents the application at the next regular council meeting, at which it is referred to the Zoning Committee for public hearing and review. For planned development applications the committee holds its own public hearing in addition to the previous public hearing held by the Plan Commission. The zoning administrator and the commissioner of planning make recommendations to the committee. Following review by the committee, the matter is presented to the full city council, which has the authority to approve amendments to the zoning ordinance subject to review by the courts. The zoning administrator is required by ordinance to maintain a public information bureau on matters arising from the zoning ordinance.

ZONING BOARD OF APPEALS
City Hall, 121 N. LaSalle St., Chicago 60602; *phone 744 0887*

The Zoning Board of Appeals was created under state law and the city zoning ordinance. It decides appeals from rulings of the zoning administrator and passes on applications for variations and variations for special uses. Decisions of the board are final, subject only to court review. The board consists of five members appointed for five-year terms by the mayor with the consent of the city council. The mayor designates the chair, who is paid $18,000 a year; the other members are paid $12,000 each.

Meetings are generally held on the third Friday of the month, but special meetings may also be held.

Written orders of the board are available at its office. In 1987, the board heard about 275 cases. A staff of five answers questions and provides explanations of zoning maps, including the legally permitted uses in various zoning districts. The board's corporate fund budget in 1988 was $224,912.

CITY FUNDING

The Chicago city budget covers only the functions performed by the city government. The Board of Education, Park District, and Chicago Community College District enact separate budgets. (Although the public library is an independent agency and has independent funds, it is included in the city budget document and appropriation ordinance.) Comparisons with other cities must be made in terms of individual services, as they may include funds for schools, parks, and colleges within their city budgets.

To get an overview of total city expenditures, one must examine all city funds. In addition to the corporate fund, there are 16 other funds supported by property taxes; 2 of these are library funds, 5 are pension funds, and 5 are note or bond redemption and interest funds (see fig. 5.6). There are also 12 nonproperty tax funds; some are for city services reimbursed by charging fees, and some are taxes earmarked for special purposes. The corporate fund, however is the main operating fund.

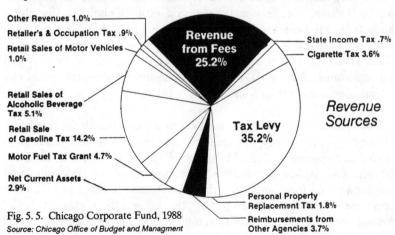

Fig. 5. 5. Chicago Corporate Fund, 1988
Source: Chicago Office of Budget and Managment

SOURCES OF FUNDS. Taxing and bonding powers of local governments are described in detail in chapter 4. Chicago uses revenue sources available to home rule governments, though any new tax enacted is generally tested in the courts, a process which may take several years. Funds also come from the state and federal governments; most of these are not included in the line-item budget of the corporate fund, except for the city's share of the state income tax. Revenue also comes from enterprise funds; from licenses, permits, fees, and franchises; from interest on investments; from sale or lease of property; and from fines. In the city's budget for 1988, it expected to have total revenues of $2,671,709,405 from all sources.

TAXES. The city's power to tax, like that of all local governments, including those with home rule powers, is limited by the state. (See chapter 4 and Home Rule section, chapter 1.) The city also receives funds arising from state and federal taxes.

The Property Tax. The tax on real estate in the city is the property tax. It is assessed and collected by the county. In 1988 the city expected to have $139,179,582 available from the sale of proceeds of daily tender notes (tax anticipation warrants) for the corporate fund, to be repaid from the following year's property tax collections. In a change in accounting procedures to a modified accrual basis, receipts of property taxes are now recorded in the budget under "Other Revenues" as "Proceeds from Daily Tender Notes."

The Municipal Utility Tax. The city's utility tax is collected as a charge amounting to 8% of gross receipts of the utilities supplying gas, electricity, and telephone services. State law provides that cities with population of over 500,000 may impose an 8% tax on natural gas use, and Chicago does so. For the telephone service, the tax is on local telephone service plus a charge to the utility for use of city property; for electrical services, it is a 5% charge on electrical services plus a franchise charge. The city expected to collect $173,154,000 in charges on gross receipts of utilities in 1988, as well as an additional $101,480,000 in compensation from them for use of city property to maintain their franchises.

Sales Taxes. Two cents of the sales tax paid on each dollar of purchases in the city goes to the city, one cent collected by the state and returned to the city, and one cent collected by the city since 1981. The state Municipal Retailers Occupation Tax (unlike the remainder of the state sales tax) includes a tax on food and drugs; the city-collected tax does not. The two taxes were expected to amount to $272,185,000 in 1988. A cigarette tax of 15 cents per pack was expected to amount to $35,220,000, and a liquor tax (per gallon: beer, 12 cents; wine, 15 cents; alcohol and spirits, 50 cents) was expected to amount to $13,325,000.

Transportation Taxes. There are four taxes which can be put under the heading of transporation taxes: (1) the motor vehicle license tax, an annual vehicle license tax (the city sticker shows you have paid it) of $50 per car, $25 for senior citizens, with expected 1988 revenue of $56,325,000; (2) the

Chicago Vehicle Fuel Tax, on aircraft and automobile fuel, with expected 1988 revenue of $79,121,000; (3) a parking tax (90 cents a day for parking in parking lots or garages), with expected revenue of $32,889,000; and (4) a motor vehicle lessor tax of 95 cents per vehicle per rental period which was expected to produce $6,000,000. A boat mooring tax of 50% of the boat mooring fees charged by the Park District was expected to produce 1988 revenues of $1,640,000. This tax was contested; it was approved by the courts in 1987, but was repealed in 1988 for 1989.

Amusement Taxes. (1) A tax of $75 per automatic amusement device was expected to bring in $1,500,000 in 1988. (2) A tax of 4% of gross receipts on admission fees to all other   amusements was expected to bring in $5,000,000.

Hotel Tax. The city's hotel tax of 3% of gross rental charges was expected to produce 1988 revenues of $16,316,000.

Employers' Expense Tax. An employers' expense tax (head tax), of $5 per employee on employers who employ 15 or more individuals within the city was expected to provide $36,200,000.

Property Transaction Taxes. (1) A tax of 6% on lease or rental of personal property became effective in 1981. (2) A tax on real property transfer became effective in 1984; its current rate is $7.50 per $1,000 of the transfer price. These two taxes were expected to produce $72,250,000 in 1988.

Shared State Revenues. The city receives a share of the following taxes collected by the state. (1) From the state income tax, the city receives its share, on the basis of population, of the one-twelfth of the state income tax which is distributed to municipalities. The city receives approximately 26% of the amount that the state distributes and expected to receive $85,000,000 in 1988. (2) From the corporate personal property replacement tax paid by corporations as part of the state income tax, the city expected to receive $33,352,000. (3) From the state motor fuel tax, 32% of which is distributed to municipalites on the basis of population, the city expected to receive $53,960,000. (4) One cent of the state sales tax (listed above) is returned to the city on sales within the city. (5) The Municipal Hotel Operators' Tax (hotel tax) is collected by the state and paid to the city. The city expected to receive $5,094,000. The income from this tax is earmarked to promote tourism and conventions.

Federal and State Grants. Block grants and categorical grants are made by the federal and state governments for specific purposes, such as health and human services, urban development, and infrastructure improvements.

The amounts depend on state and federal budgets and on success in applying for grants. (See Community Development Block Grants, below.)

Enterprise Fund Projects. The city operates five major enterprise activities, operations which are supported by user charges. These are the water fund (which supplies water to 94 suburban municipalities as well as the city); the sewer fund, established in 1980, calculated as an additional charge in 1988 of 84% of water bills; the O'Hare International Airport fund; the Midway Airport fund; and the Chicago-Calumet Skyway fund. All except the Midway fund have outstanding revenue bonds.

Licenses, Permits, Fees, Fines. Under state law, the city may not license or issue permits for revenue. Fees charged must be related to the cost of the services. The largest amount in license fees comes from licensing of alcoholic dealers, from which the city expected $11,940,000 in 1988. From other licenses, permits, and certificates, the city expected $16,580,000. Fines, forfeits, and penalties for violation of city ordinances are collected by the clerk of the Chicago municipal district court (part of the state court system) and transmitted to the city; the city expected $43,500,000 from that source in 1988. As of 1988, state legislation authorized collection of parking fines by the city Department of Revenue.

Borrowing. The city borrows in three ways: (1) Short-term borrowing through Tax Anticipation Warrants, or Daily Tender Notes, which are sold to pay for operating expenses until the property taxes are collected. The city expected to sell $139,179,582 of these in 1988. (2) Long-term borrowing through General Obligation Bonds, issued to pay for major capital improvements. The 1988 appropriation to pay principal and interest on General Obligation bonds was $81,501,000. (3) Revenue Bonds, which are also long-term borrowing, to be repaid from fees charged to users of the service. (For instance, capital improvement bonds for the water and sewer systems are repaid from water and sewer charges.)

BUDGET PROCEDURES

The city's fiscal year begins January 1. Under state law, the mayor is required to submit a budget to the city council by November 15, and the appropriation ordinance (budget) must be passed by December 31. The actual procedure of budget preparation begins much earlier in the year, however. In accordance with a 1983 executive order of the mayor, the budget director has prepared a Preliminary Budget Estimate and made it available for public review and comment. The preliminary estimates are followed by preparation of the Executive Budget, currently submitted to the city council by October 15. The council Budget Committee then holds hearings on each department's budget, and the council as a whole must approve an appropriation ordinance by the legal deadline of December 31.

Budget materials are available from the city's Office of Budget and Management, the Municipal Reference Library, and some branches of the Chicago Public Library. The budget appears in two forms, a line-item budget and a program performance budget. The line-item budget is required by state law and is a detailed item-by-item listing of every expenditure in such categories as personal services (a complete listing of positions and salaries), contractual services, travel, commodities (supplies, etc.), equipment, permanent improvements, and contingencies. The program performance budget lists expenditures by the programs to be accomplished by each department. Output is measured by work performed, services provided, or improvements made.

A third document, the Corporate/Operating Funds Revenue Estimates, is prepared by the Office of Budget and Management. It is a detailed history of each revenue source for all funds and projected estimates for each fund.

Pension Funds. There are five city annuity and benefit funds for city employees; the city's contribution is established by state law. Appropriations from the property tax and corporate personal property replacement tax for these funds for 1988 were budgeted at $218,876,000.

Capital Improvement Program. The five-year Capital Improvement Program prepared by and available from the budget office is published in the first quarter of the year. It includes all construction to be carried out within the city by all public bodies and the sources of funds for these projects. The program includes information on planned improvements to neighborhood infrastructure (new or repaved streets, alleys, sidewalks, water and sewer improvements); construction of service centers and public facilities such as senior citizen centers, health centers, fire and police stations, libraries, park facilities, schools; transportation improvements such as the new Southwest Transit Line and rehabilitation of the Loop Elevated, and airport improvements; and improvements related to business, commercial, and industrial areas.

COMMUNITY DEVELOPMENT BLOCK GRANT (CDBG) BUDGET

The Community Development Block Grant (CDBG) program is administered by the U.S. Department of Housing and Urban Development (HUD). These funds are not included in the city's line-item budget. The funds, as appropriated by Congress, are distributed by HUD on the basis of annual entitlements, based on a formula which includes population, extent of poverty, and age of housing. CDBG legislation requires that at least 51% of the funds must be used for the benefit of low- and moderate-income persons; the city must report its projects by census tracts to demonstrate compliance with this requirement.

HUD regulations require a citizen participation mechanism; the Community Development Advisory Committee (see above) reviews and comments on all proposals for CDBG funding. The Community Development and Housing Coordinating Committee, comprised of the heads of every city agency receiving CDBG funds, also reviews and comments on proposals.

CDBG funds may be used for eligible programs carried out by private as well as public agencies. Application forms are provided and explained in June, proposals are due in July; public hearings are held in September; the city council reviews and may modify the proposal in November, and the CDBG application must be submitted to HUD by December 1. The CDBG Program Year now begins on January 1.

SUMMARY OF APPROPRIATIONS FROM FUNDS BY MAJOR PURPOSES FOR YEAR 1988

FUND NO.		GENERAL EXPENSE	CAPITAL OUTLAY	DEBT SERVICE	PENSION FUNDS	SPECIFIC LEVIES FOR LOSS IN COLLECTION OF TAXES	TOTAL APPROPRIATION
	PROPERTY TAX SUPPORTED FUNDS						
100	CORPORATE FUND	1,392,168.705	5,077.281	24,936.000			1,422,181.986
324	SPECIAL SERVICE AREA NUMBER TWO	67.038				670	67.708
326	SPECIAL SERVICE AREA NUMBER ONE	3,136.000					3,136.000
342	LIBRARY FUND-BUILDINGS AND SITES	5,287.503	2,871.244	711.700		400.253	9,270.700
346	LIBRARY FUND-MAINTENANCE AND OPERATION	38,042.969	5,850	4,276.000		1,836.381	44,161.200
395	JUDGMENT TAX FUND	33,004.295		4,342.000			37,346.295
508	SPECIAL SERVICE AREA NUMBER ONE			266.000		3,000	269.000
509	NOTE REDEMPTION AND INTEREST FUND			29,375.000		1,546.000	30,921.000
510	BOND REDEMPTION AND INTEREST FUND			77,537.000		3,964.000	81,501.000
512	NOTE REDEMPTION AND INTEREST FUND			139,179.582		7,325.241	146,504.823
568	LIBRARY BOND REDEMPTION AND INTEREST FUND			19,500.000		1,026.000	20,526.000
641	PUBLIC BUILDING COMMISSION FUND	14,532.000					14,532.000
660	CITY RELIEF FUND	14,508.000		2,029.152		870.377	17,407.529
	PENSION FUNDS						
681	MUNICIPAL EMPLOYEES' ANNUITY AND BENEFIT FUND				97,051.000		97,051.000
682	LABORERS' AND RETIREMENT BOARD EMPLOYEES'				15,380.000		15,380.000
683	POLICEMEN'S ANNUITY AND BENEFIT FUND				71,221.000		71,221.000
684	FIREMEN'S ANNUITY AND BENEFIT FUND				35,199.000		35,199.000
691	PARK EMPLOYEES' ANNUITY AND BENEFIT FUND				25.000		25.000
	TOTALS--PROPERTY TAX SUPPORTED FUNDS	1,500,746.510	7,954.375	302,152.434	218,876.000	16,971.922	2,046,701.241
	NON-PROPERTY TAX FUNDS						
171	ENVIRONMENTAL CONTROL FUND	1,352,660	27,100				1,379,760
200	WATER FUND	172,471.981	33,620.777	23,537.242			229,630.000
292	PAVEMENT RESTORATION AND INSPECTION FUND	4,000.000					4,000.000
300	VEHICLE TAX FUND	55,319.120	1,005.880				56,325.000
310	MOTOR FUEL TAX FUND	53,960.000					53,960.000
314	SEWER FUND	80,344.285	17,772.162	6,128.553			104,245.000
355	MUNICIPAL HOTEL OPERATORS' OCCUPATION TAX FUND	5,500.559	36.600				5,537.159
356	SPECIAL EVENTS FUND	10,900.000					10,900.000
400	GENERAL OBLIGATION BOND FUNDS			2,700.000			2,700.000
610	MIDWAY AIRPORT FUND	15,154.035	70.659				15,224.694
701	CALUMET SKYWAY TOLL BRIDGE REVENUE FUND	6,934.790	14.530	5,800.000			12,749.320
740	CHICAGO-O'HARE INTERNATIONAL AIRPORT REVENUE FUND	210,019.920	4,602.161	93,525.529			308,147.610
	TOTALS--NON-PROPERTY TAX FUNDS	615,957.350	59,849.869	128,991.324			804,798.543
	GRAND TOTALS-ALL FUNDS	2,116,703.860	67,804.244	431,143.758	218,876.000	16,971.922	2,851,499.784
	DEDUCT INTER-FUND REIMBURSEMENTS						179,790.379
	NET TOTALS-ALL FUNDS						2,671,709.405

GENERAL EXPENSE INCLUDES APPROPRIATIONS FOR EXPENDITURES FOR OPERATION, MAINTENANCE, ORDINARY REPAIRS AND MISCELLANEOUS ITEMS OF EXPENSE.
CAPITAL OUTLAY INCLUDES APPROPRIATIONS FOR EXPENDITURES FOR PURCHASE OF ADDITIONAL AND REPLACEMENT EQUIPMENT; PERMANENT IMPROVEMENTS INCLUDING REHABILITATION AND REPLACEMENT; PURCHASE OF LAND AND EXPENDITURES INCIDENTAL TO ACQUISITION OF LAND.
DEBT SERVICE INCLUDES APPROPRIATIONS FOR REDEMPTION OF DEBT AND INTEREST ON DEBT, AND FOR REQUIRED RESERVES.
PENSION FUNDS APPROPRIATIONS REPRESENTS THE GROSS AMOUNTS OF THE CITY'S CONTRIBUTION TO THE PENSION FUNDS.
LOSS IN COLLECTION OF TAXES REPRESENTS THE AMOUNTS APPROPRIATED AS A RESERVE AGAINST THE GROSS AMOUNT OF GENERAL PROPERTY TAXES TO BE LEVIED FOR POTENTIAL LOSSES IN TAX COLLECTIONS.

Fig. 5. 6. City of Chicago Funds. Funds supported by the property tax and funds supported from other taxes and other sources of revenue are shown separately.

Source: City of Chicago Annual Appropriation Ordinance for 1988

6 Chicago Governments: Independent Agencies

Most people think of the city of Chicago as responsible for local government in the city, but in fact within the same geographic boundaries there are five separate and independent taxing bodies and a number of other independent and quasi-independent agencies. The mayor with city council approval appoints the members of the boards of many, but not all, of these agencies. But the Board of Education, the Chicago Park District, the City Colleges of Chicago, and the Chicago Public Library are independent bodies with powers granted by the state. The Chicago Transit Authority is an independent agency which gets funding from the Regional Transit Authority. The Chicago Housing Authority is an independent agency which gets funding from the U.S. Department of Housing and Urban Development. Chicago voters also elect members of the county board and county officials, the Metropolitan Sanitary District board, and judges; Chicago residents pay taxes to support these agencies and receive services from them, but their boundaries extend beyond the city. This chapter will discuss local governments other than the city itself within the city boundaries.

THE CHICAGO PUBLIC SCHOOL SYSTEM

The school district of the city of Chicago is Illinois Public School District Number 299, the largest school district in the state. It is a taxing body separate from the city. In 1917 the Illinois legislature made Chicago a unit school district in a statute, often referred to as the Otis law, which directed that any city with a population over 500,000 should constitute one school district; the law also created a Board of Examiners to certify teachers for the Chicago public schools. The School Code of Illinois (Chapter 122 of the Illinois Revised Statutes, but also published separately) contains the laws governing all of the schools of the state; Article 34 contains the Otis law and other laws that apply only to the Chicago public schools.

The Chicago public schools provide education for over 421,000 students from prekindergarten through grade 12, in 594 school units. Kindergarten is available to all children. Prekindergarten (for three- and four-year-olds) is provided in programs funded by the state and federal governments. Programs for bilingual education, special education, and disadvantaged children are partially supported by state and federal funds. The public schools serve about 12,000 children in prekindergarten, and Head Start programs of churches and private agencies serve another 6,000 children, most of whom enter public school in kindergarten.

There are special facilities for severely handicapped children; local schools provide for those whose handicaps permit mainstreaming (attendance at regular schools). Local schools and six "gifted centers" have programs for children classified as gifted. There is transitional bilingual education in 20 languages for more than 36,000 students. The school system also operates an educational public radio station, WBEZ-FM.

Desegregation and Magnet Schools. A consent decree handed down by the federal court in 1980 required the Chicago Board of Education to provide for desegregation of the Chicago public schools. As of 1987 the school population was 60.1% black, 24% Hispanic, 12.9% white, and 3% Asian, Pacific Islander, American Indian, or Alaskan native. To attract a diverse student body, the desegregation program uses magnet schools, magnet programs, community academies, scholastic academies, and special programs. However, out of 594 schools, 280 had enrollments which were 90% to 100% black. About 100 of the lowest-achieving racially identifiable schools receive special desegregation funds to improve the performance of the students and the schools. These funds are state Title I funds, part of the state school funding formula (see chapter 2). In 1987 an agreement was reached settling a suit brought by the Board of Education under the provisions of the 1980 consent decree; as a result, $87,000,000 over a five-year period in new federal funds will be earmarked for racially identifiable schools.

A magnet school has a special focus (science, mathematics, humanities, foreign language, etc.) which is integrated into the whole curriculum, and staff members are selected on the basis of the necessary skills. Scholastic academies focus on a traditional back-to-basics program. All of the magnet schools attract a citywide enrollment and admit qualified students on the basis of targeted percentages of racial groups. Magnet programs have been receiving about $4,000,000 a year in federal funds since 1985.

Some schools with regular neighborhood enrollment also have magnet programs with citywide integrated enrollment. Community academies provide for the children within their attendance area special programs similar to those of magnet schools. For some programs children are expected to read at grade level or above; those who wish to enter classical schools and regional gifted centers are tested and must be two years above grade level in reading and mathematics and reach stanine 8 or above (fall within the top 20% of students in the city). Approximately 82,600 students in 150 schools participated in desegregation programs in 1985-86.

Busing is provided for special education students and for elementary school students who participate in any voluntary transfer program and live more than a mile and a half from their school. In 1987-88 the total budget for busing was $74,739,748, of which about $45 million was for busing special education students. Special education transportation is fully reimbursed by the state. Other transportation is 40% reimbursed.

1988 State Legislation. In 1988 the state legislature passed legislation which was designed to revise the structure and procedures of the Chicago Public Schools. As of August 1988 the governor had not signed the legislation, so it was not yet law and was subject to revision by amendatory veto and subsequent action of the legislature. The legislation provided that the terms of members of the Board of Education (see below) were to end on August 31, 1989, and a 7-member interim board was to be appointed to serve until May 15, 1990, or until a new 15-member board was appointed to serve 4-year staggered terms. After July 1, 1989 the board, by majority vote of its full membership, would appoint a general superintendent to serve for three years on a performance-based contract. The legislation would give the general superintendent the power, now exercised by the board, to negotiate teacher contracts subject to board approval. A new school board nominating commission (see below) would be constituted as of July 1, 1989. It would have a membership of 25: a representative from each of the 20 district councils and 5 members to be appointed by the mayor.

The legislation also established a seven-member oversight committee to oversee the implementation of the legislation and to make annual reports to the mayor, the governor, and the General Assembly. Four committee members would be appointed by the mayor and three by the governor, all to serve without pay. (In late August the governor announced his intention to amend this section to provide that the mayor and the governor would each appoint three members and jointly choose the chair.) The committee would be dissolved in June 1994.

Provisions for parent participation (see below) were also set by the legislation. The law provided that after July 1, 1989 each school must have an 11-member Local School Council, to consist of the principal, 6 parents of children in the school, 2 community members, and 2 teachers. Each high school would also elect a nonvoting student member. The council would select a principal (accredited by the state) to serve under a three-year performance contract; the council would decide whether or not to renew the principal's contract. Each school would be given a lump-sum amount for its budget and could make decisions about the allocation of educational expenses. The principal would make up the plan, and the council could approve it or not. The council also would help develop a three-year school improvement plan and would have the power to approve it or not. Each school would have a committee of teachers to advise the principal on educational matters.

The legislation would change the name of the councils serving the districts to "District Councils," and each council would be composed of one representative from each Local School Council in its district. The council would appoint the district superintendent and decide on renewal of the superintendent's contract.

For information on the status of this or other legislation, call the office of your state representative or state senator. Citizens Information Service, *939 INFO*, will answer requests for names and telephone numbers of legislators.

CHICAGO BOARD OF EDUCATION
1819 W. Pershing Road, Chicago 60609; *phone 890 8000*
Time and location of meetings, *890 3730*

The Chicago Board of Education is the policy-making body set up by state law to appoint the general superintendent and to establish rules and regulations which have the force of law with respect to the school system. For any school purpose, the board may acquire real estate by purchase, condemnation, or otherwise, although technically real estate must be bought or sold by the city council for the board at the request of the board. The board has the power to erect or purchase through the Finance Authority (see below) buildings which are suitable for schools and to keep them in repair.

The board consists of 11 members appointed by the mayor with the consent of the city council. (See also 1988 State Legislation, above.) The mayor chooses among nominees recommended by the Citizens Nominating Committee (see below). As of August 1988, board members serve five-year terms; three were appointed in 1986, and two terms begin in each of the next four years. Terms usually begin on May 1. The mayor has no power to remove a member until the end of a term. Board members are not paid, but expenses are reimbursable, and transportation to meetings is provided.

To be eligible for appointment to the board, a person must be a U.S. citizen, a registered voter, and a resident of Chicago for the preceding three years. Board members failing to resign from any federal, state, or local government office (other than notary public or National Guard) within 30 days of appointment to the board are deemed to have vacated their appointments. Board members must fill out an economic interest form.

At the annual meeting, on the fourth Wednesday of May, the members of the board elect from among themselves a president and a vice-president. The president presides at board meetings and acts in emergency matters when the board is not in session. To be final, all such actions must be ratified by the board at an open meeting. The vice-president presides in the absence of the president.

Meetings. The board meets on the second and fourth Wednesdays of the month unless otherwise decided. Meetings are preceded by a public participation segment beginning at 10:30 A.M. for a daytime meeting and 6 P.M. for an evening meeting. Members of the public who wish to speak must sign up. Each speaker is allotted two minutes, but up to four other signed-up speakers may yield time to one spokesperson. Any subject may be addressed as long as individuals are not mentioned by name.

The regular business meeting of the board begins at 1:30 P.M. at a daytime meeting and immediately following the public-participation segment at an evening meeting. The meetings of the board and its committees are open to the public except when real estate, personnel, or litigation are to be discussed. The board then meets in executive session, but all final action must be taken at an open meeting. Meetings usually take place at board headquarters, but each year some board and committee meetings are held in public schools.

CITIZENS NOMINATING COMMITTEE FOR THE BOARD OF EDUCATION. An advisory commission on school board nominations was set up in 1946, revised in 1969, and subsequently allowed to lapse. In 1984, by executive order, the mayor appointed the Citizens Nominating Committee for the Board of Education. The committee, which may have up to 25 members, serves at the pleasure of the mayor when Board of Education members are to be appointed. Committee members are chosen to represent community and civic organizations and the diverse constituencies of the city. (See also 1988 State Legislation, above.) The committee seeks applicants, conducts interviews, and submits to the mayor the names of at least three persons for each vacancy.

CHICAGO PUBLIC SCHOOLS FINANCE AUTHORITY

In 1979, because of the precarious financial condition of the school system, the state legislature created the Chicago Public School Finance Authority, an oversight body empowered to require that the Board of Education operate under balanced annual budgets and to sell long-term bonds such as those needed for new buildings. The five members are appointed, two by the governor, two by the mayor, and a chair jointly by the governor and the mayor. Members serve five-year terms without compensation other than expenses. They review the budget, and if they reject it, schools cannot open. In fiscal 1988, the authority agreed that the board had demonstrated its financial stability by having balanced budgets, and the authority ceased to review the board's three-year financial plans.

PARENT PARTICIPATION

A policy statement of the Board of Education in 1987 stressed the need for parent and community involvement in the schools. Staff is directed to plan cooperatively with parents and community to improve the quality of education in each school and to resolve problems.

Local School Improvement Councils. State legislation of 1985 requires that each school have a Local School Improvement Council (LSIC). Under rules issued by the Board of Education, following state law, 70% of the members of the LSIC must be parents of children enrolled in the school. The remaining members may be students, faculty, and residents living within the school attendance boundaries. Each LSIC draws up its own bylaws specifying membership qualifications. LSIC members elect officers; the president must be a parent. The LSIC is empowered to disapprove individual items in the discretionary budget of the school principal and to participate in the selection of the principal, teachers, and administrative staff. It may make recommendations on school curriculum. It may not raise money, except to meet basic expenses of the LSIC. (See also Local School Council description under 1988 State Legislation, above.)

District Education Advisory Councils. Every school in a district is entitled to representation on its elementary or high school District Education Advisory Council (DEAC). Each local school elects two delegates to the DEAC; one must be a member of the LSIC and the other a member of the Parents and Teachers Association (PTA) or other local school organization. Other members of the DEAC may include school personnel, representatives of community organizations, and members-at-large. Elementary schools may send representatives to their high school DEAC. The chair of a DEAC must be the parent or guardian of a pupil in the district and may not be an employee of the school system. Officers must be installed by November 15. The councils have the right to disapprove proposed expenditures from the district superintendent's discretionary fund and the supervising engineer's contingency fund. They also advise on district priorities, including budget development, educational policy, and in-service training of staff. (See also District Councils, under 1988 State Legislation, above.)

Principal Nominating Committees. When a vacancy occurs for a principal, the district superintendent meets with the LSIC to establish a Principal Nominating Committee. At least 60% of the committee members and the chair they select must be parents of the children in the school. Membership must reflect the ethnic and racial diversity of the school. The committee is provided with a list of qualified applicants for the position of principal and may interview them at the school. The committee names at least three nominees and gives the reasons for its choice. The General Superintendent is not bound by the recommendations, but in practice has followed them except in unusual circumstances. (See also Local School Councils, under 1988 State Legislation, above.)

ECIA Councils. The Board encourages parent participation in decision making for programs funded under Chapter 1 of the federal Education Consolidation and Improvement Act (ECIA, formerly ESEA). For these programs there are local, district, and citywide councils of parents of children receiving ECIA services and community members. ECIA Councils are among the groups designated to be represented on the Local School Improvement Councils (see above).

Multi-Lingual/Multi-Cultural Education Councils. A citywide Advisory Council on Multi-Lingual/Multi-Cultural Education represents groups interested in providing special programs for students with limited ability to speak English. There are also local councils, which may be part of LSICs, and district councils representing schools with such students.

Other Parent Groups. Although there is no mandate for establishing advisory councils to serve the needs of special education programs, many schools and districts have self-organized groups of these parents. Parents of children enrolled in Head Start and Child-Parent Centers are required to take an active part in those programs. Parents of children in the Effective Schools Program participate in a Local School Planning Team.

Volunteer Programs. The policy of the Board of Education is to encourage volunteers to assist in the schools. A consultant on the staff coordinates such efforts. Volunteer work ranges from providing special programs to parent patrols to clerical assistance.

Adopt-a-School Program. In the Adopt-a-School Program, begun in 1981, a business or institution adopts a specific school and, in consultation with the principal and LSIC, provides appropriate enrichment programs, such as career guidance. In 1986-87 there were 245 such adoptions.

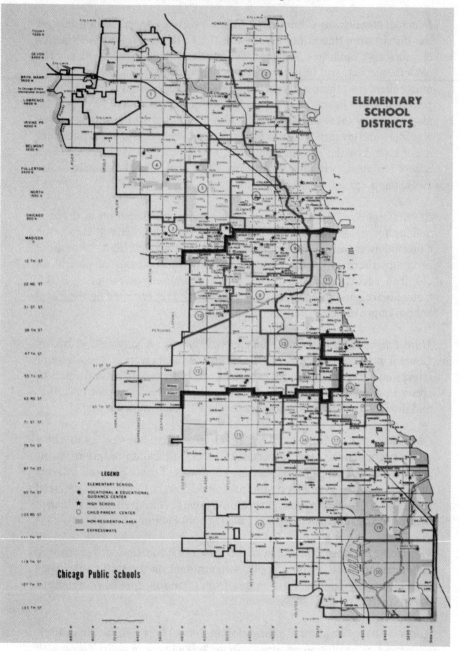

Fig. 6. 1. Chicago School District map. There are 20 elementary school districts in the Chicago Public School system. Elementary School Districts 1-7 are in the North High School District, 8-13 in the Central District, and 14-20 in the South District

Source: Chicago Public Schools.

CHICAGO PUBLIC SCHOOLS ADMINISTRATION

To distinguish between the functions of the schools and their administrators and the Board of Education and its members, in 1983 the board designated the name "Chicago Public Schools" for the schools, staff, and school administrators. The legal name "Board of Education of the City of Chicago" refers to the governing body and its legal documents.

Board Appointments. The Board of Education appoints the general superintendent to a four-year term under a contract which in 1985 provided for a salary of $100,000 a year plus an increment of up to $10,000 a year if performance is deemed satisfactory. The secretary of the board and the heads of the departments of internal audit, law, and finance are chosen by the board and report directly to it. These departments are independent of the superintendent. The chief financial officer, a position required by state law since 1980, is appointed by the board with approval of the Finance Authority; this officer prepares and supervises the budget and financial plan and oversees expenditures.

Administrative Organization. The general superintendent is responsible for all departments not noted above and for providing leadership to the system. A deputy superintendent is in charge of the day-to-day operation of the schools. An associate superintendent of instructional services is responsible for curriculum, vocational education, special education, multilingual education, and early childhood programs. An associate superintendent in charge of funded programs is responsible for programs provided by the state and federal governments for students with specific problems.

An associate superintendent in charge of the Office of Human Resources deals with personnel, employee relations, and training and development. One assistant to the general superintendent supervises Management Services. Another assistant to the general superintendent is responsible for the Department of Operations Analysis and Planning and the Department of Research and Evaluation. Four additional smaller departments are Governmental Relations, Communications, Affirmative Action, and Operation Services.

The Division of Visual Education selects and distributes audiovisual equipment and materials. The Bureau of Telecommunications and Broadcasting operates radio station WBEZ-FM.

Textbooks. Textbooks are lent without charge to students. A staff committee appointed by the principal selects textbooks and other materials for each school. Board policy encourages parent participation in the process. The selection is made from an approved list adopted by the board, and additional books may be approved if necessary. Lists for approval are compiled and revised by committees of teachers, principals, and community members. Computer programs are offered at all high schools and some elementary schools.

Districts. Elementary schools are grouped geographically into 20 districts, each administered by a district superintendent. High schools are grouped into 3 districts, north, central, and south, each administered by a district superintendent.

Personnel. Each school has a principal who is responsible for that school's operation. When there is a vacancy, the LSIC of the school may recommend its choice for principal through a Principal Nominating Committee (see above). Teachers are hired and promoted according to the provisions of the Illinois School Code and the rules of the Board of Education, as administered by the Board of Examiners (see below). In the 1986-87 fiscal year, the full-time equivalents of 25,643.9 teachers and principals were at the local schools, and 705.5 were at central and district offices.

The term "career service personnel" covers employees who are not teachers or administrators. In 1986-87 there were 16,532.9 employees working under 250 job descriptions, including engineers, auditors, data-processing programmers, architects, lawyers, doctors, editors, writers, clerks, custodial workers, tradesmen, cooks, nurses, and teachers' aides. Of the career service staff, 93% function at local schools. When vacancies occur, announcements are posted, and applicants must provide credentials and pass examinations. The local school or office seeking the employee conducts interviews and chooses from among the qualified applicants.

Board of Examiners. The Board of Examiners was created by state law (the Otis Law) to certify teachers and principals for the Chicago public schools. Subsequently it was given the responsibility for certifying career service employees of the schools. The Board of Examiners is made up of the general superintendent, a vice-chair, and a secretary. As of June 30, 1988, the Board of Examiners no longer has responsibility for certification of teachers and administrators, but its certification of career service will continue. After mid-1988, the teachers will be certified through the state certification process.

School Funding. The total budget for the school system for 1987-88 was $1,865,086,322. Funds from the state provided 47% of the budget, funds from the federal government 13%, local property taxes 33%, and other sources 7%. General state aid is based on average daily attendance, number of low-income pupils, assessed valuation of property in the district, and the amount appropriated by the legislature and approved by the governor. Categorical state aid is partial reimbursement for programs such as special education, vocational education, bilingual education, and driver education.

Federal funds are for specific programs such as special education, vocational education, bilingual education, and food services. Federal funds and state categorical funds must be spent for the designated purposes and cannot be transferred to other purposes.

The school tax on real estate in Chicago is at the full limit permitted by the state. The legislature can grant a higher school tax rate, or a higher rate can be approved by referendum.

Budget Procedures. The fiscal year of the Board of Education is September 1 to August 31. Between January and April, local school budgets are presented at community meetings (public notice is required). The board must present its three-year financial plan to the Finance Authority by May 1 and submit a balanced final budget to it by August 1; the authority must approve the budget before schools can open.

A revised final budget may be developed after fall labor negotiations; public hearings are required. The board must adopt the final budget within the first 60 days of the fiscal year (before November 1). The City Council approves the tax levy ordinance.

Information. Some departments and schools prepare publications about their operations. As of 1987, there is no central location within board headquarters where all publications are available, and there is no complete listing. Under its 1987 policy statement on community involvement in the schools, the board has promised timely response to written requests for information about performance, management, and finances.

CITY COLLEGES OF CHICAGO

226 W. Jackson Boulevard, Chicago 60606-6998; *Information Phone 855 3033*

Community College District 508 is a tax-levying body whose boundaries are those of the city of Chicago. There are eight community colleges in the system, collectively known as the City Colleges of Chicago. They are part of a system set up under the state Public Junior College Act of 1965, which provided that grades 13 and 14 (equivalent to the first two years of college) be made available to every student in the state through formation of junior (now community) college districts.

In Chicago, a junior college system administered by the Chicago Board of Education had begun in 1911, when college-level courses were first offered at Crane Technical High School. This system was transferred to the City Colleges of Chicago, which started operation on July 1, 1966. The colleges in the system are as follows:

Chicago City-Wide College, 226 W. Jackson Boulevard
Daley College, 7500 S. Pulaski Road
Kennedy-King College, 6800 S. Wentworth Avenue
Harold Washington College (formerly Loop), 30 E. Lake Street
Malcolm X College, 1900 W. Van Buren Street
Olive-Harvey College, 10001 S. Woodlawn Avenue
Truman College, 1145 W. Wilson Avenue
Wright College, 3400 N. Austin Avenue (A new campus is planned at Montrose and Narragansett Avenues.)

The district offers television courses for college credit over its station, WYCC (Channel 20), 7500 S. Pulaski Road, and it operates the Dawson Technical Institute, 3901 S. State Street, where technical programs are available to adults. In addition, free courses for adults are offered at 1,200 sites, providing Adult Basic Education (ABE), English as a Second Language (ESL), and General Educational Development (GED) to enable adults to complete requirements for a certificate equivalent to a high school diploma. Evening high school courses are given by Chicago City-Wide College and offered throughout the city.

Student enrollment in spring 1987 was 112,437, with a full-time equivalency of 54,151. Just under half of the students were enrolled in credit courses toward an associate degree, some of these leading to career employment skills and others to transfer to four-year colleges. The remainder were enrolled in adult continuing education courses or learning skills programs.

Admission. The City Colleges of Chicago are open-admission institutions. Applications are welcomed from graduates of accredited high schools, holders of GED certificates, transfers from other colleges and universities, and part-time students 18 years or older who have not completed high school but qualify for college-level work. The consent of the department chair is required to enroll in some classes that require specified background and experience.

Tuition. As of April 1988, tuition for Chicago residents was $26 per credit hour, plus fees and charges. For out-of-district Illinois residents, basic tuition was $60.35 per credit hour; for out-of-state and foreign students, it was $86.20 per credit hour. Senior citizens may enroll free for up to six credit hours during late registration for courses where seats are available. Public aid recipients may enroll free for up to five credit hours.

BOARD OF TRUSTEES. The City Colleges are governed by an unpaid board. Seven are appointed by the mayor with city council approval, and a nonvoting student board member is elected by fellow students, each year from a different college. The trustees meet at noon on the first Tuesday of each month at the central administrative offices, 226 W. Jackson Boulevard. Meetings are open to the public.

The trustees appoint a chancellor, usually for a three-year term, at an annual salary of $89,078. The chancellor appoints the presidents of the constituent colleges with the approval of the board.

Personnel. As of spring 1988, there were some 1,150 full-time faculty members and many part-time instructors who taught adult or continuing education or specialized courses. Beginning teachers must have a master's degree in the specific area applied for. There are approximately 1,000 administrative and support employees. No civil service examinations are required for employment.

Funding. The budget for the 1988 fiscal year was $268,609,982. Of this, 38% came from the Illinois Community College Board, 36% from the property tax, 13% from the federal government, 9% from tuition and fees, and 4% from other sources.

Budget Procedures. A public hearing on the Tentative Budget is required and is usually held in July; this budget must be made available for public inspection for at least ten days before the hearing. Public notice of the hearing is required. The Final Budget Appropriation Resolution is usually passed in August. In 1986, for its 1987 budget, an additional hearing was required under the state Truth in Taxation law, which mandates a public hearing if a local government appropriation requires an increase of 5% or more in its property tax levy. Under state law, the final budget must be passed by the board and the tax levy ordinance approved by the city council by September 30.

CHICAGO PARK DISTRICT

425 E. McFetridge Drive, Chicago 60605; *phone 294 2200*
For addresses and telephone numbers of individual park facilities, see
Chicago Park District listing in white pages of Chicago telephone directory.

The Chicago Park District is a separate local governmental body, independent of the city of Chicago except that the mayor appoints its Board of Commissioners. The district may levy property taxes, make special assessments, and issue bonds within limits set by state law. It may enact and enforce ordinances, rules, and regulations for the government and protection of park property, and it may acquire lands and properties by gift,

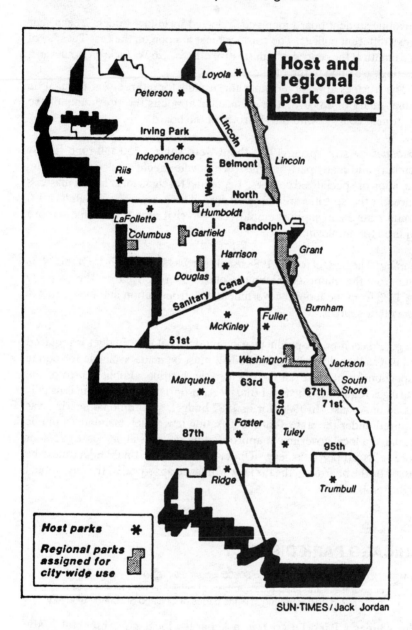

Fig. 6. 2. Chicago Park District map. Each host park is to have an advisory council representative of the community to help on planning and maintenance. Individual parks may have
their own councils, as well.

Source: Chicago Sun Times, © 1988

purchase, or condemnation without the approval of any other governmental body. As of 1988, however, the district was referring plans for lakefront development to the Chicago Plan Commission for approval under the city's Lakefront Protection Ordinance. Ordinance and regulation-making powers are limited to district grounds, but for tax and referendum purposes the district has the same boundaries as Chicago.

In 1838, a year after Chicago received its charter, the first of Chicago's parks was established; this was Dearborn Park, on what is now South Michigan Avenue, at the site of the present Cultural Center of the Public Library. By 1934 there were 22 separate park districts in the city, incorporated by the state legislature in that year into one district with its own taxing power. The Functional Consolidation Act of 1959 transferred to the city control of all boulevards (which had previously been under Park District control) and police personnel, formerly Park District police.

In 1988 the park system included 7,309 acres and consisted of 563 parks, 251 field houses, 31 bathing beaches, 6 golf courses, 713 tennis courts (6 indoor), 8 yacht harbors, 11 launching ramps for small boats, 90 swimming pools (31 indoor) and lagoons, 3 public garages, the Lincoln Park Zoo, and the sports stadium at Soldier Field. The district offers a broad variety of summer and winter sports, sports instruction, recreation programs, and arts and crafts programs to the general public and special activities for mentally and physically handicapped youngsters. Free concerts in Grant Park and in neighborhood parks are held in the summer.

McCormick Place East, under the jurisdiction of the Metropolitan Fair and Exposition Authority, is on Park District land. In addition, eight major museums are on park property, partially funded by a separate tax levy. The total for this levy in 1988 was $38,031,708, of which $12,102,000 was to be for capital improvements. In 1988 operating support for the museums amounted to $25,929,708, divided as follows:

Museum of Science and Industry	$5,890,089
Field Museum of Natural History	5,890,089
Art Institute of Chicago	5,890,089
John G. Shedd Aquarium	4,224,416
Chicago Historical Society	973,608
Chicago Academy of Sciences	925,950
Adler Planetarium	1,876,170
Du Sable Museum	259,297

BOARD OF COMMISSIONERS. The mayor appoints, with city council approval, the five members of the district's board. They serve staggered five-year terms and are not paid. Two are appointed by the board to serve on the district's Civil Service Board and are paid $500 a year. The board elects its own president and appoints an executive vice-president (replacing the former general superintendent). The board generally meets in the board room of the district office at 10 A.M. on the second and fourth Tuesdays of each month, or at the call of the president or any other commissioner. Meetings are open to the public; information on the place and time of the meetings is available by telephoning the district's office.

Administration. A restructuring of the park district was announced in 1988. The plan organized the system into 13 "host park" clusters and 4 "regional park" clusters. Each host park will have a management center responsible for maintenance and recreation programs for the community and for neighborhood parks, playgrounds, playlots, swimming pools, and landscaped areas within its boundaries.. The regional park clusters are Grant and Burnham Parks; Lincoln Park; South Shore Cultural Center and Jackson and Washington Parks; and Columbus, Douglas, Garfield, and Humboldt Parks. The restructuring included initiation of civil service testing for Park District employees.

Funding. State law limits the district's corporate fund to a rate of 66 cents on each $100 of equalized assessed valuation (EAV) and its aquarium and museum fund to 15 cents on each $100 EAV. The 1988 district total budget was $285,953,144, from the property tax, the personal property replacement tax, and activity and program revenues. The 1988 corporate budget (Operating Fund) was $149,989,570. There were 3,818 full-time employeees and from 1,400 to 1,600 additional part-time and seasonal employees. The salary of the executive vice-president was $85,200.

Budget Procedures. District rules provide that a preliminary budget must be completed by October 1. Budget recommendations and a proposed appropriation ordinance must be submitted to the board by November 1. The proposed budget must be available for public inspection for a minimum of ten days, and at least one public hearing must be scheduled before December 28. The board must approve the budget by December 31. Community meetings on the proposed budget may be held before the legal deadline.

CHICAGO PUBLIC LIBRARY

Central Library, reference and research temporary facility, 400 N. Franklin St., Chicago 60610.

Cultural Center, 78 E. Washington St., Chicago 60602.

General Information phone, *269 2800.* (See also information services, below.)

The Chicago Public Library is in some ways a part of Chicago city government and in others an independent taxing body, established under

The Library System

Fig. 6. 3. Chicago Public Library branch library map
Source: Chicago Public Library

state law and city ordinance. Its board is appointed by the mayor, and its budget and bonds are passed by the city council, but it has a tax levy which appears separately on the property tax bill and the power to select its own staff within city guidelines.

The Chicago Public Library is the major public library in the metropolitan area, serving not only city residents but also many persons who live outside of the city, through contracts with suburban libraries in the library systems. (See chapter 2.) The library and its 82 neighborhood branch libraries, 2 regional libraries, and 2 cooperative state libraries (the Illinois Regional Library for the Blind and Physically Handicapped and the Library for the Illinois State Psychiatric Institution) constitute a consolidated library system which serves as one of the 4 library research and information centers established by the Illinois Library Systems Act of 1965.

In 1834, one year after the founding of the city, Chicago residents established a subscription library. By 1871 it had 30,000 volumes; all were destroyed in the Chicago fire of that year. Over 8,000 volumes were received after the fire as a result of an appeal made in the British Parliament to British authors, publishers, and societies to contribute books to a "Free Library of Chicago." In 1872 the state legislature passed the Free Public Library Act of Illinois; in April 1872 the city council enacted an ordinance establishing the Chicago Public Library; and the library opened, in an abandoned water tower, on January 1, 1873.

Expansion. Discussion on the need for expansion of the Central Library Building began in 1972. The present Cultural Center, which houses part of the library collection, is the original public library building that was dedicated on the 25th anniversary of the Chicago fire. The building has been renovated and has been designated as a landmark. It includes meeting rooms and exhibit space, and concerts and cultural events are held there. A temporary facility for research and reference materials is at 400 N. Franklin St. A new and expanded reference and research library is scheduled to be completed by 1991 at a site bounded by State and Van Buren Streets, Plymouth Court, and Congress Parkway.

Collections. The Central Library research and reference center includes a computer-assisted reference center, and in general it houses the library's materials on business, science, technology, history, social sciences, education, Head Start, government publications, and newspapers. The Cultural Center collections include fiction, literature and language, children's books, foreign language materials, and the film/video center. Some special collections are housed at the Cultural Center, including collections on art; book arts; Chicago authors, theater, and history; neighborhood history; the Columbian Exposition; and the library archives.

A research collection of Afro-American history and literature is housed at 9525 S. Halsted St. (call *881 6900* for hours). A Secondhand Prose Bookstore is at 4544 N. Lincoln Ave. (call *728 8923* for hours).

Library Services. As of December 31, 1986 the library had 4,764,673 volumes in its collection and 1,082,994 registered cardholders. Total circulation in 1986 was 8,134,798 items issued and 6,652,433 used in the library. Besides books, the library circulates audiocassettes, videocassettes, periodicals, pamphlets, sheet and bound music, films, slides, pictures, and records.

The library provides information centers to answer public questions; it also provides services for senior citizens and the physically challenged (the medically, visually, mobility, and hearing impaired, and the developmentally disabled). It presents lectures, concerts, films, and exhibits. Its learning programs include great books programs, children's story hours, computer-assisted instruction (and microcomputers in some locations), homework centers, homebound services, interlibrary loan, literacy tutoring, and (in cooperation with Chicago City Colleges) English as a Second Language, Study Unlimited, General Educational Development, and literacy classes. The library and its branches also provide voter registration for Chicago citizens.

Information Services. The library offers a variety of telephone information services. *DIAL-LAW, 644 0800,* and *DIAL PET, 342 5738,* provide tape-recorded information. Others answer individual questions:

Business Information Center, *269 2814*

Card Catalog Information, *269 2807*

Career Information Center, *269 2814*

Computer-Assisted Reference Center (computer literature search, by appointment, minimum charge $5), *269 2915*

Head Start Resource Center, *744 4449*

Education and Philosophy Information Center, *269 2929*

Newspapers and General Periodicals Center, *269 2913*

Out of Town and Foreign Telephone Directories, *269 2954*

Science/Technology Information Center, Patent Desk, *269 2865*

Social Sciences and History Information Center, *269 2929*

Spanish Information Services, *269 2940*

Volunteer Services, *269 2995*

Library Cards. Residents of Chicago, including children able to write or print their names, may be issued free library cards. Persons who own property in the city but do not live there may receive a free card on presentation of a current real estate property tax bill.

Suburban residents who have a suburban library card from a library that has a reciprocal borrowing arrangement with the Chicago Public Library also may receive free Chicago library cards. If a suburban resident lives in an unincorporated area, has no local library, or the local library has no reciprocity with the Chicago library, a fee of $30 is charged for a card.

Library Hours. Library hours are 9 A.M. to 7 P.M., Monday - Thursday; 9 A.M. to 6 P.M., Friday; and 9 A.M. to 5 P.M., Saturday. Libraries are closed on Sundays (except for scheduled events at the Cultural Center) and on the following holidays: New Year's Day, Martin Luther King's birthday, Lincoln's birthday, Washingon's birthday, Pulaski Day, Memorial Day, Independence Day, Labor Day, Thanksgiving, and Christmas.

CHICAGO PUBLIC LIBRARY BOARD. The Library Board establishes policy and appoints the Library Commissioner. The nine-member board is appointed for three-year terms by the mayor with the consent of the city council. Board members serve without pay.

Board meetings are open to the public; they are held at 9:30 A.M. on the second Tuesday of each month, usually at the Cultural Center. (For information on meetings, call *269 3057.*)

Administration and Funding. The library is headed by a commissioner, whose salary in 1988 was $95,000 a year. Two new positions were added in the 1988 budget, that of deputy commissioner and chief librarian (at $72,000 a year), and that of deputy commissioner of finance and administration (at $55,000 a year).

The 1988 budget provided for 983 full-time employees and 282,440 hours of work by part-time employees. Under city ordinance, the library must comply with the city Department of Purchasing guidelines for contracts and purchase orders.

Money for library support comes from two property tax levies: the city council may levy a tax of 22 cents per $100 of equalized assessed valuation (EAV) for library maintenance and operation, and up to 3 cents per $100 EAV for construction and equipment of new buildings. In addition, the library receives state funds for its services as a research and reference center. The 1988 operating budget was $44,161,200, and the building and site fund budget was $9,270,700.

CHICAGO BOARD OF ELECTION COMMISSIONERS

City Hall, 121 N. LaSalle St., Chicago 60602; *phone 269 7900*
Registration verification, *269 7936* or *269 7923*
Polling place information, *269 7976*
Election Central (complaint line for election days only), *269 7870*

The Chicago Board of Election Commissioners is an independent board whose members are appointed by the Cook County Circuit Court and whose budget comes in part from the county and in part from the city. Its structure and responsibilities are set by state law. It administers all elections within the city, sets precinct boundaries, appoints election judges, and is responsible for voter registration and the house-to-house canvass conducted after precinct registration day. In 1986 there were 1,475,556 registered voters in Chicago; 841,085 of them voted in the general election.

In 1988 there were 2,908 precincts within the city, each containing (as nearly as practicable) 400 to 600 registered voters. Five election judges from the major political parties are appointed in each precinct; the party with three judges in even-numbered precincts has two in odd-numbered precincts. For information on registering to vote, see chapter 3

The law provides for a three-member board, appointed by the Circuit Court, serving staggered three-year terms. Of the three members, there must be at least one from each of the two major political parties. The board elects a chairman and secretary from its own membership and appoints an executive director.

The costs of conducting elections (payment for judges of election, registrars, computer time, printing of ballots, costs of canvassing, rental of polling places, transportation of voting equipment) is paid by the city for municipal elections and by the county for nonmunicipal elections. The county pays the salary of the chairman ($59,604 in 1988), the other two commissioners ($33,948 each), and the executive director ($53,240). In 1988, a nonmunicipal election year, the city corporate fund appropriation for the board was $11,270,487, which provided for 164 employees and the salary of the attorney of elections ($62,244). Additional employees are hired temporarily at election time.

CHICAGO HOUSING AUTHORITY (CHA)

22 W. Madison St., Chicago 60602; *phone 791 8500*
Applications, *791 8528*

The Chicago Housing Authority is an independent municipal corporation organized under Illinois law and funded by the U.S. government, with a board appointed by the mayor and approved by the city council. It was organized in 1937 to build and operate public housing in Chicago for

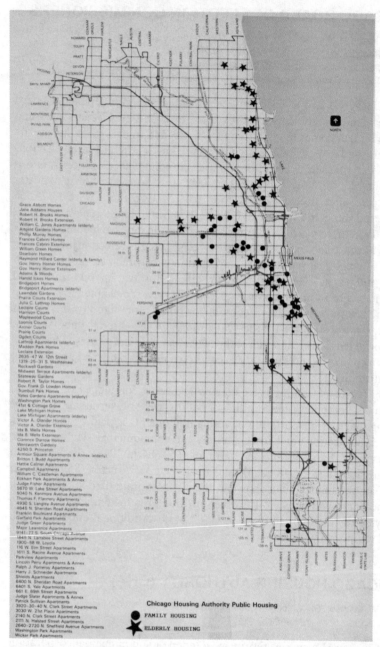

Fig. 6. 4. Chicago Housing Authority map. Locations of public housing are shown.

Source: Chicago Housing Authority

persons whose incomes are insufficient to obtain "decent, safe, and sanitary dwelling" in the private market (U.S. Housing Act of 1937). Most CHA housing has been constructed under terms of federal housing legislation which calls for a "decent home and suitable living environment for every American family" (U.S. Housing Acts of 1949 and 1968).

HOUSING PROGRAMS. As of December 1985, CHA housed more than 145,000 persons, 4.8% of the city population, in six programs. It also gives space to social agencies for programs in education, child development and counseling, domestic life, employment, health, and recreation.

1. *Family Housing.* Begun in 1937, the CHA family housing program is the second-largest such program in the nation. It consists of 30,555 apartments designed primarily for families with children. These units house about 111,000 persons in 153 highrise and 1,030 lowrise buildings. Families whose income is less than 50% of the median income in the Chicago area are eligible; rent is 30% of the adjusted gross family income.

2. *Senior Housing.* Begun in 1959, the largest senior housing program in the nation is managed by the CHA. The program provides housing for 10,500 people in 9,974 apartments, at an average rent of $69 a month.

3. *Section 8 Existing Housing Assistance Payments.* "Section 8" refers to a section of the federal housing law. The Section 8 program began in 1976 and provides rent subsidies to 3,945 low-income families and 2,821 elderly living in privately owned and managed rental housing. Qualified persons receive subsidy certificates for residences they choose (which must comply with housing quality standards). Applications for family Section 8 subsidies were discontinued in 1985, as the waiting list was then more than 10 years old; the current waiting list is 40,000 families and 5,000 elderly.

4. *Section 8 Moderate Rehabilitation.* Under Section 8, one program provides funds for moderate rehabilitation of privately owned rental properties, provided the owner contracts with CHA to rent to low-income tenants under the Section 8 program for 15 years after the renovation is completed. Rents are based on the cost of owning and operating the rehabilitated property. The average cost of the rehabilitation is over $11,000 per unit. Financing is generally provided by private lenders, though in some cases partial financing is provided by the city's Department of Housing, using Community Development Block Grant funds.

5. *Section 8 Substantial Rehabilitation.* Another Section 8 program consists of eight developments, with 1,938 units, originally constructed in the 1950s

with city and state funds. In 1978 CHA provided for substantial rehabilitation and upgrading of the aging developments, and in 1981 management of the units was consolidated under CHA.

6. *Scattered Sites.* The scattered site program began in 1975. It provides housing in new or rehabilitated units in sites throughout the city, as opposed to large concentrations of public housing units in a single area. In 1987 CHA stated that it would provide 2,223 units for 8,000 residents; this was expected to cost $100,000,000. The scattered site program was placed into receivership in 1987, following a class action suit which charged racial discrimination in the location of public housing and CHA's inability to meet a court order concerning acquisition, building, and rehabilitation of scattered sites. As of the end of 1987, 3,900 units had been completed, and HUD had authorized and funded 292 additional units.

Locations. Senior citizen housing is in 51 buildings scattered throughout the city. Section 8 housing and scattered site housing is also dispersed. Management addresses for the large housing developments are as follows (ZIP codes in parentheses):

> Abla Homes, 1324 S. Loomis (60608)
> Altgeld Gardens, 940 E. 132nd St. (60627)
> Cabrini-Green Homes, 418 W. Oak (60610)
> City/State Development, 2616 S. King Drive (60616)
> Dearborn Homes, 2960 S. Federal (60616)
> Hilliard Center, 2030 S. State (60616)
> Horner Homes, 1834 W. Washington (60612)
> Ickes Homes, 2400 S. State (60616)
> Lathrop Homes, 200 Diversey Pkwy. (60647)
> Lawndale/Leclaire Homes, 4410 S. LaPorte (60638)
> Madden Park Homes, 3750 S. Ellis (60653)
> Rockwell Gardens, 2500 W. Jackson (60612)
> Stateway Gardens, 3640 S. State (60609)
> Robert Taylor Homes
>   Area 1, 4700 S. State (60646)
>   Area 2, 4525 S. Federal (60609)
>   Area 3, 4946 S. State (60646)
>   Area 4, 5323 S. Federal (60609)
> Trumbull Park Homes, 2437 E. 106th St. (60655)
> Washington Park Homes, 4440 S. Cottage Grove (60653)
> Wells Homes, 454 E. Pershing Road (60653)
> Wentworth Gardens, 3770 S. Wentworth (60609)

Application. Applicants for any CHA program fill out registration forms available at the CHA Central Rental Office, 22 W. Madison St., open Monday through Friday, 8:30 A.M. to 4 P.M. An applicant is placed on a waiting list if eligible. The waiting list for apartments in requested family developments is about 8,000 and for elderly housing about 5,000. Applications for family Section 8 subsidies were discontinued in 1985, because of the length and age of the waiting list.

Eligibility. Families (or individuals) whose income is less than 50% of the median income for that size family in the Chicago area are eligible for admission to CHA developments (and Section 8 housing, when that waiting list is reopened). They pay an amount based on their income, and rents are limited to 30% of the adjusted income of the household. Tenants may remain in the program until their portion of the rent is equal to the contract rent. Maximum incomes are stated in terms of "very low income" and "lower income." Persons with incomes more than the very low income, up to the lower income amounts, may be admitted only with prior approval by the U.S. Department of Housing and Urban Development (HUD).

TABLE 6.1. 1987 INCOME LIMITATIONS FOR ADMISSION TO CHA HOUSING PROGRAMS

Number of Persons	Very Low Income	Low Income
1	$12,900	$20,600
2	14,700	23,550
3	16,550	26,500
4	18,400	29,450
5	19,850	31,300
6	21,350	33,150
7	22,800	34,950
8 or more	24,300	36,800

Source: Chicago Housing Authority

Administration. Federal housing legislation, U.S. Department of Housing and Urban Development (HUD) policies, and court decisions all affect public housing administration. CHA policies are formulated and directed by its board, appointed for five-year terms by the mayor with the approval of the city council. Six board members are unpaid, but the chair is paid $31,200 a year. An executive director is appointed by the board at a salary in 1987 of $84,000 a year.

Funding. The CHA has no taxing power and receives no real estate tax funds. Its operating costs are paid from rents (1987 expected income of $42,614,260) and allocations of federal housing moneys from HUD (1987 requested allocation of $98,642,190). Its expected operating expenses for that year were $141,942,560. As of August 1987, CHA had 1,966 employees in administration, maintenance, and the crafts; 334 employees were part of special programs, and 79% of those were CHA residents.

Funds for major rehabilitation come primarily from the Comprehensive Improvement Assistance Program (CIAP) of HUD. In recent years Congress has provided annual appropriations for this fund. In the past, CHA was able to use Section 8 Substantial Rehabilitation funds to rehabilitate the City/State apartments, originally built with city and state funds; these funds cannot be used to rehabilitate public housing built with federal funds. New construction funds come through public temporary loan note sales. Financing of older developments was provided with 40-year bonds, but recently financing has been provided by the Federal Financing Bank. Principal and interest are paid by HUD.

Tenant Participation. Elections are held in all CHA developments to select building, development, and central advisory councils. A tenants' central advisory council, composed of presidents of the local advisory councils, was formed in 1970 and reorganized in 1976. Tenant hearing boards hear grievances about eviction notices and CHA assessments of tenants for damages.

Board Meetings. The CHA Board meets on the second Tuesday and fourth Monday of each month at 9:30 A.M. Meetings may be held in the Board Room at 22 W. Madison St. or at a development center. Information on meeting dates, times, and locations is available by calling *791 8500*; agendas, minutes, and annual reports are also available.

CHICAGO DWELLINGS ASSOCIATION (CDA)

Chicago Housing Authority, 22 W. Madison St., Chicago 60602; *phone 791 8500*

The Chicago Dwellings Association (CDA) is a private, not-for-profit corporation which may receive funds to carry out construction, rehabilitation, or purchase of buildings for middle-income housing. It may rent or sell this housing. CDA owns three high-rise buildings (managed by the Chicago Housing Authority): one for families, Midway Gardens, 727 E. 60th St.; one for the elderly, Drexel Square, 51st St. and Drexel Boulevard; and one for professional personnel in the West Side Medical Center, 1929 W. Harrison St. The CHA Board acts as board of the CDA.

METROPOLITAN FAIR AND EXPOSITION AUTHORITY

McCormick Place on the Lake, 2300 S. Lake Shore Drive, Chicago 60616; *phone 791 7000*

State law in 1955 created the Metropolitan Fair and Exposition Authority as an independent body to be responsible for McCormick Place, the

3,600,000-square-foot trade fair and convention center at Lake Shore Drive and 23rd Street. The authority is empowered to promote, operate, and maintain fairs, expositions, and conventions and to construct buildings within Cook County. It has the power to sell bonds with the consent of the legislature.

The main exposition hall, McCormick Place East, is built on Park District land on the lakefront. The first McCormick Place, which opened in 1961, was destroyed by fire in 1967. Its replacement, opened in 1971, contains about 760,000 square feet of exhibit space, the Arie Crown Theater, 3 smaller theaters, 28 meeting rooms, and 7 restaurants. McCormick Place West was formerly Donnelley Hall, a printing plant acquired by the city in 1977. The Public Building Commission converted the area into 330,000 square feet of exhibit space; the authority leased and managed it, and in 1986 acquired it through a lease purchase agreement. McCormick Place North provides an additional 525,000 square feet of exhibit space; it was authorized in 1984 and, though not then completed, opened for its first exhibit in 1986. To build the north structure and to refinance existing bonds, the legislature in 1984 authorized $252,000,000 in dedicated state tax revenue bonds, the debt service to be paid by an increase in the state hotel tax and a new soft drink tax. In 1985 an additional bond issue of $60,000,000 was authorized.

The authority prepares and publishes three-year financial plans. The plan issued for 1987-89 reports an operating budget of $4,800,000, with income from rentals, service charges, and commissions expected to provide about 87.7% of the operating costs; the remainder is provided by a state appropriation from cigarette tax funds. There were 550 full-time equivalent positions budgeted for 1988. Debt service for 1987 (principal and interest) amounted to $32,568,313.

Board. The board consists of 12 members, appointed for five-year staggered terms. A board member may not be a public official or an employee of the Chicago Convention and Tourism Bureau. The governor appoints 6 members of the board, with the consent of the state senate, and the mayor of Chicago appoints 6. (The law does not require city council approval of the mayor's appointees.) Board members select a chairman and secretary and appoint the general manager. Board members serve without pay.

ILLINOIS SPORTS FACILITIES AUTHORITY

First National Plaza, suite 2785, Chicago 60603; *phone 793 1991*

In 1987 state law set up an authority to build a sports stadium. The area of its authority is coterminous with the city of Chicago. It was given power to build and maintain one stadium; its property is to be tax-exempt; and it can issue bonds. It was required to give 30-day notice of the proposed location of the stadium. Effective in March 1988, the authority levied a 2% hotel operators tax on hotels in Chicago (in addition to the city hotel tax). From August 1988, the authority is also to receive $5,000,000 a year from the state hotel operators tax (collected throughout the state) and $5,000,000 a year from Chicago's share of the state income tax which is distributed to municipalities (see chapter 4).

The authority is governed by a seven-member unpaid board serving three-year staggered terms. The governor appoints the chairman. The governor and the mayor each appoint three members; each must approve the other's appointments, and the governor's appointments must be with the consent of the state Senate.

ILLINOIS INTERNATIONAL PORT DISTRICT

12800 S. Butler Drive, Chicago 60633; *phone 646 4400*

The 1951 state legislature created the Chicago Regional Port District and changed the name to the Illinois International Port District in 1986. The district has two locations: one at 130th Street and the Calumet Expressway, and one at 95th Street at the lakefront on the Calumet River. It is a municipal corporation for the development of commerce through Calumet Harbor and Lake Calumet, charged with fostering, stimulating, and promoting shipment of cargoes and commerce through the port and maintaining the port and harbor facilities. Any changes in harbor plans or development of port facilities must be submitted for approval to the state Department of Transportation.

The port handles 10% of the annual maritime tonnage coming into Chicago, 155 ships and 1,980,540 tons in 1987. The district's Foreign Trade Zone license was approved in 1973, and there is an industrial park area for international operations. In 1977 the legislature provided for a $10,000,000 loan from the Capital Development Fund to pay for acquisition of a 190-acre lakefront site at the mouth of the Calumet River for building a container and cargo dock. Docks, transit facilities, warehouses, grain elevators, and tank farms have been developed on port district property. The district owns the public terminal facilities, but state law provides that all facilities are leased and operated by private business. About 1,000 people are employed by the businesses that lease and operate the facilities.

Board of Directors. The governing body of the district is a nine-member board appointed for staggered five-year terms; four are appointed by the governor with the advice and consent of the senate; five are appointed by the mayor with the advice and consent of the city council. The governor's appointees must be approved by the mayor and the mayor's by the governor.

The board appoints the executive director and selects its own chairman. Board meetings are open to the public and are usually held on the third Friday of each month, at the board room of the Metropolitan Sanitary District, 100 E. Erie St., Chicago.

Finances. To finance the original development of the port, revenue bonds totaling $24,000,000 were sold, to be paid from charges to users of the facilities. However, in 1986 the state appropriated $5,100,000 from general revenue funds to establish an escrow account to repay bonds due in 1995.

In 1988, the district had 10 full-time and 2 part-time employees. Specialists for engineering and legal work are paid on a fee-for-service basis. In the 1986-87 fiscal year, salaries and fringe benefits amounted to $430,775. The operating budget for the port's 1987 fiscal year was $1,567,525. In that year the gross income from rentals and fees was $2,438,000; of this, $490,240 was used to pay interest on revenue bonds.

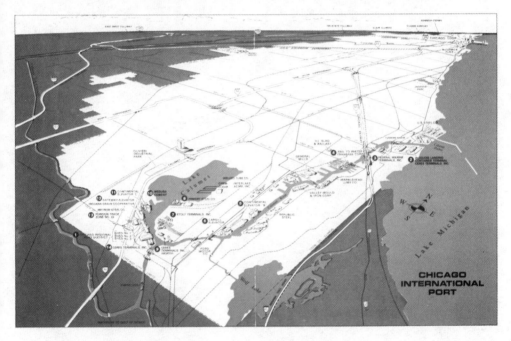

Fig. 6. 5. Chicago International Port Facilities
Source: Chicago International Port District © by PROSPECTO MAP CO., Richmond, IL 60071, 1983 edition

7 Cook County Governments: The County

Residents of Cook County are served by a multiplicity of governments and separate taxing bodies, including the government of Cook County itself, the Forest Preserve District, the Metropolitan Sanitary District, their municipalities, their townships, and their special districts. Some county and regional services are provided for the whole county, including the city of Chicago; others are provided for suburban Cook County (sometimes excluding other municipalities which provide those services for themselves); others are provided to unincorporated areas of the county, where the residents are not part of any city, town, or village government. This chapter describes the government of the County and of the Forest Preserve District, also governed by the county commissioners.

COOK COUNTY

The county is the most traditional and universal form of local government in the United States. It originated in England after the Norman Conquest, when the local unit of government, the shire, came to be called the county. The chief executive officer was known as the shire-reeve, a title later shortened to sheriff. The English settlers brought their county organization with them, and it took root, especially in the southern colonies. Before the Norman Conquest the shire in England had considerable autonomy, subject to limited control by the central government. A more centralized government characterized the period after 1066, and the English county came to be considered primarily an administrative district for the central government. The same view applied to the early American county. Until recently, it was generally held that counties existed only for the purposes of general political government in states.

In general, the state creates counties to render governmental services to rural areas and creates municipalities to govern those areas that are essentially urban. Thus, people who live in the county's unincorporated areas (about one-fourth of the total county area) receive directly from the county many services that a municipality provides within the boundaries of a city or village, for instance, police protection and zoning regulation. These services are supported by general county funds, though the county receives sales tax and a share of the state income tax for residents of these areas and licenses vehicles in these areas (see County Funding, below). Understanding county government is further complicated by the fact that some services are provided only to suburban areas (including the unincorporated areas) and others are provided for the entire county.

The Cook County Board of Commissioners is the main governing body of Cook County, but nine other county officials are also elected; these independently elected officials set policy for the offices to which they are elected. The county board, however, approves their budgets. The Illinois Constitution specifies that the county board president, members of the county board, the county clerk, the sheriff, the state's attorney, and the treasurer must be elected. Under the constitution other Cook County officials could be elected or appointed, but as of 1988 the following are also elected: assessor, two members of the Board of (property tax) Appeals, recorder of deeds, and superintendent of the educational service region. The clerk of the circuit court and circuit court judges are also elected.

The Cook County budget of $984.5 million for 1988 provides funding for about 23,000 employees; more than 10,000 of these are employed by the independently elected county officials or by agencies reporting to the court system (see chapter 9); another 9,300 are employees of the Cook County Health Facilities, which has a separate tax levy.

COOK COUNTY BOARD OF COMMISSIONERS
County Building, 118 N. Clark St., Chicago 60602; *phone 443 6398*

The Cook County Board of Commissioners is the legislative body of the county, and the president of the board (separately elected as a commissioner) is the county's chief executive officer. The board also serves as the board of the Cook County Forest Preserve District, a special purpose taxing district. The board levies taxes, passes ordinances, approves all county purchases over $5,000, and adopts the annual budget for the entire county government. The board also levies taxes for the Circuit Court of Cook County, a part of the state court system partially supported by the state. Many functions of the county are performed by the other elected county officials, over whom the county board has no control except in the passage of their budgets and approval of bond issues, contracts, and special large expenditures.

For the suburban areas, the county provides health, highway, economic development, and environmental control services., For unincorporated areas the board passes and enforces regulatory ordinances on Dutch elm disease and animal control and on building and zoning. (The sheriff provides police services to unincorporated areas.) Restaurant and liquor licenses in unincorporated areas are issued by the president of the board.

As of 1988, 10 members of the board are elected at large from Chicago and 7 members are elected at large from suburban Cook County. All are elected for four-year terms. The constitution specifically authorizes election of members of the board from the two districts, but it also specifies procedures for change: (1) a different method of election can be approved by a majority of votes cast in each of the two districts in a referendum, or (2) the board can divide the county into single-member districts from which a resident of each district would be elected. If the referendum method is used, the method of election can be altered by the board or by another referendum. The board can change the method of election only once; thereafter any change can be made only by referendum.

Vacancies. If a vacancy occurs in the office of commissioner, the remaining members from that commissioner's district (Chicago or suburban Cook County) choose a successor. County officials are not subject to recall by the voters. However, the election laws provide that any elective office shall become vacant if the incumbent is convicted of an infamous crime under Illinois law or any offense involving a violation of the oath of office. The county board may fill vacancies in county elective office.

Meetings. Board meetings are usually held on the first and third Mondays of the month at 10 A.M. in room 567 of the County Building. Special meetings may be called by the president or by one-third of the members. In a rule adopted in 1971, the board provided that individuals may address the board after submitting a written request at the beginning of the meeting to the secretary of the board.

Pay and Staff. The president of the board of commissioners is paid $74,000 a year, the chairman of the finance committee is paid $43,500, and the other 15 commissioners are each paid $40,000. Each commissioner (except the president) may appoint a secretary and an administrative assistant. A secretary to the board serves at the pleasure of the board, at an annual salary of $76,500. The total staff of the commissioners, committees, and secretary for 1988 (not including the president's staff) was 58, with a corporate fund appropriation of $2,183,043.

PRESIDENT
OF THE COOK COUNTY BOARD OF COMMISSIONERS
County Building, 118 N. Clark St., Chicago 60602; *phone 443 6400*

In addition to presiding at county board meetings, the president of the Cook County Board of Commissioners, as chief executive of the county, is responsible for the administration of the county government, except for the responsibilities held by other elected officials. With the consent of the board, the president appoints the heads of county departments falling under the board's jurisdiction. State law provides that the president of a home rule county (such as Cook) is the appointing officer for special taxing boards whose jurisdictions extend over more than one township within the county. In 1969 the legislature gave the president the responsibility to submit an executive budget to the board committee on finance; this budget is prepared by the county budget director and approved by the president. The president also serves as the liquor control commissioner in unincorporated areas and can grant or revoke licenses.

The president has the same voting power as other members of the board and cannot vote a second time as presiding officer to resolve a tie. The president has the power to veto an entire appropriation or any item in it and can veto any ordinance, resolution, or motion. A four-fifths vote of all members elected to the board can override a veto. If the president takes no action within six days on a motion or resolution, the measure takes effect without the president's signature.

The president of the board runs as a candidate for commissioner from either Chicago or suburban Cook County and also runs at large in the whole county for the office of president. In 1973 the board adopted an ordinance which no longer required the president of the board also to run as a commissioner, but since that date candidates have chosen to run as both. If a vacancy occurs in the office of president, the method of filling the vacancy depends on how much time remains in the term. If more than 2 years and 60 days remain in the term, the governor must call a special election on the date of the general election; the voters then elect one of the county board members president. If less than that time remains of the term, the other members of the board elect one of their number as replacement, to serve until the next general election.

The 1988 budget provides for 14 employees in the office of the president, which includes the office of inquiry and information and the real estate management division. The total 1988 appropriation from the corporate fund for this office was $574,297. (There is also a Bureau of Administration; see below.)

DEPARTMENTS ADMINISTERED BY THE PRESIDENT OF THE COUNTY BOARD

Under the office of the president, an administrative chart of the county shows the Bureau of Administration, headed by a chief administrative officer responsible for departments dealing with management of information systems, planning and development, personnel, position classification, budget and management, and central services. Nineteen additional offices or departments are shown as reporting directly to the president. These include three financial departments (the auditor, comptroller, and purchasing agent), five which fall under the Cook County Health Facilities budget (the medical examiner, public health, Cook County

Hospital, Oak Forest Hospital, and Cermak Health Services; see Cook County Health Facilities, below), and four which serve the court system (the Juvenile Temporary Detention Center, Supportive Services, the Law Library, and the Judicial Advisory Council; see chapter 9, Courts). The seven others reporting to the president are the Department of Building and Zoning; the Zoning Board of Appeals; the Department of Construction, Maintenance and Operations; the Environmental Control Bureau; the Department of Animal Control; the Highway Department; and the Veterans Assistance Commission.

BUREAU OF ADMINISTRATION

County Building, 118 N. Clark St. Chicago 60602; *phone 443 4660*

The Bureau of Administration was established in 1969. The chief administrative officer directs six budgetary units: Budget and Management Services, Central Services, Management Information Systems (data processing), Personnel, the Position Classification Agency, and Planning and Development. There are also a number of subdivisions within the office of the chief administrative officer with the following responsibilities:

Employee Assistance Program, a diagnostic and referral service.

Human Relations and Contract Compliance, which recommends rules for minority set-aside programs and investigates racial complaints in unincorporated areas.

President's Office of Employment Training (POET), which administers federally funded employment training programs in suburban Cook County.

Economic Development, Planning, and Administration of Programs: the chief administrative officer serves as chairman of the Cook County Community Development Advisory Council and cochairman of the Cook County Economic Development Advisory Committee. The Cook County Office of Economic Development was established in 1983 and added to the corporate budget in 1987. It conducts economic planning and research and publishes the *Annual Update of the County's Overall Economic Development Program*.

The Budget and Management Services Department assists with preparation of the county budget, audits work performance, reviews transfers of funds, and provides management assistance to other county departments.

The Department of Central Services provides warehousing, microfilm, offset printing, photocopy, telephone, and messenger service for all county offices. The director also acts as chair of the Local Records Commission.

The Department for Management of Information Systems provides computer services for county departments and elected officials, including those for property assessment, property tax extensions and collections, budget preparation, payroll, purchasing, voter registration, and vote tabulation.

The Department of Personnel: the jurisdiction of the county Civil Service Commission (see below) and the Department of Personnel is limited by statute to employees under the county Board of Commissioners, excluding employees of elected or appointed officials whose method of classification or compensation is otherwise provided by law.

The Department of Personnel is responsible for implementing the policies set by the Civil Service Commission for employee recruitment, testing, and processing, including medical examinations, administration, certification, and record keeping. It also handles the employee safety program. It obtains the services of experts to serve as examination consultants on a voluntary basis. These experts serve on advisory committees, make recommendations on examination materials, and serve on oral examination committees interviewing applicants for classification.

COOK COUNTY CIVIL SERVICE COMMISSION. A civil service commission for the county was established by state law in 1895. It has jurisdiction over employees under the Cook County Board of Commissioners, except for those at Cook County Hospital, Oak Forest Hospital, and Cermak Health Services, who are under the jurisdiction of the Health and Hospitals Governing Board. By court decision, the commission has no jurisdiction over the employees of other elected county officials.

The duties of the commission are to formulate rules for examinations, appointments, and removals, and to publish them. It is responsible for conducting civil service examinations and maintaining lists of eligible applicants in order of merit, and it acts as a quasi-judicial body to conduct hearings of grievances or actions brought against employees by department heads. Civil service employees may be removed from office only if written charges are filed by the department head and an investigation is conducted; employees have the opportunity to be heard in their own defense at a public hearing.

Public competitive examinations are conducted for county civil service positions. To take an examination, the applicant must file an application and pay a fee. The Civil Service Commission lists applicants by order of their test achievement and furnishes the list to the county board president, who in turn certifies the highest-standing candidate to the appointing officer for employment. Certain positions are by law exempt from civil service examination, such as attorneys and other professional categories.

The commission consists of three members, not more than two of whom may be of the same political party. The members are appointed by the president of the county board to serve staggered three-year terms. They are prohibited from paid employment in any other governmental position, and their salaries are determined by the county board. In 1988 the chair was paid $26,124 a year and the other two commissioners $20,988 each. The commissioners determine for themselves who shall be chair, vice-chair, and secretary.

Position Classification Agency. A separate agency establishes and maintains a position classification plan for county employees. Unlike the Personnel Department and the Civil Service Commission, the Position Classification Agency has jurisdiction over the employees of elected county officials as well as those under the Cook County Board; it does not, however, classify or set wage scales for hospital employees.

Department of Planning and Development. Each of the six counties in northeastern Illinois has a plan commission and planning department. In Cook County (unlike the other counties, which have separate commissions), the county board members are the constituted plan commission. The Department of Planning and Development assists in preparation of state and federal grant applications, acts as county liaison with other planning agencies, works with the Cook County Zoning Board of Appeals to review effects of the zoning ordinance, and develops a land-use inventory. The department is the administrative agency for the Cook County Community Development Block Grant (CDBG) program, the Rental Rehabilitation Program (RRP), and other grants under the federal Housing and Community Development Act. The department prepares and implements the Housing Assistance Plan and oversees all activities funded by CDBG.

Community Development Block Grant Program. The county's CDBG program includes the population of 136 units of local government which are municipalities of population under 50,000 and townships. The selection of projects is competitive. About 98% of the CDBG grant is spent for activities which principally benefit low- and moderate-income persons; the remainder is used to eliminate slum and blight. Between 1975 and 1988, Cook County was allocated $184,253,890 for CDBG purposes.

TABLE 7.1. BUREAU OF ADMINISTRATION

	Employee Positions	Corporate Fund
Office of Chief Administrator	25	$913,459
Data Processing	140	9,933,181
Planning and Development	8	260,275
Budget and Management	17	872,072
Personnel	36	1,248,819
Central Services	105	2,576,590
Position Classification	29	1,045,909

COUNTY COMPTROLLER

County Building, 118 N. Clark St., Chicago 60602; *phone 443 5601*

The county comptroller is the chief fiscal officer of the county. (See also County Treasurer, below.) The office of the comptroller reviews, audits and settles all debts and credits in which the county is concerned, and it is the bookkeeping agency for the county. The comptroller is appointed by the president of the county board, with the consent of the board, at an annual salary of $80,000. In 1988 this office had 55 employee positions and a corporate fund budget of $1,572,791.

COUNTY AUDITOR

County Building, 118 N. Clark St., Chicago 60602; *phone 443 6511*

The county auditor is responsible for auditing financial records of all county departments. The office of the auditor also audits the books and records of retail and wholesale businesses to verify the receipts of taxes on new motor vehicles, alcoholic beverages, gasoline, and cigarettes. The auditor maintains a record of all parcels of land in the county on which property taxes are delinquent. The auditor is appointed by the president of the Cook County Board with the consent of the board at an annual salary of $80,000. In 1988 there were 64 positions in this office and its corporate fund budget was $1,970,261.

PURCHASING AGENT

County Building, 118 N. Clark St., Chicago 60602; *phone 443 5370*

Cook County government has had a central department of purchases since 1943; it was established by state law and is subject to the state Purchasing Act. Contracts and purchases of $5,000 or more must be approved by the county board. The department is responsible for purchases and contracts for all county agencies except the Forest Preserve District. The head of the department, called the purchasing agent, is appointed by the president of the county board with the consent of the board, at an annual salary of $62,767; the department's 1988 corporate fund budget was $1,947,997; it had 80 employee positions.

DEPARTMENT OF CONSTRUCTION, MAINTENANCE, AND OPERATIONS

2323 S. Rockwell, Chicago 60608; *phone 890 2660*

The Department of Construction, Maintenance, and Operations is responsible for maintaining, operating, servicing and repairing county properties and equipment throughout the county, including suburban courtrooms, the Criminal Court building, and the Cook County Juvenile Center. It is not responsible for operation and maintenance of the hospitals. The highest administrative position listed in the 1988 budget is that of superintendent of mechanics, at $56,101 a year. There were a total of 269 employee positions and a corporate fund budget of $15,008,413.

VETERANS ASSISTANCE COMMISSION
739 S. Winchester Ave., Chicago 60612; phone 666 2910

The Veterans Assistance Commission administers emergency assistance to indigent veterans who served 90 days or more in the U.S. armed services during wartime, who were honorably discharged, and who have lived in Illinois for a year or more. It is also required by a state law originally passed in 1907 (Chapter 34, 6201-03) to provide for burial of deceased soldiers, sailors, and marines, and their parents, wives, widows, widowers, and minor children, if they die in Cook County without being able to pay funeral expenses. The benefit does not apply to relatives if they were receiving public assistance at the time of death. Burial expenses are limited to $600.

The commission is made up of three members appointed by the president of the Cook County Board for three-year terms without pay. Its 1988 budget, from corporate funds, was $147,841 (of which $25,000 was designated for burials), and it had two employees.

DEPARTMENT OF ENVIRONMENTAL CONTROL (suburban)
1500 Maybrook Court, Maywood 60153; phone 865 6165

The Department of Environmental Control has jurisdiction over the county outside Chicago. In 1965 the county board adopted an air pollution ordinance, amended since then to meet the requirements of the state environmental agency. A formal agreement with the state was adopted in 1975; it was designed to coordinate monitoring of air quality, to deal with air pollution emergencies, and to maintain surveillance of emission sources. A noise and vibration control regulation was added in 1972, limiting noise levels within specific times for vehicles, buildings, and scavenger operations. The department inspects industrial plants, responds to and initiates complaints, and issues permits for new construction, open burning, and demolition. The department expected to generate $1,000,000 in revenue in 1988. It is administered by the environmental control director, who is appointed by the president of the county board with the consent of the board, at an annual salary of $55,991. The 1988 budget provided for 47 employee positions and a corporate fund appropriation of $1,620,702.

DEPARTMENT OF HIGHWAYS
County Building, 118 N. Clark St., Chicago 60602; phone 443 7842

There are over 10,000 miles of roads in Cook County, most of them maintained by municipalities or the state. Townships maintain about 500 miles of roads in the county. The Cook County Department of Highways is responsible for design and construction of highway improvements on the 600 miles of roads which comprise the county highway system. The department is also responsible for general supervision and approval of township and road district highway improvements. The department is headed by the highway superintendent, who must be qualified by a competitive examination given by the Illinois Department of Transportation. The county board selects a superintendent from a list of candidates for a six-year term, renewable without further examination. The 1988 salary of the superintendent was $76,209.

During 1987 the total awards for highway improvement projects were $50,439,156. Funding for the department comes from the property tax, the motor fuel tax, federal funds, and the proceeds of bond issues. The 1988 highway fund budget for planning, maintenance, and repair provided for 775 employees and a total appropriation from that fund of $39,035,297, and 8 employees and a budget of $246,330 for traffic safety programs, including driver education.

DEPARTMENT OF ANIMAL CONTROL (unincorporated areas and some suburban municipalities)
1500 Maybrook Drive, Maywood 60153; phone 865 6050

The Department of Animal Control patrols, picks up loose dogs, and enforces leash laws in unincorporated areas. It is the animal care agency for areas which do not have health departments certified by the state for rabies control. Young dogs and cats must be vaccinated annually; older dogs may have a one-year or a three-year vaccination. The department sells rabies tags to licensed veterinarians. Revenue generated by the department for 1987 was $670,118. The department is headed by an animal control administrator at a salary of $29,506 a year and a business manager at a salary of $38,544 a year. In 1988 it had 15 additional employees and a budget of $737,725 from the Animal Control Fund.

DEPARTMENT OF BUILDING AND ZONING
(unincorporated areas)
County Building, 118 N. Clark St., Chicago 60602; phone 443 7670

The Department of Building and Zoning administers and enforces zoning and building standards for proposed and existing residential, commercial, and industrial areas in the unincorporated parts of the county. It reviews plans and inspects sites for flood protection and verifies that public road, public health, and sanitary facility permits required by other governmental agencies are obtained. The department also handles annual inspections for fire and other safety factors in multifamily, mixed-occupancy, and commercial units. The commissioner of the department is appointed by the president of the Cook County Board with the consent of the board at an annual salary of $58,198; in 1988 there were 69 employee positions and an annual budget of $2,370,039. Income in 1987 from permits and inspection fees amounted to $1,582,142.

ZONING BOARD OF APPEALS (unincorporated areas)
County Building, 118 N. Clark St., Chicago 60602; *phone 443 7681*

The Zoning Board of Appeals is responsible for holding public hearings and deciding appeals on rezoning decisions of the Department of Building and Zoning. A chairman (paid $26,124 a year) and four members (paid $20,988) are appointed by the president of the county board. In 1988 there were five additional employees and a total corporate budget of $306,726.

COOK COUNTY HEALTH FACILITIES

Cook County health facilities include Cook County Hospital, Oak Forest Hospital, Cermak Health Services, the Cook County Department of Health, and the Office of the Medical Examiner. The Cook County Board is responsible for their operation. The Health Facilities Committee of the board oversees the administration of Cook County and Oak Forest Hospitals; the other three departments report directly to the president of the board unless a particular issue is delegated to the committee.

There is a separate budget and separate tax levy for the Cook County Health Facilities. Hearings on this budget are conducted along with those for the county budget, following the same procedures. In addition, suburban Cook County residents pay a separate tax for the Suburban Tuberculosis Sanitarium, which is not part of the Cook County Health Facilties.

The County Health Fund estimated resources for 1988 amounted to $385,566,467. Of this, 53.4% ($206,056,625) was expected to come from property taxes, 1.7% ($6,500,000) from the personal property replacement tax, 6% ($23,000,000) from the county cigarette tax, and 36.3% ($140,000,000) from Medicare, public assistance, and other payments for patient care. The remainder was from fund balances and miscellaneous income.

COOK COUNTY HOSPITAL

1835 W. Harrison, Chicago 60612; *phone 633 6000*

Cook County Hospital, one of the largest public hospitals in the nation, provides health care primarily to the medically indigent, the uninsured, and the unemployed. Patients pay part of the cost when possible. The federal and state governments pay costs for persons on Medicare, Medicaid, and public assistance. The hospital is located in the West Side Medical Center.

The hospital was established in 1832 and provided medical services in various Chicago locations until 1876, when a facility was built at the Harrison Street address. The original facility was replaced, and the current main building opened in 1914. In the fall of 1987 the hospital administration submitted Phase V of a long-range plan to the County Board. (Phases I-IV were reports researched and submitted by private and governmental groups.) Phase V proposed replacement of the current 1,108-bed facility with a modern facility of 696 to 813 beds. The board voted approval of the concept, but in 1988, in view of proposals to use existing beds in other hospitals, the proposal was under reconsideration.

The hospital includes the Fantus Health Center for outpatients, named for Dr. Bernard Fantus, who established the first blood bank in the U.S. at Cook County Hospital. Specialized services include burn care, neonatal intensive care, and trauma care. The hospital provides training opportunities for medical schools, nursing schools, and other health professional training programs.

Fig. 7. 1. Cook County Hospital
Source: Cook County Hospital

Outpatient Services. The hospital provides family practice and internal medicine physicians on an outpatient basis at three other Chicago locations:

Englewood Neighborhood Health Center, 641 W. 63rd St., Chicago 60621; *phone 723 1814*

Salvation Army Freedom Clinic, 1515 W. Monroe St., Chicago 60607; *phone 733 0500*

South Lawndale Clinic, 2611 S. Lawndale, Chicago 60623; *phone 521 0750*

Patients may receive follow-up services either at the above three clinics or at four clinics run by other agencies:

Bethel Wholistic Health Center, 4215 W. Washington Blvd., Chicago 60621; *phone 826 7474*

Near North Health Services, 1276 N. Clybourn, Chicago 60623; *phone 337 1073*

North Lawndale Christian Health Center, 3860 W. Ogden, Chicago 60623; *phone 521 5006*

Englewood Health Clinic, 641 W. 63rd St., Chicago 60621; *phone 925 1232* (a separate clinic from the Englewood Neighborhood Health Center, listed above at the same address)

The hospital is headed by a director, who is appointed by the Cook County board, at an annual salary in 1988 of $99,000. There were 6,486 employees, including 350 attending physicians, 500 medical residents, 1,100 registered nurses, and 300 licensed practical nurses. The 1988 budget for the hospital was $274,792,042. About 38% was expected to come from repayments for Medicare, Medicaid, and other third-party payments, and 62% from tax revenues. In addition, in 1987 the Cook County Board authorized $60,000,000 in renovation and modernization expenditures.

OAK FOREST HOSPITAL
15900 S. Cicero Ave., Oak Forest 60452; *phone 687 7200*

Oak Forest Hospital, with 994 beds, is a health care center for the chronically ill. It was founded in 1910 as the Oak Forest Infirmary, to feed and house the destitute. In 1957 it became the Oak Forest Hospital. The hospital is 25 miles south of Chicago's Loop, on a 350-acre site in Oak Forest. It is open to all Cook County residents. The hospital's acute care section has 145 beds; its physical rehabilitation unit has 74; its chronic disease unit has 669; and its intermediate care facility has 106 beds. The hospital also administers three community family health centers, with fees based on ability to pay.

Outpatient clinics of Oak Forest Hospital are in the following locations:

Cottage Grove Medical Center, 1647 Cottage Grove Ave., Ford Heights 60411; *phone 758 7077*

Woody-Winston Medical Center, 650 E. Phoenix Center Dr., Phoenix 60426; *phone 687 7050*

Lincoln Memorial Medical Center, 3518 W. 139th St., Robbins 60472; *phone 687 6720*

The hospital is headed by a director, who is appointed by the Cook County board, at an annual salary in 1988 of $95,000. The 1988 budget provided for 2,300 positions and a total cost of $75,795,512, with estimated revenues from Medicare, public assistance, and private payers of $38,500,000.

CERMAK HEALTH SERVICES
2800 S. California, Chicago 60608; *phone 890 9300*

Cermak Health Services, formerly known as Cermak Hospital, is located at the Department of Corrections and provides health services to detainees and inmates, except for those requiring surgery or having serious illnesses. (Such patients are sent, under guard, to Cook County Hospital.) All inmates are examined and evaluated on entry into the Department of Corrections. Services provided include psychiatric and psychological, medical and dental, and eye examinations. The hospital has 64 beds and was budgeted in 1988 for 241 employees and a total budget of $8,456,104 from the Health Facilities Fund. Revenue generated in 1987 amounted to $456,104. The hospital is headed by an administrative director, at a salary of $51,314 and a medical chief of staff at $92,988; the chair of the psychiatry department is the highest paid staff member, at a salary of $100,008.

COOK COUNTY DEPARTMENT OF PUBLIC HEALTH (Suburban)
1500 S. Maybrook Drive, Maywood 60153; *phone 865 6100*

The Cook County Department of Public Health provides health and inspectional services to Cook County except for residents of Chicago, Evanston, Skokie, Oak Park, and Stickney Township, each of which has its own state-recognized health department. Its service area includes unincorporated areas and 130 municipalities, with a population of 2,248,594. The department provides medical, dental, hearing, and vision clinics; inspection of day-care centers, restaurants and food establishments, mobile home parks, motels, septic tanks and septic tank cleaners, seepage systems, water supply, solid waste disposal, and swimming pools; vital statistics (including filing of birth and death certificates); communicable disease control; home nursing visits; and an AIDS education program.

A Refugee Clinic is available to all refugees living in suburban Cook, DuPage, Lake, and Kane Counties (*phone 865 6119*). A WIC program offers supplemental foods and nutrition education for pregnant and nursing women, infants, and children through age five (*phone 865 6100*). Vision and hearing screening is available for preschool children (*phone 865 6120*).

The department's other health clinic programs are administered through four district offices, each of which provides services at a variety of locations. Most clinics require appointments. Services are free to suburban Cook County residents, except for family planning clinics, which in 1987 inaugurated a sliding-fee payment scale (most charges are $1). Certain clinic programs have financial eligibility requirements; these are adult health, WIC, dental, family planning, school-age, and well-child clinics.

North District Office.
5600 W. Old Orchard Road, Skokie 60077; *phone 470 7227*

The North District Office serves the townships of Barrington, Elk Grove, Hanover, Maine, New Trier, Niles, Northfield, Palatine, and Schaumburg. It provides dental clinics in Des Plaines and Skokie for adults and children over the age of three; a family planning clinic in Mount Prospect; immunization clinics in Des Plaines, Streamwood, and Wheeling; blood pressure screening (*phone 470 7227*); well-child clinics in Des Plaines, Hanover Park, Palatine, and Wheeling; and adult health, school age, maternal, and sexually transmitted disease clinics in Mount Prospect.

West District Office.
507 Washington Blvd., Maywood 60153; *phone 344 6052*

The West District Office serves an area from Schiller Park on the north to Willow Springs, Justice, and Bridgeview on the south. In Maywood it has dental, family planning, immunization, well-child, maternal, sexually transmitted disease, and school age clinics. In Forest Park it has a family planning clinic and an adult health clinic. There is another immunization clinic in Brookfield, and another well-child clinic in Melrose Park, and there are three adult health clinics, in River Grove, Forest Park, and Bellwood. Blood pressure screening is available; *phone 344 6052.*

Southwest District Office.
5410 W. 95th St., Oak Lawn 60453; *phone 423 7500*

The Southwest District Office serves an area from Evergreen Park, Home Town, Oak Lawn, and Hickory Hills on the north to Calumet Park, Blue Island, Robbins, Crestwood, and Orland Park on the south. In Markham it has dental, family planning, immunization, adult health, and sexually transmitted disease clinics. In Hickory Hills it has family planning, school age, and maternal clinics. In Harvey it has dental and sexually transmitted disease clinics. In Alsip it has a well-child and a maternal clinic. There is another dental clinic in East Chicago Heights, and another family planning clinic in Calumet Park. Well-child clinics are also held in Blue Island, Chicago Ridge, and Orland Hills. Blood pressure screening is available; *phone 423 7500.*

South District Office.
Sixth District Circuit Court Building, 165th and Kedzie Parkway, Markham 60426; *phone 210 4500*

The South District Office serves an area from the Chicago city line, Riverdale, Dixmoor, Posen, Midlothian, Oak Forest, Tinley Park, and Westhaven on the north to the county line on the south. Like the Southwest office, it also provides services in Markham and Harvey for the residents of its area. Dental clinics are held in Markham, Harvey, and East Chicago Heights. Family planning clinics are held in Markham, Chicago Heights, and Harvey. Immunization clinics are held in Markham, South Holland, and Sauk Village. Well-child clinics are held in Chicago Heights, Harvey, Markham, Park Forest, Tinley Park, and South Holland. Adult health clinics are held in Markham and Chicago Heights. Maternal clinics are held in Alsip, Markham, and Harvey. Sexually transmitted disease clinics are held in Markham and Harvey. A school-age clinic is held in Markham. Blood pressure screening is available; *phone 210 4500*.

Administration and Funding. The department is headed by a chief medical officer appointed by the county board, at a salary in 1988 of $75,444. Its 1988 budget provided for 152 employees, funded by $5,199,160 from the county's hospital fund. In 1987 the department generated $593,585 in revenue. Budget hearings are conducted at the same time as the county budget hearings, with the same timetable.

OFFICE OF THE MEDICAL EXAMINER
2121 W. Harrison St., Chicago 60612; *phone 666 0500*

The Office of the Medical Examiner was established by the Cook County Board of Commissioners in 1976; it replaced the previous elected office of coroner. The office is charged with determining the cause of death in all violent or unexplainable deaths, and it performs autopsies, post mortem examinations, and other tests. The medical examiner, who is appointed by the president of the Cook County board with the advice and consent of the board, must be a forensic pathologist (a medical board-certified physician who specializes in determining the cause of death in compliance with civil and criminal law). In 1988 the office had 123 employees, The medical examiner was paid $107,040 a year, and the budget, from the county Health Facilities Fund, was $4,589,234.

COURT SYSTEM AGENCIES
On the table of organization acompanying the 1988 appropriations ordinance, four agencies which serve the courts are listed as reporting to the president of the Cook County Board. The functions of these agencies are described in chapter 9. (Other agencies serving the courts but included in the Cook County appropriation ordinance are listed as reporting to the judiciary.) The number of employees and the 1988 budgets of the four agencies reporting to the president are as follows:

TABLE 7.? COURT SYSTEM AGENCIES
REPORTING TO BOARD PRESIDENT

	Employees	Budget
Juvenile Temporary Detention Center	318	$8,903,106
Department of Supportive Services	27	742,272
Law Library	56	2,794,797
Judicial Advisory Council	3	116,603

DEPARTMENTS ADMINISTERED
BY INDEPENDENTLY ELECTED OFFICIALS

COOK COUNTY TREASURER

County Building, 118 N. Clark, Chicago 60602; *phone 443 5100*
  1500 Maybrook Square, Maywood 60153; *phone 865 6007*
  16501 S. Kedzie Ave., Markham 60426; *phone 210 4120*
  5600 Old Orchard Road, Skokie 60077; *phone 470 7240*

The treasurer of Cook County is elected for a four-year term. The treasurer is the custodian of all revenues, both public and private, required to be held by the county for Cook County government, the circuit court of Cook County, and the state. This office is also responsible for the collection of property taxes and their distribution to more than 800 taxing agencies in the county. (Tax bills refer to the "Cook County collector," but this is the treasurer's office.) Taxpayers may protest their property tax bills to the treasurer.

The treasurer's office is responsible for selecting banks for deposit of county funds, subject to approval of the county board. The treasurer reported revenue of $21,784,403 from penalties on delinquent taxes and investment earnings and $2,778,734 in collections of inheritance taxes (see chapter 4) in 1987.

The salary of the treasurer in 1988 was $62,000 a year. There were 223 employee positions and an appropriation from the county's corporate fund of $6,853,349.

COOK COUNTY CLERK

County Building, 118 N. Clark St., Chicago 60602; *phone 443 5656*

Under the Illinois Constitution, the office of county clerk must be filled by election. Illinois law gives the county clerk responsibilities to act as clerk of the county board and as election authority for suburban Cook County, to issue licenses, extend taxes, keep vital statistics records, and maintain a variety of other records.

CLERK OF THE COUNTY BOARD. In its capacity as Clerk of the County Board, the clerk's office prepares notices of board meetings and agendas, acts as clerk at board meetings, and prepares minutes for publication. This part of the clerk's office receives and processes legal notices, contracts and bonds, county leases, county invoices over $5,000, Torrens payments (see below), county ordinances, resolutions and proclamations, and zoning, building, road and bridge, and county hospital matters.

Tax Redemption Division. The Tax Redemption Division processes annual sales of delinquent property taxes, scavenger sales, forfeitures, and special assessment sales. It also seeks to redeem, for citizens, property sold or forfeited for delinquent real estate taxes.

Tax Extension Division. Tax levy ordinances from all local taxing bodies within the county are received by the county clerk, who is then responsible for checking to see that they conform to state tax rate limitations. After receiving the equalization formula (see chapter 4), the clerk extends the tax rates to meet the tax levy (apportions the taxes among taxpayers for each taxing district).

Division of License and Registration. The Division of License and Registration issues marriage licenses and certifies notary public commissions, private detectives, and magistrates. Persons conducting businesses in a name other than their own (called an assumed name) must register with this division.

Ethics and Financial Disclosure Section. The office which receives and makes available statements filed under the state Governmental Ethics and Campaign Disclosure laws (see Preface) is the Ethics and Financial Disclosure Section of the clerk's office.

Map Division. A division of the clerk's office keeps detailed maps, assigns permanent real estate index numbers, and maintains records of the boundaries of election and taxing districts within the county.

Vital Statistics Division. Vital statistics, the records of births, marriages, and deaths in Cook County, date back to 1871.

Revenue from fees for the above services for 1987 was $3,062,430. For 1988, 184 employee positions were budgeted and the corporate fund appropriation was $4,452,558.

ELECTION DIVISION (suburban)
County Building, 118 N. Clark St., Chicago 60602; *phone 443 5150*
    Polling places, *443 5188*
    Voter registration, *443 5166*

The section of the clerk's office which has responsibility for conducting elections in suburban Cook County is the Election Division. In 1986 there were 1,218,321 registered voters in suburban Cook County; 635,285 of them voted in the 1986 general election.

The election division sets suburban precinct boundaries, secures polling places, selects election judges and provides training courses for them, conducts voter registration, deputizes municipal and township clerks to be registrars, and trains and certifies members of private organizations as registrars. It prints ballots and maintains voting equipment, and it receives election results, canvasses them, and announces them.

The expenses of this section vary from year to year, depending on whether an election is scheduled; they are paid from the corporate fund and from election funds. In 1988 the corporate fund appropriation was $2,016,091 for the county clerk's election division and $194,015 for the Chicago Board of Elections. (The county corporate fund pays the salaries of the commissioners and executive director of the Chicago Board of Elections.) From election funds, the county clerk's election division was budgeted for $10,287,436; $5,567,893 was budgeted for election costs in Cook County municipalities; and there was an additional special purpose appropriation of $699,088. There were 96 employees budgeted. Since the consolidation of elections, the county pays the costs of suburban municipal elections from a tax levy on suburban Cook County. Judges of election are paid out of the Election Account.

The 1988 salary of the county clerk was $62,000. The total number of employees in all divisions was 280.

COOK COUNTY SHERIFF
Public Information Office, rm. 704, Richard J. Daley Center, 50 W. Washington St.,
   Chicago 60602; *phone 443 6444*
   Sheriff's Police phone, *458 1000*
   Complaints, *865 4700, Internal Affairs*

The sheriff is elected to a four-year term and can be reelected. A candidate may not be a person convicted of a felony, bribery, perjury, or other infamous crime. The duties of the sheriff are set forth in Chapter 125 of the Illinois Revised Statutes. The salary of the sheriff in 1988 was $80,000 per year; the appropriation for the sheriff's office was $126,718,560; there were 4,408 employee positions. Of these, 46 employees and a budget of $1,399,355 were for the sheriff's office. In addition, there are five major departments under the sheriff's direction:

COOK COUNTY SHERIFF'S POLICE DEPARTMENT. The enforcement of law in unincorporated areas of Cook County is the responsibility of the sheriff's police. In incorporated areas, the sheriff works with local police or assumes responsibility when requested or when the need is evident. The fugitive warrant division of the Sheriff's Police Department serves warrants for arrest in criminal fugitive cases. The Internal Investigation Unit investigates complaints against police. In 1988 the police department's budget was $23,866,357 from the corporate fund, with 564 positions.

COURT SERVICES DEPARTMENT. The Civil Process Division of the Court Services Department processes court orders issued by the county circuit court, including wage garnishment orders, eviction notices, summonses to appear in court, and seizure of property under court order.

The Courtroom Services Division is responsible for maintaining order and security in the courts. This division also supervises the Child Support Division, which is responsible for serving court orders and for apprehension of defendants who fail to respond to child support orders. In 1988 this department had a corporate fund budget of $31,202,026 and 1,376 budgeted positions.

YOUTH SERVICES DEPARTMENT. The Youth Services Department provides resources for delinquency prevention and attempts to divert young people from the juvenile justice system by working with law enforcement agencies, schools, and youth service agencies. In 1988 this department had 14 employees and a corporate fund budget of $431,259.

CUSTODIAL DEPARTMENT. The Custodial Department provides security and performs household functions for the County Building, the Criminal Courts buildings at 2600 S. California and 1340 S. Michigan, and suburban court buildings. In 1988 this department had 388 positions and a corporate fund budget of $8,595,047.

DEPARTMENT OF CORRECTIONS
2700 S. California Avenue, Chicago 60608; *phone 890 7100*

The Department of Corrections is responsible by state law for detention of persons 17 years of age and older awaiting trial (who are denied or cannot pay bail) and those convicted of crimes and sentenced to up to one year in jail. (Those convicted of felonies under state law are committed to state prisons, and those convicted of crimes under federal law to federal prisons.) The department is located on a 50-acre site on the southwest side of Chicago. It had an average daily population in 1987 of 5,000 inmates, with an official total capacity for 4,703 males and 364 females.

The Department of Corrections is charged with establishing diagnostic, classification, and rehabilitation programs. Male inmates are classified and assigned, within limits of available space, to one of the eight divisions; female inmates are all assigned to Division III.

Division I, the former Cook County Jail, was built in 1912 and renovated in 1982. It is a maximum security facility with a capacity for 776 male inmates. Division II is the former city House of Corrections; as a less secure setting, it houses males held on lower bonds. It has capacity for 792, in two large dormitories and a third building for inmates who are enrolled in the Substance Abuse Treatment Center. Division III (the Women's Division) was completed in 1973. It houses all females in custody and has a capacity for 364. Division IV was opened in 1975; it has a capacity for 704 male inmates.

Division V, completed in 1978, houses the reception, classification, and diagnostic center where all incoming and outgoing inmates are processed.

It has a capacity for 992 males. The department's administrative offices are also in this building.

Division VI was opened in 1979. It also has a capacity for 992 male inmates, those deemed in need of a maximum security setting. Two gymnasiums are located in this division, as well as the department's training academy for correctional officers. Division VII houses approximately 500 work-release inmates (persons sentenced to periodic imprisonment who must live part-time at the jail). Division VIII was completed in 1985 and has a total capacity of 939 males. It provides housing for diabetics and inmates unable to cope with the general jail population or in need of prolonged psychiatric observation.

Cermak Health Services is also located on the grounds of the Department of Corrections, but is part of the Cook County health system and is funded from the County Health Facilities Fund. It offers on-site medical, psychiatric, and dental services and eye examinations to inmates and has 64 beds. Inmates requiring surgery or who have serious illnesses are sent to Cook County Hospital, where they must have 24-hour guards.

The sheriff has sole responsibility for hiring and firing the director of the Department of Corrections. In 1988 the director's annual salary was $57,500. The corporate fund budget was $61,224,516, and there were 2,009 positions budgeted.

Department of Corrections Board. A five-member board is appointed by the sheriff with the consent of the Cook County Board of Commissioners for five-year staggered terms to recommend policy and establish rules; it has no executive or administrative duties. Persons appointed to the board receive $100 per meeting and must have experience in law, medicine, social work, penology, or corrections. Board meetings are open to the public and are usually held bimonthly on Fridays at noon in the sheriff's office or at the Department of Corrections.

COOK COUNTY SHERIFF'S MERIT BOARD
Room 1079, County Building, 118 N. Clark St., Chicago 60602; *phone 443 7938*

The Cook County Sheriff's Merit Board solicits, tests, and certifies applicants for positions of full-time courtroom deputy sheriffs, sheriff's police, and correctional officers at the Department of Corrections. Applicants are given a written examination, a psychological test, and urinalysis, and background and fingerprint checks are made. Merit Board members review the files. The list of those certified is sent to the sheriff's office where candidates are appointed to fill vacancies. Correctional officers are given preference for openings in the sheriff's police force.

The board also administers promotional examinations and holds hearings on serious disciplinary cases for sheriff's police, correctional officers, and full-time deputy sheriffs.

The County Board of Commissioners appoints the three members of the board to serve for two-year terms at a salary of $600 per month. In 1988, there were 11 employees, including an executive director, and the corporate fund budget was $395,289.

STATE'S ATTORNEY

500 Richard J. Daley Center, 50 W. Washington St., Chicago 60602; *phone 443 5440*

Civil Division, *443 5450*

Consumer Fraud unit, *443 4600*

Nursing Home Hotline, *443 4377*

Community unit, *443 5598*

Criminal Division, 2600 S. California, Chicago 60608; *phone, 890 6200*

Gang Hotline, *890 3454*

Narcotics Hotline, *890 6600*

Victim-Witness Assistance, *890 7200*

The state's attorney is elected to a four-year term and takes office the first Monday in December following the election. A candidate for this office must be a licensed attorney. If a vacancy occurs in the office, the Cook County board appoints a successor until the next general election.

The state's attorney is the chief law officer of Cook County and is both a county officer and an officer of the state of Illinois; the state pays one-third of the salary of the state's attorney. This office initiates actions and indictments and prosecutes civil and criminal suits in the Cook County circuit court whenever the state or county is concerned. The office also provides legal counsel to Cook County officials and agencies and is the prosecuting authority for the state police and secretary of state for cases arising within Cook County.

Geographically, the department is divided into the same six districts as the Municipal Department of the Circuit Court; each district courthouse (in Chicago, Skokie, Maywood, Chicago Ridge, Markham, and a new court-house planned for completion in 1988 in Rolling Meadows) contains a state's attorney's office to handle traffic cases, misdemeanors, and felonies occurring within the district. Operationally, the office is divided into five bureaus:

General Criminal Prosecutions Bureau. The General Criminal Prosecutions Bureau is staffed by more than 400 assistant state's attorneys, who must be licensed attorneys. It includes the following subdivisions: felony trial, juvenile, sex crimes prosecutions, criminal appeals, traffic (which also prosecutes boating and snowmobile offenses), D.U.I. (driving under the influence), and general trial (Municipal).

Civil Action Bureau. The Civil Action Bureau is the section of the office which acts as legal advisor to county government and represents it and its officials in civil legal proceedings. The bureau takes action to collect debts owed to the county, pursues condemnation actions, and represents the county's interest in probate proceedings. It advises county officials in employee discipline and discharge cases, and it defends county agencies in any actions brought against them.

Special Prosecutions Bureau. The Special Prosecutions Bureau is responsible for matters which require special investigative and prosecutorial techniques, such as granting immunity to potential witnesses, and the use of the grand jury to obtain testimony, documents, or evidence. As of 1988, the bureau includes the following units: arson, financial and government fraud, gangs, narcotics, public integrity, and organized crime.

Investigations Bureau. The Investigations Bureau is partially staffed by sheriff's police as well as by state's attorney's investigators. It assists in preparing cases for trial. It also investigates allegations of crime such as complex financial crimes, police brutality, corruption, narcotics, welfare and vote fraud, organized crime, street gang crime, and criminal housing law violations. It offers assistance in conducting investigations to the 133 law enforcement agencies in the county. It serves subpoenas and locates victims and witnesses and provides for their presence in court.

Public Interest Bureau. The Public Interest Bureau responds to consumer fraud complaints and enforces housing and nursing home standards. It brings paternity suits and enforces child support orders. It is responsible for commitment hearings, involuntary admissions, and mental health emergency writs. It also enforces environmental safety laws, utility regulations, and obscenity laws.

Funding. The salary of the state's attorney in 1988 was $75,000, one-third paid by the state. There were 992 employee positions and a corporate fund appropriation of $36,477,781.

ASSESSOR

County Building, 118 N. Clark St., Chicago 60602; *phone 443 5303*
  Taxpayer Assistance, *443 7550*
  Homeowners Exemption, *443 7500*
  Senior Citizens Exemption, *443 6151*

Markham Branch, 16501 S. Kedzie Ave., Markham 60426; *phone 210 4100*

Maywood Branch, 1500 Maybrook Square, Maywood 60153; *phone 865 6032*

Skokie Branch, 5600 Old Orchard Road, Skokie 60077; *phone 470 7237*

The Illinois Constitution provides that county assessors may be either appointed or elected; in Cook County the assessor is elected for a four-year term. The powers and duties of the office are established by state law.

The assessor's office is responsible for the quadrennial assessment of all real property in the county, for the original assessment of any improvements added between assessments, for reviewing complaints of taxpayers, and for administering residential exemption and business incentive programs.   The assessor, however, has no authority to assess railroad property or capital stock. As of 1987 the total equalized assessed valuation of property in Cook County was more than $39.3 billion. The assessment process and exemptions are described in chapter 4.

The salary of the assessor in 1988 was $74,000 a year. There were 423 employee positions and a corporate fund budget of $13,604,703.

BOARD OF APPEALS (Property Tax Appeals)
County Building, 118 N. Clark St., Chicago 60602; *phone 443 5542*

A two-member elected board has responsibility for reviewing taxpayer's complaints about valuation of their property and exemptions. The Board of Appeals has the power to correct factual mistakes, to review certificates of error (issued by the assessor), and to order the assessor to revise and correct the assessed value of property. The board processed more than 25,000 complaints in 1987.

Members of the board are elected for four-year terms and are paid $43,500 a year. In 1988 there were 49 additional positions budgeted and a corporate fund appropriation of $1,457,457.

RECORDER OF DEEDS
County Building, 118 N. Clark St., Chicago 60602; *phone 443 5050*

The Recorder of Deeds is elected for a four-year term; the Illinois Constitution does not require that this office be elective. State law (Chapter 115, Illinois Revised Statutes) sets forth the duties of the office; they are to keep records of legal documents ("all forms of documents the public sees fit to record," according to the statement of duties in the appropriations ordinance) and to administer the Torrens system of land title administration.

Most of the documents recorded are related to land deeds, mortgages, releases of mortgages, ordinances of annexation, tax liens, and plats of survey. Other legal documents kept on record include incorporation of new businesses, dissolution of corporations, chattel mortgages, military discharge certificates, certificates of divorce and annulment, and some wills. Fees are charged based on the size of the document. There is no charge to senior citizens for copies of deeds needed to apply for the Homestead or Circuit Breaker property tax reduction.

The Torrens system of land title registration was adopted in 1897 by Cook County; it serves to guarantee land titles registered in the county. Each title is guaranteed by a cash indemnity fund and by the full resources of the county.

The 1988 salary of the recorder was $50,000. There was a corporate fund budget of $6,043,601, which provided for 275 positions. Revenue for 1987 from fees was $17,558,259.

SUPERINTENDENT OF EDUCATIONAL SERVICE REGION
33 W. Grand Ave., Chicago 60610; *phone 644 7114*

The 1870 state constitution authorized election of a superintendent of schools in each county, but this office is not mentioned in the 1970 constitution. Until 1969, this office was known as the Cook County superintendent of schools.

The voters of Cook County (Chicago and suburbs) elect the superintendent of the educational service region (ESR) for a four-year term. A candidate for the office must have a master's degree and 20 credit hours in education, a supervisory or administrative certificate issued by the state, at least four years of teaching experience, and (unless running for re-election) experience in full-time teaching or supervising in public schools for at least two years of the four preceding the candidacy.

The duties of the office are defined in the Illinois School Code. For all 144 public school districts in Cook County, including Chicago, the office distributes federal and state aid and processes reports to the state. The primary responsibilities of the office are enforcement and services. Enforcement activities include visiting school facilities to observe compliance with the law, examining the books of school treasurers, enforcing school bus and safety regulations, issuing bus driver permits, investigating school dropout cases, and filing court cases for truancy.

Services include teacher certification and placement assistance, administering General Education Development tests (GED) for high school and grade school equivalency diplomas, and providing training for teachers and other school personnel. GED applications are processed in the mini-civic centers of Markham, Maywood, and Skokie. In 1986 the office conducted a pilot truant alternative program in Maywood, leading to a 52% reduction in truancy.

The salary of the superintendent in 1988 was $55,000 a year, of which $9,500 was paid by the county and the remainder by the state. There were 57 employees and a corporate fund appropriation of $1,647,163.

COUNTY FUNDING

The Cook County budget covers the activities of the county itself, including expenses for the Circuit Court of Cook County and all the independently elected county officials, but not for the Forest Preserve District (which has a separate budget). The budget document (Annual Appropriation Bill), 988 pages for fiscal 1988, includes the corporate fund and 33 additional restricted funds. The largest of the restricted funds is that for the county health facilties, which has a tax levy separate from that of the county. The county has a separate fund for county employees' annuities and benefits. Its 1988 appropriation was $66,014,000.

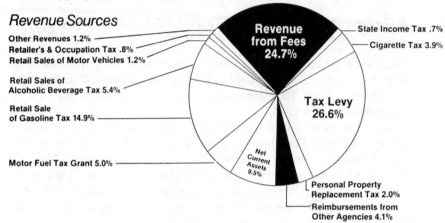

Revenue Sources

Other Revenues 1.2%
Retailer's & Occupation Tax .8%
Retail Sales of Motor Vehicles 1.2%

Retail Sales of
Alcoholic Beverage Tax 5.4%

Retail Sale
of Gasoline Tax 14.9%

Motor Fuel Tax Grant 5.0%

Revenue from Fees 24.7%

State Income Tax .7%
Cigarette Tax 3.9%

Tax Levy 26.6%

Net Current Assets 9.5%

Personal Property Replacement Tax 2.0%
Reimbursements from Other Agencies 4.1%

Fig. 7. 2. Cook County Corporate Fund.
Source: Message of the President submitting Executive Budget

SOURCES OF FUNDS. Taxing and bonding powers of local governments are described in chapter 4, Financing Local Government. Cook County uses revenue sources available to a home rule county. In addition to taxes, funds come from the state and federal governments, fees for services, from interest on investments, from sale or lease of property; the county can collect fees for licenses, permits, and franchises and income from fines in unincorporated areas where no municipality is collecting such charges.

Taxes: Unincorporated Areas. Three taxes are collected in the unincorporated areas by the state and distributed to the county (the state collects the same taxes for municipalities and distributes the funds directly to them). These are the County Retailers Occupation Tax (general sales tax, one cent per dollar) collected from unincorporated areas, the one-twelfth of the state income tax distributed according to population, and the unincorporated areas' share of the Personal Property Replacement tax. A tax on motor vehicles is collected by the county only in unincorporated areas; in June 1988 amounts ranged from $1.00 a year for vehicles owned by senior citizens to $95.00 a year for large trucks

Countywide Taxes. Two property tax levies which support county services are listed on the tax bill, one for the County of Cook and one for the Cook County Health Facilties. The county collects four additional taxes on retail sales: on sales of new motor vehicles; on alcoholic beverages; on cigarettes; and on gasoline. In addition, a portion of the estate taxes collected by the state government from Cook County estates is paid to the county.

EXHIBIT A   COOK COUNTY, ILLINOIS

                              COUNTY HEALTH FUND

                  ESTIMATED REVENUES AND OTHER RESOURCES AVAILABLE
                              FOR FISCAL YEAR 1988

1988 PROPERTY TAX LEVY (RATE 52.31 CENTS PER HUNDRED DOLLARS).......
(BASED ON AN ESTIMATED VALUATION OF $39,384,823,306)................$ 206,056,625
PERSONAL PROPERTY REPLACEMENT TAX..................................   6,500,000

REVENUE FROM PATIENT FEES
                         COUNTY   OAK
                         HOSPITAL   FOREST   TOTAL

MEDICARE $24,000,000 $15,500,000 $39,500,000
PUBLIC ASSISTANCE   64,500,000   17,000,000   81,500,000
PRIVATE PAYORS
AND CARRIERS   13,000,000   6,000,000   19,000,000

                     101,500,000   38,500,000   140,000,000

MISCELLANEOUS REVENUE (EXHIBIT D)..................................   3,800,000
CIGARETTE TAX..   23,000,000
FUND BALANCE AVAILABLE FOR APPROPRIATION...........................   6,209,842

        TOTAL ESTIMATED RESOURCES.................................$ 385,566,467

EXHIBIT B   1988 EXECUTIVE BUDGET SUMMARY

                          FUNDING COUNTY BUDGET

            Budget Recommendations are made from the following
            Financial Resources:

            Property Tax Levy - Corporate $148,326,729.
            Non-Property Tax Revenue - Corporate   273,617,414.

            Property Tax Levy - Highway   26,188,391.
            Non-Property Tax Revenue - Highway   13,093,236.
            Property Tax Levy - Bond and Interest   51,226,050.
            Property Tax Levy - County Employees
              Annuity and Benefit Fund   59,405,998.
            Non-Property Tax Levy
              Annuity and Benefit Fund   6,608,002.
            Property Tax Levy
              Cook County Juvenile Temporary
              Detention Center Rental Fund   3,333,160.
            Non-Property Tax Revenue
              Cook County Juvenile Temporary
              Detention Center Rental Fund   365,000.
            Property Tax Levy
              Circuit Court Law Enforcement
              Facilities Rental Fund   331,640.
            Non-Property Tax Revenue
              Circuit Court Law Enforcement
              Facilities Rental Fund   37,000.
            Election Fund Levy   16,904,417.

                                                       $599,437,037.

Fig. 7. 3. Cook County Budget. These are summary pages from 1988 Cook County Budget
Documents. Exhibit A is from the Executive Budget Recoommendations for the Cook Coun-
ty Health Program; Exhibit B is from the Message of the President submitting the Executive
Budget. These are separate documents.

Federal and State Grants. The county listed anticipated revenues of $26,419,686 for 1988 from 36 federal, state, and private grants. These included a Community Development Block Grant (CDBG) of $6,877,950, 19 grants for various health programs, 4 grants for job training, 7 grants connected with law enforcement or the court system., an economic development grant, and an air monitoring grant.

Licenses, Permits, Fees, Fines. The county charges for various licenses it issues, such as marriage licenses and notary certificates. It charges fees for services: the income expected from patient fees from Cook County and Oak Forest Hospitals for 1988 was $140,000,000; the sheriff's office expected to collect $9,600,000 in charges for issuing summons and other legal processes. It issues building and zoning permits and charges inspection fees in unincorporated areas. The city of Prospect Heights and the village of Palatine reimburse the county for police services. Altogether, the county expected 25.2% of the 1988 corporate fund budget of $421,944,143 to be paid by revenue from fees, and 36.3% of the county health facilities budget of $385,566,467 to come from patient care payments.

Borrowing. Like all local governments dependent on property taxes, the county borrows on a short-term basis through tax anticipation warrants. As a home rule unit, the county has the powers to issue long-term bonds, which are generally for capital expenses. It appropriated $51,226,050 for bond and interest payments in 1988.

Budget procedures. Unlike that of other local governmental bodies, the Cook County fiscal year is not an exact calendar year. It begins on the first Monday in December and runs through the Sunday before the first Monday in December of the following year (December 1, 1986 to December 6, 1987; December 7, 1987 to December 4, 1988). Thus different fiscal years include different numbers of days. The county also does not adopt its budget before the beginning of the fiscal year. State law provides that it must be adopted within the first quarter of each fiscal year (roughly by March 1).

Development of the budget begins with departmental requests, review by the board president and budget staff, and preparation of an executive budget by the budget director. The county's Annual Appropriation Bill includes both line item and program budgets for each department. The county comptroller must submit an estimate of revenues for the coming year by November 1. The executive budget is submitted to the board's committee on finance, which holds hearings with each department and may amend the budget. The board may amend the budget during the year but may not exceed the appropriations for a fund without approving a supplemental appropriation supported by an estimate of resources.

Public hearings are required by state law and are held in February before the budget goes to the county board for possible amendment and final approval. Budget recommendations, the comptroller's report, Health Facilities financial statements, and information on public hearings are available from the county board offices at 118 N. Clark St., Chicago 60602.

COOK COUNTY FOREST PRESERVE DISTRICT

536 N. Harlem Ave., River Forest 60305; *phone 261 8400*

The Cook County Forest Preserve District is a separate, independent taxing body, but the Cook County Board of Commissioners acts as the Forest Preserve District Board of Commissioners. The district is a belt of 66,961 acres of forest reservations, including 42 lakes, in suburban Cook County, roughly in a semicircle surrounding the city. It provides recreational areas, nature centers, and educational programs; the Brookfield Zoological Park and the Botanic Garden are in the Forest Preserves. About 40,000,000 visitors use the preserves each year.

The movement for a forest preserve system followed a 1904 report of the Outer Belt Park Commission, made up of city and county officials and private citizens, and the 1909 publication of the Burnham Plan for the city of Chicago. State legislation was passed in 1913, and the district was organized in 1915. Its charter gave the district power to "acquire lands containing forests and land connecting such forests and to maintain, preserve, restore, and restock such lands together with their flora, fauna, and scenic beauties in their natural condition as nearly as may be for the education, recreation, and enjoyment of the people." Recreational development of the area grew out of a 1929 report by a citizen advisory committee, a 1931 referendum approving a bond issue for improvements, and the work of the Civilian Conservation Corps beginning in 1933.

As of 1988, plans are to develop full utilization of 18% of the forest preserves and leave the remaining area in its natural state. The district may issue acquisition bonds until it holds a total of 75,000 acres, but recent land purchases have been made with the assistance of federal grants. In addition to Brookfield Zoo and the Botanic Gardens, the district maintains the following recreational facilities:

10 golf courses
3 swimming pools
124 baseball fields
5 winter sports areas
cross-country skiing through most of the preserves
187 miles of trails for hikers and horseback riding
40 fishing centers, including 6 boat ramps
52 miles of trails for bicycle use only
2,200 picnic areas and 190 picnic groves
6 tent camping sites
3 organized youth group cottage camping facilities
the Chicago Portage National Historic Site

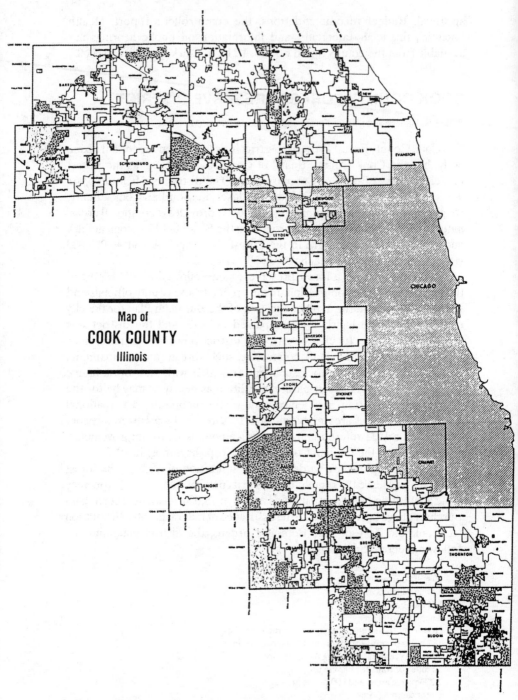

Fig. 7. 4. Forest Preserve District map
Source: cover of 1988 Cook County Budget Recommendations.

Forest preserve maps and trail maps are available from the district office. Picnic sites may be reserved; reservations for any time during a year are accepted beginning on the first working day of the year.

Educational Services. The district's Conservation Department is responsible for wildlife management and public instruction. The wildlife management program is particularly concerned with deer, raccoon, and beaver, and the fisheries management program supervises the 42 lakes with 1,724 acres of water. The district cooperates with public and private school systems to provide workshops, field trips, and courses for teachers in outdoor science education. Four nature centers, a museum of living examples of forest preserve fauna, and an adult education center provide opportunities to study plant and animal life of marshy meadows and sand dunes:

Little Red Schoolhouse, Palos Preserves
River Trail Nature Center, south of Wheeling
Sand Ridge Nature Center, Dhabbona Woods, near 159th St. and Torrence Ave.
Crabtree Nature Center, south of Barrington
Trailside Museum of Natural History, Thatcher Woods
Adult Education Center, Camp Sawagau, Palos Hills

Organization and Finance. The president of the county board is also president of the Forest Preserve District and appoints the superintendent. The superintendent's salary is $95,000 a year. In 1988, the district had 891 regular employees and 344 seasonal employees hired as needed.

In an area coterminous with Cook County, the district levies taxes for operating expenses, retirement of bonds and payment of interest, and for construction and development. Under state law it levies additional taxes for three agencies which have separate boards and are not accountable to the district: the Employees' Annuity and Benefit Fund, the Zoological Fund, and the Botanic Garden Fund. The Brookfield Zoo is operated by the Chicago Zoological Society and the Botanic Garden by the Chicago Horticultural Society; both raise additional funds from other sources.

The district may incur bonded indebtedness, which is limited by the legislature to 0.345% of the assessed valuation of the county. The legislature also set limits on the amount that can be raised by taxes. The total 1988 appropriation of $78,691,722.64 was divided as follows:

Corporate Fund	$27,337,622.45
Construction and Development Fund	7,339,948.70
Bond and Interest Fund	7,651,250.00
Real Estate Acquisition Fund	10,818,642.49
Employees Annuity and Benefit Trust	1,629,000.00
Zoological Fund	17,075,403.00
Botanic Garden Fund	6,839,856.00

The income was from four sources: property tax levy, $46,252,777.86; corporate personal property replacement tax, $3,703,000; miscellaneous income, $12,982,044; surplus, $15,753,900.78.

The Forest Preserve District's fiscal year, slightly different from that of the county, runs from January 1 to December 31. State statute requires adoption of an appropriation ordinance within 60 days after the start of the fiscal year (by February 29 or March 1). The state law does not require public review and hearings on the budget, but the Finance Committee of the district board usually holds public hearings on the same day that the county board schedules its public hearings.

Forest Preserve District of Cook County Advisory Committee. An unpaid nine-member advisory committee undertakes research and makes recommendations to the district's board. Its membership is appointed for life, and vacancies are filled by the committee with the consent of the district's board. Staff is provided by the district.

Cook County Clean Streams Committee. A volunteer committee was established by the Forest Preserve commissioners in 1953, with a mission to detect violations of the laws prohibiting pollution of streams and rivers. Watershed committees, appointed by the Clean Streams Committee, voluntarily patrol rivers and streams and forward information about violations to the responsible agency, such as the Metropolitan Sanitary District or the U.S. Army Corps of Engineers. If a violator fails to comply, the case is referred to the state's attorney or the attorney general. Anyone interested in clean streams may volunteer to become a member of the committee, which meets six times a year at the Forest Preserve headquarters. The expenses of the committee, including a paid executive secretary, are part of the Forest Preserve District budget.

8 Cook County Governments: Independent Agencies

In addition to the County and the Forest Preserve District, there are in Cook County (as within the city of Chicago) a number of other governmental agencies, with a variety of boundaries and a variety of functions. This chapter describes Sanitary Districts, transportation districts, and the Public Building Commission, which serve all of Cook County, and three agencies which are independent bodies serving suburban Cook County.

METROPOLITAN SANITARY DISTRICT OF GREATER CHICAGO (MSD)

100 E. Erie, Chicago 60611; *phone 751 5600*
Emergency and night service, *751 6555*

The Metropolitan Sanitary District of Greater Chicago (MSD) is a municipal corporation with taxing and bonding powers, governed by an elected board of commissioners. It is responsible for collection, treatment, and disposal of wastewater from an area of 872 square miles that includes most of Cook County. It is also charged with protecting the water quality of Lake Michigan. It serves over 5,100,000 people and serves industries which contribute waste equivalent to that of an additional 4,500,000 people. MSD sewer permits are required for new residential, commercial, and industrial developments, except in the city of Chicago..

Before a sanitary district was created, raw sewage emptied directly into the Chicago River and ultimately flowed into Lake Michigan. This practice contaminated the water supply and caused a great epidemic after a severe rainstorm in 1885. The Illinois legislature established a Drainage and Water Supply Commission to study water supply and waste disposal, and in 1889 the Chicago Sanitary District was formed. It was charged with collecting and disposing of sewage, protecting the water supply, and regulating navigation in the area's waterways. In 1955 its name was changed to Metropolitan Sanitary District of Greater Chicago to reflect the increased area it served.

In 1900 the new district undertook the creation of the 30-mile-long Sanitary and Ship Canal. The canal connected the Chicago River to the Des Plaines River, thereby reversing the flow of the Chicago River since the Des Plaines River is lower than Lake Michigan. This feat caused the American Society of Civil Engineers in 1955 to name the MSD one of the seven engineering wonders of the U.S.

Waste Treatment. Municipal sewers collect waste and rainwater and discharge them into the MSD system. MSD has enforcement powers which permit it to monitor and regulate the quality of discharges into the wastewater system and waterways within Cook County. Industries may be required to pretreat their wastes to meet MSD regulations. Waste discharges into Lake Michigan are prohibited, although raw sewage and rainwater may be discharged directly into the rivers and Lake Michigan when rainstorms are so severe that the treatment facilities cannot handle the flow and widespread flooding of urban areas is imminent. (See below, Flood Control.)

The MSD treatment program is one of the largest in the world. About 1.5 billion gallons of water a day are treated in seven treatment plants. The four older plants provide primary and secondary treatment which can remove 90% or more of the contaminants; three newer plants provide primary, secondary, and tertiary treatment which can remove 99% of the contaminants.

The MSD uses a treatment process called the activated sludge process. This process produces a purified liquid effluent and a solid called sludge. After treatment by anaerobic digestors, the sludge is dried, at which point it looks like topsoil. This sludge is a "soil amender" which can be used for plantings that remain outside the food chain. The dried sludge is recycled through bulk distribution to both the public and private sector for use in development of recreational parks, restoration of roadway medians and shoulders, maintenance and improvement of grounds, and landscaping projects. The city of Chicago uses dried sludge in the closure of landfill at 103rd St. and Doty Avenue which will become a recreation area. Since 1987 sludge has been trucked to Fulton County under a plan to reclaim strip-mined areas. The district purchased 15,528 acres there in 1970 and has been reclaiming it, first through the use of liquid sludge and since 1987 through dried sludge. The reclaimed area is farmed under contract for producing nonfood crops.

Flood Control: Tunnel and Reservoir Plan (TARP). As population has grown, there has been less open land to absorb rainwater and greater amounts of sewage. The Tunnel and Reservoir Plan (TARP) was adopted in 1970 to solve the problem of discharges of sewage and rainwater into the rivers and lake during severe storms. Phase I of TARP consists of a system of reservoir tunnels dug 240 to 300 feet deep into bedrock below Chicago and nearby suburbs. Four completed sections total over 50 miles. The largest of these sections is the Mainstream System, 31 miles long and capable of holding a billion gallons of water. Rainwater and sewage is held in the tunnels until it can be treated. The MSD reports that, when it is completed, TARP Phase I will eliminate 80% of the combined sewage pollution problem in the Chicago area. The completed portion of the TARP Phase I took almost ten years to construct and cost $1.2 billion.

Phase II of the TARP project has been under the jurisdiction of the U.S. Army Corps of Engineers. It is a system of huge basins intended to collect and hold flood waters after very heavy rainfalls. The water would be held in these basins until it could be treated. As of 1988, acquisitions of rights-of-way and preliminary designs were under way. Construction depended on appropriation of federal funds.

Water Quality Monitoring. The MSD conducts patrol boat surveillance and water sampling from Glencoe, Illinois to Hammond, Indiana. It also monitors water quality with respect to the Zion Nuclear Power Plant. As of 1987, it reports biological, chemical, and radioactivity levels that meet standards set for drinking water by the U.S. Environmental Protection Agency. MSD publishes the *Lake Michigan Water Quality Clean Water Quarterly*, which reports the results of its monitoring, including studies of aquatic life and the effects of festivals held at the lakeshore in Chicago.

Administration. The MSD is managed by an elected board of nine commissioners, three elected at large every two years by the voters of the district. They serve six-year terms. If a vacancy occurs, the governor appoints a replacement to serve the remainder of the term. The commissioners elect a president and vice-president. They appoint the general superintendent, the treasurer, and the three members of the Civil Service Board. The general superintendent is the chief executive officer and appoints department heads.

Meetings. The MSD Board meets in the boardroom at 100 E. Erie, usually on the first and third Thursdays of each month at 10 A.M. Meetings are open to the public.

Department of Personnel and Civil Service Board. A civil service system was created by the legislature in 1889 when the district was established. Positions are classified, and competitive examinations are held for both initial appointment and for promotion. An examination must be held for any position filled by a temporary worker, and an eligibility list must be posted within 60 days of the temporary appointment. In 1987 about 80%

of the approximately 2,300 MSD employees had civil service status, principally those working in maintenance and operation of the treatment plants. The remainder of the employees are in general administration, personnel, law, research and development, finance, and surveillance and enforcement.

Funding. The Metropolitan Sanitary District is supported chiefly by user charges, if the property tax for the Sanitary District listed on a home owner's real estate tax bill is considered to be a user charge. Industry and other large users of services, such as hospitals and universities, pay a separate user charge. There are also surcharges for treatment of special wastes. Some income is derived from leasing MSD property not in immediate use. (Other land not in immediate use is shared with local park districts for recreation use or dedicated to nature preserves.) Several million dollars of the MSD energy needs are supplied as a byproduct of its primary operations. Electricity is generated by a hydroelectric power plant on the Illinois River in Lockport. A burnable gas is obtained and reused as part of the sludge treatment process at several plant locations.

The total MSD budget for 1988 was $624,148,000; it employed 2,358 persons. Salaries for commissioners are set by the state legislature. In 1988, four commissioners were paid $30,000 a year and two were paid $32,000, the president was paid $39,500, the vice-president $37,000, and the finance chair $35,000. The general superintendent's salary was $107,514. The MSD construction program is funded by federal and state grants and the sale of bonds. In 1988, the district expected grant receipts of $161,719,000.

Budget. Preparation of the Sanitary District budget begins in August and September. In October an Initial Budget is published and presented to the board. The Finance Committee holds meetings open to the public in November, and then publishes a Tentative Budget, which must be available to the public for ten days. Public hearings are held in late November or early December. The Final Budget must be adopted before January 1.

THORN CREEK BASIN SANITARY DISTRICT
700 West End Avenue, Chicago Heights 60411; *phone 754 0525*

The Thorn Creek Basin Sanitary District, formerly the Sanitary District of Bloom Township, serves Steger and Crete in Will County and Chicago Heights, South Chicago, and Park Forest in Cook County (as of spring 1988 it was annexing the village of Homewood). The district was formed in 1928; at that time a sewage treatment plant served Chicago Heights. The plant, built in 1907, was one of the first municipal treatment plants in Illinois. The present plant can serve up to 110,000 persons; as of 1988 it was serving 85,000.

The district is headed by a three-member elected board of trustees, serving three-year staggered terms at salaries of $3,000 a year. There are 34 staff members. The 1988 budget was $3,445,835, and the tax rate was 9 cents per $100 of equalized assessed valuation.

PUBLIC BUILDING COMMISSION (PBC)
50 W. Washington St., Chicago 60602; *phone 744 3090*

The Chicago Public Building Commission (PBC), while it is listed as a city agency and appears in the city budget, is an independent governmental entity, not a department of the city. It serves the city and six other local governments under 1955 state legislation which authorizes the creation of the commission to construct governmental and school buildings and lease them to local governments. The commission was created by the city of Chicago in 1956; it finances construction for the city of Chicago, the Chicago Board of Education, the Chicago Park District, the Chicago Community College District, the Metropolitan Sanitary District, the Forest Preserve District, and Cook County. The commission has the power, on request from these governmental bodies, to issue revenue bonds to acquire, construct, reconstruct, and equip buildings and facilities to be leased to the governmental unit. It requires the governmental unit to provide for a property tax to pay the rentals; under the law, such property taxes are not subject to statutory limitations. Administrative expenses and interest and principal on the revenue bonds are paid out of rental charges to the governmental bodies using the buildings.

The commission has 11 members, who serve five-year terms; 6 are appointed by the mayor, and 1 member by each of 5 other municipal bodies. Commissioners are not paid.

The commission has 21 employees; it is headed by an executive director, who has a salary of $71,548. An additional 190 employees are responsible to the executive director for maintenance of the Daley Center. The commission submits an annual operating and maintenance budget for the Daley Center to the city council and the county board. The commission's budget for 1988 showed anticipated lease income of $80,398,067.

REGIONAL TRANSPORTATION AUTHORITY (RTA)
1 N. Dearborn, Chicago 60602; *phone 917 0700*

In 1972 the governor of Illinois appointed a task force to study public transportation systems in northeastern Illinois, and this task force proposed a Regional Transportation Authority to serve the six-county area of Cook, DuPage, Kane, Lake, McHenry, and Will counties. The RTA was authorized by legislation in 1973 and approved by referendum in 1974. It serves an area of 3,700 square miles with an estimated 1986 population of 7,300,000.

In 1983 the state legislature restructured the RTA and gave it responsibility for financial oversight and regional coordination of mass transportation. The Chicago Transit Authority (CTA), commuter railroads (Metra), and suburban bus systems (PACE) are all under RTA unified control and are funded by RTA.

The RTA has no power to levy a property tax but does have power to levy a sales tax (in 1988 1% in Cook County and 0.25% in the other five counties), to sell revenue bonds of up to $400,000,000 for capital improvements, and to receive grant funds from the federal Urban Mass Transportation Administration (UMTA) and the state for operating assistance, for new facilities, and for research and demonstration projects.

Under the reorganization operating responsibilities were decentralized, but the RTA was given strong budgetary review powers. A formula was established allocating 85% of the sales tax receipts directly to the three service boards, and a new state funding source, the Public Transportation Fund (PTF), equal to 25% of the sales tax receipts was provided to the RTA for allocation to the service boards. As a condition for receiving state funds, the system as a whole must recover at least 50% of total operating expenses from fares and other system-generated revenues.

RTA Board. State law establishes an RTA Board of 13 directors, appointed for five-year staggered terms. The mayor of Chicago appoints 4 with the consent of the city council; 1 is the chairman of the Board of the Chicago Transit Authority; 4 are appointed by suburban members of the Cook County Board; 1 is appointed by the chairman of the DuPage County Board; 2 are jointly appointed by the chairmen of the county boards of Kane, Lake, McHenry, and Will counties. For the term ending July 1, 1989, the governor appoints the chairman; after that the chairman is appointed from outside the board membership by the other 12 directors with the concurrence of 9 directors. Each board member except the CTA chairman is paid $25,000 a year.

A majority of the directors constitute a quorum, but 7 votes are required for approval of contracts, adoption of rules, or passage of resolutions or ordinances.

Budget and Finance. Each year by December 31 the RTA must adopt both a five-year plan and an annual budget. In August the RTA holds hearings on its preliminary budget projections, including estimates of the "recovery ratio," the percentage of operating costs that CTA, PACE, and Metra are expected to recover from fares. By September 15, the RTA must advise each of the subsidiary agencies what their subsidies will be and what their recovery ratio must be. Then the subsidiary agencies hold public hearings, and they must transmit their proposed budgets and financial plans to the

RTA by November 15. The RTA holds hearings in early December for the three budgets of CTA, PACE, and Metra. At least one public hearing on the RTA's five-year plan must be held in each of the six counties. The five-year plan must also be presented to the Northeastern Illinois Planning Commission (NIPC) and the Chicago Area Transportation Study (CATS) for review and comment. The final budget of the RTA is presented to the state legislature and the governor. Budget materials and information on public hearings are available from the RTA director of public affairs at the RTA offices.

Sources and amounts of funds. Total RTA expenses for 1988 were budgeted at $32,720,621. This includes an administrative budget of $4,995,641, with 72 employees; nonadministrative costs (for insurance, marketing, travel information, etc.) of $8,574,980; and regional capital financing costs of $19,150,000.

Advisory Board. An advisory board is made up of the chairs of the advisory boards of the CTA, PACE, and Metra. It meets quarterly. The RTA Board must meet with the Advisory Board at least once every four months.

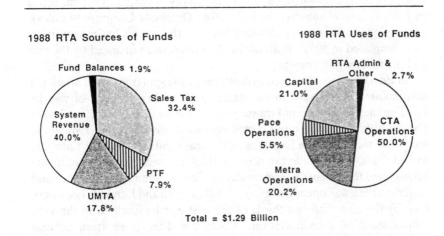

1988 RTA Sources of Funds

Fund Balances 1.9%
Sales Tax 32.4%
System Revenue 40.0%
PTF 7.9%
UMTA 17.8%

1988 RTA Uses of Funds

RTA Admin & Other 2.7%
Capital 21.0%
Pace Operations 5.5%
CTA Operations 50.0%
Metra Operations 20.2%

Total = $1.29 Billion

Fig. 8. 1. RTA funds
Source: Regional Transportation Authority Budget

CHICAGO TRANSIT AUTHORITY

Merchandise Mart Plaza, P.O. Box 3555, Chicago 60654; *Phone, Complaints, 664 7200*
Travel Information, Chicago, *836 7000*
Travel Information, suburbs, *1-800 972 7000*
CTA maps, *664 7200, extension 3318*
Hearing impaired TDD, *226 3708*
Special Services Program for mobility-limited persons, *527 1700*

The Chicago Transit Authority (CTA) serves the city of Chicago and 37 suburbs, with a total population of 3.7 million. It operates the second-largest public transportation system in the United States. The system in 1987 included 6 rapid transit routes with 215 miles of track, 143 stations, and 1,200 rapid transit cars. There were 133 bus routes covering 2,090 route-miles of 2,247 buses; there were 12,900 posted bus stops.

Created by 1945 state legislation (Chapter 11 2/3, 30, 311, 701), the CTA began operating in 1947, after acquiring the properties of the bankrupt privately owned Chicago Rapid Transit Company and the Chicago Surface Lines. In 1952 the CTA became the sole operator of transit when it purchased the Chicago Motor Coach Company.

Under state law the CTA has the right to acquire, construct, maintain and operate local transportation facilities within the city of Chicago and through the city to some suburbs.

Rapid Transit Lines. The rapid transit system has been developed over a long period. The downtown State Street subway (4.9 miles) was completed in 1943. A second subway, the Milwaukee-Dearborn-Congress (4 miles), connecting the Milwaukee elevated line with the central business district, was completed in 1951. Both of these subways were financed by the city and the federal government.

In 1958 Chicago pioneered in combining rail rapid transit and multilane automobile expressways in the same grade-separated right-of-way by building the Congress rapid transit route in the median of the Eisenhower Expressway. A second rapid transit operation was opened in 1969 in the median of the Dan Ryan Expressway; this was combined with the Lake line to Oak Park. A five-mile extension of the CTA west-northwest route via subway and the Kennedy Expressway median between Logan Square and Jefferson Park was opened in 1970. The Dan Ryan and Kennedy lines were built by the city, with two-thirds of the cost met by funds from the U.S. Department of Transportation. Chicago's share came from general obligation bond funds approved by Chicago voters under the 1966 Capital Improvement Bond Referendum.

The Skokie Swift (five miles in six and a half minutes) service between Howard Street in Chicago and Dempster Street in Skokie was inaugurated in 1964 as a federally aided mass transportation project.

In 1984 the CTA began direct rapid transit service to O'Hare International Airport, continuing the Kennedy Expressway route to the airport. It was planned and engineered by the city and the CTA and was built by the city Department of Public Works. Funding came from the federal and state governments.

In 1987 construction began on the Southwest Rapid Transit Line to Midway Airport which is expected to begin operating in 1993. Planning for this line began in 1977. The city has responsibility for financing, design, construction, and property acquisition. The CTA is involved in technical aspects of design and construction, as well as specifications for and the purchase of transit vehicles. The cost is expected to be $496,000,000, of which the federal government will pay 85% and the state 15%.

CTA Board. The Chicago Transit Authority Board is a seven-member board, with four members appointed by the mayor, subject to approval by the City Council and the governor, and three appointed by the governor, subject to approval by the Illinois Senate and the mayor. Board members are appointed to seven-year terms. They are paid $25,000 a year, except for the chair, who is paid $50,000 a year. The chair is elected by the board and becomes a member of the board of the Regional Transportation Board. In the event of a vacancy another chair is elected by the board.

It is the responsibility of the board to operate and contract for service, to establish service and fare levels, to prepare an annual balanced budget and multiyear financial plan for approval by the Regional Transportation Authority (RTA), to prepare a capital plan for review by the RTA, and to negotiate labor contracts.

The CTA's executive director is selected by the board, is responsible for day-to-day operations, and is paid $110,000 a year.

Citizens Advisory Board (CAB). An advisory board which serves without pay is appointed by the Chicago Transit Board for two-year terms. The Citizens Advisory Board (CAB) elects a chair, who becomes a member of the RTA's Citizens Advisory Board. The CAB holds monthly meetings which are open to the public in the board room (room 734) of the CTA offices. Every three months, as required by law, the CAB meetings are joint meetings with the Chicago Transit Board.

Funding. The CTA divides its expenses into two main categories, operating and capital.

The operating budget for 1988 was $653,624,000. Part of the costs are paid from what is called System-Generated Revenue, which includes fares, investment income, and advertising revenue. Part is from funding from the RTA, usually slightly less than one-half of the budget. The RTA specifies what percentage of operating expenses must be recovered from

System-Generated Revenue; this is called the recovery ratio requirement. Regionally the recovery ratio must exceed 50%, and typically the CTA's recovery ratio is about 51%.

Each year before the CTA can receive state or federal operating assistance the city of Chicago must agree to contribute $3,000,000 and Cook County $2,000,000. This funding is counted as part of the System-Generated Revenue.

Budget. The CTA's fiscal year runs from January 1 to December 31. In mid-May the departments are asked to submit goals, programs, and objectives for the following year. In early July the departments estimate their specific, detailed staffing and funding needs for the next year, based on present levels. At the end of July, the CTA submits to the RTA an estimate of present-year results and the needs for the next year. By September 15, by law, the RTA must set "budget marks" (an estimate of how much funding will be available and what the recovery ratio must be) through a preliminary RTA budget.

The CTA then develops a preliminary proposed budget and holds public hearings. The CTA Budget Committee and Board may then review and modify the proposed budget. A final proposed budget must be submitted to the RTA by November 15. A two-year financial plan is also submitted. After November 15, the RTA goes through its own process of review and public hearings and must adopt a consolidated regional budget. The CTA board then makes any necessary modifications in its budget and adopts a final budget of its own.

In 1988 the CTA had 13,163 positions budgeted. About 10,000 are employed in operations and maintenance. Salaries represent over 70% of the operating budget. Hiring is done through letters of application.

Capital Budget. The CTA capital budget for 1988 was $89,156,000. Funds come from the federal and state governments and the RTA. The CTA develops a five-year Capital Improvement Program and submits it to the RTA. The RTA reviews the CTA's program and develops a consolidated regional capital program, which it then must submit to the Chicago Area Transportation Study (CATS), the metropolitan planning organization required by the federal government.

Once the Capital Improvement Program is approved, the CTA submits grant applications to funding agencies. Capital programs have typically been 75% to 80% financed by the federal Urban Mass Transportation Administration (UMTA) and by a local share of 20% to 25%. The local share has generally been a combination of Illinois Department of Transportation and RTA funds. In recent years, the RTA has provided all of the funds for some capital programs.

Meetings. CTA board meetings are open to the public. They are held at 10:30 A.M. the first Wednesday of the month in the CTA board room on the seventh floor of the Merchandise Mart.

METRA (METROPOLITAN RAIL)
547 W. Jackson Blvd., Chicago 60606; *phone 322 6900*
Travel Information 322 6777

The commuter rail division of the Regional Transportation Authority (RTA) was established by law in 1983. Its board of directors organized in 1984 and introduced the name "Metra" to provide identity for commuter rail service in northeast Illinois. Metra is charged with providing public transportation by rail either through direct ownership and operation or through purchase-of-service contracts. It receives revenue from customers and funding from the RTA.

Metra routes serve over 100 communities at 233 local and downtown rail stations, 68 of which are in the city of Chicago, and the remainder in Illinois suburbs. Service extends to 1 station in Wisconsin and 19 in Indiana, but these operations are not supported by Illinois taxes. Metra has purchase-of-service agreements with the Burlington Northern, the Chicago and Northwestern, and the Norfolk and Western railroads and shares a three-way contract with the Northwest Indiana Commuter Transportation District and the Chicago, South Shore and South Bend Railroad. Passenger coaches and locomotives are owned by Metra or leased to it by suburban mass transit districts. Metra acquired ownership of all commuter facilities of the now-defunct Rock Island Railroad and the Milwaukee Road. In 1987 it acquired the commuter facilities of the Illinois Central Gulf and renamed the service Metra/Electric.

Board. The law provides for a seven-member board; none of its members may be an employee of a transportation agency or (unlike the PACE board) a governmental official or employee. Members serve four-year staggered terms. One director is appointed by the chairman of the DuPage County Board; two, who must not live in Cook County or DuPage County, are appointed by vote of the chairmen of the county boards of Kane, Lake, McHenry, and Will counties; three, who must live in suburban Cook County, are appointed by the suburban members of the Cook County Board; one Chicago resident is appointed by the mayor of Chicago. The chairman is elected by the board, with the approval of at least five members. The chairman is paid $25,000 a year, the other members $15,000, and all are reimbursed for expenses.

The law governing Metra provides for reapportionment of the board after each federal census, but it also provides that appointments must be based on morning boardings of the commuter rail services (reserving, however, at least one appointment by the mayor of Chicago).

The board appoints the executive director; appointment or dismissal requires the concurrence of six of the seven directors.

Budget and Finance. The board must prepare an annual budget and a financial plan for the following two years; these must be based on RTA estimates of funds available. Before submitting the budget and financial plan to the RTA, Metra must hold a public hearing in each of the counties it serves. The budget must be submitted to the RTA by November 15; the RTA may require modifications. The Metra budget is finally passed as part of the RTA budget. Metra's 1988 budget projects a ridership of 64,000,000 and a recovery ratio from income of 54% of costs. Its total budget for the year was $374,326,000; it had 1,942 employees, not including those working for the carriers from whom Metra purchased services.

Citizens Advisory Board. A ten-member citizens advisory board is appointed for two-year terms by the Commuter Rail Board. Members serve without compensation and meet quarterly with the Rail Board.

INDEPENDENT AGENCIES
SERVING SUBURBAN COOK COUNTY

PACE SUBURBAN BUS SERVICE
550 W. Algonquin Road, Arlington Heights; *phone 364 7223*

PACE was established as part of the Regional Transportation Authority (RTA) by state law in 1983 with jurisdiction over public transportation by bus within the metropolitan area, other than that provided by the Chicago Transit Authority (CTA) or commuter rail (Metra). It receives funding from the RTA and is delegated the powers given to the RTA to contract for or initiate bus service in the suburbs.

It serves an area of 3,446 square miles with a population of 4,200,000 and has about 36,000,000 riders a year. About half of the service is provided by PACE-owned carriers, 43.5% by publicly owned carriers (municipal or transit districts), and 6.4% by private contract carriers. PACE subsidizes 61 paratransit services which carry over 1,100,000 passengers, about 3% of its ridership. There are three types of paratransit services: Dial-a-ride, curb-to-curb service with lift-equipped buses; shared-ride taxi services, through contracts with private operators; and fixed-route deviation services, where a bus will deviate from its fixed route on request.

Board. The governing body of PACE is a 12-member board, appointed for four-year terms; terms of those appointed from Cook County expire in 1989,

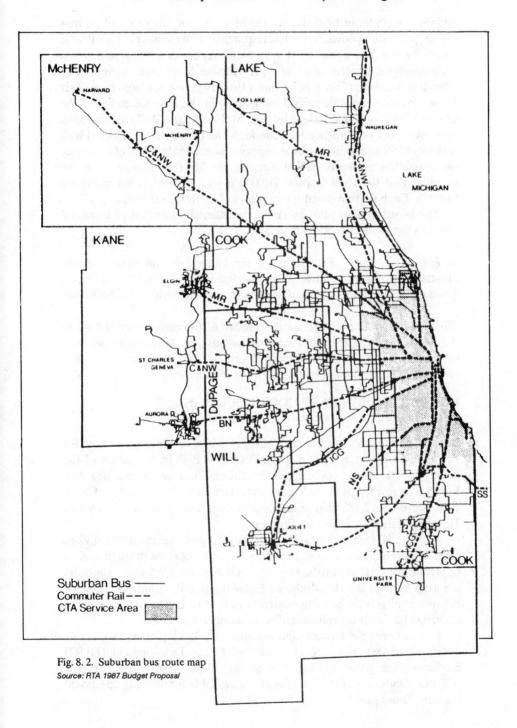

Fig. 8. 2. Suburban bus route map
Source: RTA 1987 Budget Proposal

and the remainder in 1990. Unlike the Metra board, whose members may not be government officials, the law requires that all members of the PACE board except the chair must be chief executives of municipalities. Membership is structured to be representative of all areas served. The suburban members of the Cook County Board appoint 6, 1 from each of six Cook County regions described (at length) in the law; the chairs of the county boards of Kane, Lake, DuPage, McHenry, and Will counties each appoint 1 from their respective counties. The board chair is elected by a majority of those making the board appointments. In the event of a vacancy the appointing authority of that directorship fills the vacancy. The law provides that the chair is paid $15,000 a year and the other members $10,000. Each is reimbursed for expenses of up to $5,000 a year.

The board appoints the executive director; appointment or dismissal requires the votes of eight directors.

Budget and Finance. Provisions for the budget and financial plan are identical with those of Metra, above. In 1988 PACE had 1,228 employees, a budget for operations of $71,100,000, and a capital budget of $25,000.000.

Citizen Advisory Board. The law establishes a 10-member unpaid Citizen Advisory Board appointed by the Suburban Bus Board to serve for two-year terms. The citizen board selects its chairman from its membership. It is required to meet with the PACE Board at least quarterly.

HOUSING AUTHORITY OF COOK COUNTY (HACC)
59 E. Van Buren St., Chicago 60605; *phone 939 0742*

The Housing Authority of Cook County provides low-income housing for suburban Cook County. It was established in 1946 by resolution of the county board under provisions of the Illinois Housing Authorities Act. Funds are provided by the U.S. government under the Housing Act of 1937. HACC provides 2,182 units in its developments and 4,654 units through its Housing Assistance Payments Program.

HACC's Housing Assistance Payments Program (Section 8) provides subsidized rentals for low- and moderate-income persons through leasing of private housing. A certificate program is used for 3,909 units; vouchers are used for 686; and the Moderate Rehabilitation Program, under which the owner of private housing contracts to rent to low-income tenants in exchange for funds for rehabilitation, accounts for 59 units.

The authority modernizes and maintains its developments through its operating budget, the U.S. Housing and Urban Development (HUD) modernization program, and Community Development Block Grant (CDBG) funds. As of 1987, no funds are available for building additional low-rent housing.

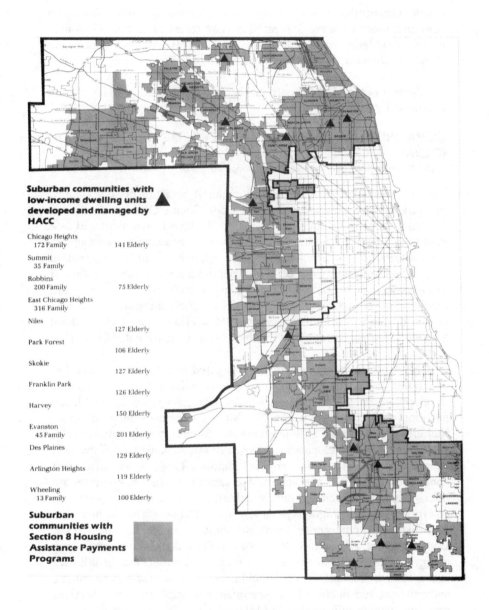

Suburban communities with low-income dwelling units developed and managed by HACC

Chicago Heights
172 Family   141 Elderly

Summit
35 Family

Robbins
200 Family   75 Elderly

East Chicago Heights
316 Family

Niles
       127 Elderly

Park Forest
       106 Elderly

Skokie
       127 Elderly

Franklin Park
       126 Elderly

Harvey
       150 Elderly

Evanston
45 Family   201 Elderly

Des Plaines
       129 Elderly

Arlington Heights
       119 Elderly

Wheeling
13 Family   100 Elderly

Suburban communities with Section 8 Housing Assistance Payments Programs

Fig. 8. 3. Housing Authority of Cook County map
Source: Housing Authority of Cook County

Board. The president of the Cook County Board appoints five unpaid commissioners to serve staggered 5-year terms. The commissioners establish budgets, review programs and operations, and appoint an Executive Director. The authority has a staff of 115.

Meetings of the HACC board are held on the second Monday of each month, at 1 P.M., subject to call.

COMMUNITY AND ECONOMIC DEVELOPMENT ASSOCIATION (CEDA)
224 N. Desplaines St., Chicago 60606; *phone 207 5444*

The Community and Economic Development Association of Cook County, Inc. (CEDA) was first created as the Cook County Office of Economic Opportunity by the county board in 1965. In 1966 it was chartered as a private, nonprofit corporation. It is, however, the community action agency for suburban Cook County, originally established under the federal Economic Opportunity Act of 1964. That act authorized the creation of local community action agencies to identify and solve the causes and condition of poverty. As of 1987, support for community action agencies comes through Community Services Block Grants and other federal government programs, administered by the state Department of Commerce and Community Affairs.

CEDA offers programs which are targeted to low-income and other disadvantaged populations; such programs include those in economic development and jobs, education, housing, emergency services, health and nutrition, and human services. CEDA's economic development program includes job training and placement, summer youth employment, entrepreneurship development, and a revolving loan fund for small business expansion. Its education program includes Head Start, adult and community education, and scholarship assistance. Its housing program offers housing counseling, home weatherization, and minor repairs. Its emergency services programs provide transitional housing for the homeless and displaced, emergency food and shelter for the homeless, U.S. Department of Agriculture food commodities distribution, and home energy assistance. Its health and nutrition program includes health care clinics at three of its sites, a supplemental food program for women, infants and children, and an effort to reduce infant mortality. Its human services program includes information and referral, family case management, day care, and senior services. In providing services, CEDA is affiliated with three related corporations.

Community Action Services, Inc., is a nonprofit corporation which provides bus transportation for preschool children.

Community Enterprises, Inc., is a for-profit corporation designed to create new businesses in economically distressed areas.

Community Nutrition Network is a for-profit corporation which operates the meals program for senior citizens.

CEDA's services are delivered through nine Community Development Areas, each served by a community service center:

Blue Island Community Service Center, 12812 S. Western Ave., Blue Island 60406; *phone 371 5840*

Chicago Heights Council for Community Action, 1203 West End Ave., Chicago Heights 60411; *phone 754 4575*

East Chicago Heights Community Service Center, Inc., 1647 Cottage Grove Ave., Ford Heights 60411; *phone 758 2510*

Evanston Neighbors at Work, 1229 Emerson, Evanston 60201; *phone 328 5166*

Harvey Area Community Service Center, 53 E. 154th St., Harvey 60426; *phone 339 3610*

CEDA/Robbins Human Resource Center, 3518 W. 139th St., P.O. Box 116, Robbins 60472; *phones 371 1522, 371 1220*

Southwest Development Association, 6246 S. Archer Road, Summit 60501; *phone 458 2736*

Proviso-Leyden Council for Community Action, Inc., 1108 W. Madison St., Maywood 60153; *phone 450 3500*

CEDA Northwest Self-Help Center, Inc., 120 W. Eastman, Arlington Heights 60004; *phone 392 2332*

Board of Directors. CEDA is governed by a 33-member board serving 5-year staggered terms. Two members are chosen by the county board; 9 are chosen by townships and municipalities; 9 are chosen by the boards of the community service centers, and 1 each by the Head Start community council and the Senior Citizen council; 11 are appointed by social agencies. Each community service center has an advisory board which conducts an annual open forum on community issues; these send delegates to CEDA's annual Community Congress, which identifies priorities. An annual *Report to the People* is published in conjunction with the congress.

Funding. During its 1986-87 fiscal year, CEDA's funding, from federal, state, county, township, and municipal sources amounted to $20,560,203, with an additional $1,684,449 in contributions of food, goods, services, and volunteer-hours. It had 286 full-time employees, 49 part-time, and 94 temporary. Its summer youth employment program provided 8-week summer jobs for about 1,100 low-income youths aged 14 to 21.

SUBURBAN COOK COUNTY TUBERCULOSIS SANITARIUM DISTRICT
Hospital, 55th St. and County Line Road, Hinsdale 60521; *phone 323 5800*

A tax-levying body organized in 1949, the Suburban Cook County Tuberculosis Sanitarium District provides residents of suburban Cook County with cost-free care for tuberculosis and complications associated with tuberculosis. Programs cover case-finding, prevention, diagnosis, and treatment. Tuberculosis treatment boards of neighboring counties may send patients requiring hospital care to the Hinsdale facility; cost for treating those patients is paid by the referring board. There is no referral system for care in the hospital for Chicago residents.

In 1973 the district was authorized to accept patients other than tuberculosis cases, as long as the cost for such patients was paid for. The hospital now serves the general public with all hospital services except obstetrics.

In 1987 there were 187 active cases of tuberculosis and 52 with atypical tuberculosis infection. A total of 58,000 clinic visits were made by suburban residents in 1987. In addition to the hospital, there are the following clinics:

Main Clinic, 7556 Jackson Blvd., Forest Park 60130; *phone 323 5800*

Medical Clinic, 15948 Halsted St., Harvey 60426; *phone 333 5630*

Park Ridge Clinic, 1999 Dempster St., Park Ridge 60068; *phone 825 6672*

Little Company of Mary Hospital, 2800 W. 95th St., Evergreen Park 60642; *phone 422 6200*

Evanston Civic Center, 2100 Ridge, Evanston 60204; *phone 323 5800*

X-ray facility, Fridays only, Oak Lawn Fire Station, 9437 Cook Ave, Oak Lawn 60457; *phone 323 5800*

Board. A five-member board of directors is appointed by the president of the county board. They serve unpaid, staggered, three-year terms. Meetings of the board are open to the public and are held on the second Wednesday of each month at 2 P.M. at the Suburban Hospital and Sanitarium in Hinsdale.

Funding. The budget for the district for 1987-88 was $2,599,734. The tax rate was 1.3 cents per $100 equalized assessed valuation.

9   The Courts

Civil and criminal cases may be brought to the federal or the state courts, depending on the nature of the case. Some kinds of cases originate in the federal courts; others may be appealed from state to federal courts. All courts in Chicago and Cook County are part of the federal or state systems.

FEDERAL COURTS IN COOK COUNTY

SEVENTH CIRCUIT OF THE U.S. COURT OF APPEALS

Dirksen Federal Building, 219 S. Dearborn, Chicago 60604; *phone 435 5850*

The Seventh Circuit of the U.S. Court of Appeals includes Illinois, Indiana, and Wisconsin. The U.S. Court of Appeals for the circuit is in Chicago. It has 13 active judges and 5 senior judges. Judges are appointed for life by the president, with the advice and consent of the U.S. Senate, and may be removed only by impeachment procedures. The salary of an appeals court judge is $95,000 a year.

U.S. DISTRICT COURT FOR THE NORTHERN DISTRICT OF ILLINOIS

Dirksen Federal Building, 219 S. Dearborn, Chicago 60604
    Phone information, civil cases, *435 5691*
    Criminal cases, *435 5695*
    Bankruptcy, *435 5693*
    Naturalization records, *435 5697*

Illinois is divided into three U.S. court districts. Cook County is in the Northern District of Illinois, and the District Court for that district is in Chicago, as is the U.S. Bankruptcy Court for that district. The District Court for the Northern District of Illinois is a trial court which includes 21 active judges and 4 senior judges. They, too, are appointed by the president for life, with the advice and consent of the U.S. Senate, and can be removed only by impeachment. The salary of a district court judge is $89,500 a year.

STATE COURTS

The courts which conduct trials on state laws and municipal ordinances in Illinois are state courts. Cook County is the First Judicial District of the Illinois Appellate and Supreme Courts.

QUALIFICATION AND ELECTION OF JUDGES

A candidate for judge must be a citizen, a licensed attorney, and a resident of the district or circuit from which he or she seeks election.

Candidates to fill vacancies run on a partisan ticket against opposition. The 1970 Illinois Constitution provides that judicial candidates be nominated at primary elections or by petition and elected at the general or judicial elections. In the event of a vacancy, the Supreme Court makes an appointment. A judge serving by appointment who wishes to continue must be nominated and elected at the next general election. At the end of the first elected term of office, a judge may run for reelection without opposition and without party label. To do so, a judge must file a declaration of candidacy at least six months before the date of the general election. Judges running for reelection appear on a special ballot, separate from the party ballots, called the Judicial Retention Ballot. Voters may vote yes or no to retain each judge. A judge must recieve yes votes from three-fifths of the voters who vote on the question in order to remain in office.

Circuit Court Judges. There are 177 elected circuit court judges in the Circuit Court of Cook County, elected for six-year terms: 94 are elected countywide, 56 are elected by Chicago voters, and 27 are elected by Cook County voters outside of Chicago. As of May 1988, the salary of a circuit court judge is $80,599.

Associate Judges. Additional judges of the Circuit Court (179 of them in 1987) are appointed by the elected circuit court judges for terms of four years. To be reappointed an associate judge needs the affirmative votes of three-fifths of the elected judges. Associate judges have the same powers as circuit judges except for felony case trials. They may hear felony cases only if they are designated to hear such cases by the chief judge and authorized by the Illinois Supreme Court. Appeals from decisions of associate judges are taken directly to the appellate court, just as are appeals from decisions of a circuit judge. As of May 1988, the salary of an associate circuit court judge is $75,118.

ILLINOIS SUPREME COURT

The Illinois Supreme Court is the highest state court. It may review decisions appealed from the lower courts, and it has original jurisdiction in certain kinds of cases specified in the Illinois Constitution. The Supreme Court supervises and administers all of the state courts, and the court appoints an administrative director to assist the chief justice. The Supreme

Court may assign a judge to serve temporarily in any state court. Three of the seven Supreme Court judges are elected for ten-year terms by the voters of Cook County. The salary of a Supreme Court judge is $93,266 a year.

The Supreme Court ordinarily meets in Springfield, although court may be held in Chicago for some cases.

ILLINOIS APPELLATE COURT, FIRST DISTRICT
Richard J. Daley Center, 50 W. Randolph, Chicago 60602

The state Appellate Court reviews cases appealed from the Circuit Courts in Cook County. In the first district there are five divisions of four judges each. Each division has a presiding judge, with a term of one year. Cook County voters elect 18 Appellate Court judges for ten-year terms. Two Circuit Court judges are assigned to Appellate Court duty as well. The salary of an Appellate Court judge is $87,780 a year.

CIRCUIT COURT OF COOK COUNTY
The Circuit Court functions through two major departments, the County Department and the Municipal Department. The County Department is organized by kinds of cases dealt with, and the Municipal Department is organized geographically to deal with other types of cases. The elected clerk of the Circuit Court serves both departments, as do the elected Cook County sheriff and the appointed public defender.

Funding. The Cook County corporate fund pays $500 of each judge's salary, and the state pays the remainder. The Juvenile Court has a county corporate fund budget separate from the other parts of the court; in 1988 its budget was $13,502,655. The corporate fund budgets for the other courts were $4,494,417 for the judiciary and $8,580,162 for the office of the chief judge. All court buildings are funded by the county. Budget hearings for the county court funds are held as part of the Cook County budget hearings.

COUNTY DEPARTMENT
Criminal Division, 2500 S. California, Chicago 60608; *phone 890 7100*
Juvenile Division, 100 S. Hamilton, Chicago 60612; *phone 738 8200*
All other divisions: Richard J. Daley Center, 50 W. Randolph, Chicago 60602; *phone 443 4591*

The County Department has seven divisions, and each has a presiding judge and an associate clerk. The responsibilities of the divisions are as follows:

Chancery Division. The Chancery Division hears suits for injunction (orders that persons either do a particular act or refrain from doing it), interpleader (cases in which two litigants sue to determine who is the rightful claimant against a third party), construction of wills and trusts, mortgage foreclosures, and dissolutions of partnerships and corporations. Cases in this division are likely to have multiple litigants.

County Division. The County Division hears cases involving adoptions, inheritance tax, election supervision and contests, real estate taxes, municipal organization, and mental health proceedings.

Criminal Division. The Criminal Division hears felony cases (crimes for which the penalty is one year or more in a state prison).

Domestic Relations Division. The Domestic Relations Division hears cases on divorce, alimony, separate maintenance, annulment, child custody, and all related matters. This division offers a marriage and family counseling service to litigants.

Juvenile Division. The Juvenile Division hears cases involving delinquent minors under the age of 17, minors under the age of 18 who are dependent, neglected, or otherwise in need of supervision, and child abuse. (See below for description of procedures with juveniles.)

Law Division. The Law Division hears civil actions for recovery of money in excess of $15,000. Most cases are personal injury suits resulting from automobile accidents.

Probate Division. The Probate Division hears cases involving proof of wills and administration of estates of deceased persons, minors, and disabled persons.

MUNICIPAL DEPARTMENT

The Municipal Department hears civil actions for recovery of money or property where the amount claimed is $15,000 or less. These include landlord and tenant cases, wage garnishment, and citations. It also hears criminal prosecutions, quasi-criminal actions, and cases of traffic offenses. It is divided geographically into six districts. The First Municipal District serves Chicago, and Districts 2 through 6 serve suburban Cook County.

District 1

Office of Presiding Judge, Room 1303, Richard J. Daley Center, 50 W. Randolph, Chicago 60602; *phone 443 6132*

Traffic Court, 321 N. La Salle St., Chicago 60610; *phone 822 3604*

Pro Se Court, Room 1308, Richard J. Daley Center, 50 W. Randolph, Chicago 60602; *phone 443 3484*

District 1 branches are specialized courts, such as Law Jury, Housing, Felony, Narcotics, Criminal Jury, and Women's Courts. Bond Court is in session seven nights a week, and four Holiday Courts allow defendants to make bond on Saturdays, Sundays, and court holidays. In Pro Se Court individuals may file cases involving claims of $1,000 or less without the assistance of a lawyer.

District 2. District 2 serves the townships of Evanston, New Trier, Northfield, and Wheeling, and parts of Palatine and Niles. The courthouse is at 5600 Old Orchard Road, Skokie 60077; *phone 470 7500*

District 3. District 3 serves the townships of Barrington, Hanover, Schaumburg, Elk Grove, Maine, Norwood Park, and Leyden, and parts of Palatine and Niles. Administrative offices, as of mid-1988, are at 7166 Milwaukee Avenue, Niles 60648; *phone 647 7310*. A new central courthouse, scheduled to be completed in 1988, will be at Euclid and Wilke, Rolling Meadows 60008.

District 4. District 4 serves the townships of Proviso, River Forest, Riverside, Oak Park, Berwyn, and Cicero. The courthouse is at 1500 Maybrook Drive, Maywood 60153; *phone 865 6000*

District 5. District 5 serves the townships of Lyons, Stickney, Worth, Lemont, Palos, and Orland. Court is held in municipalities within the district. Administrative offices are at 10500 S. Oxford, Chicago Ridge 60415; *phone 857 8850*. A new central courthouse is scheduled to be completed in 1989 at 7600 W. 103rd St., Bridgeview 60455.

District 6. District 6 serves the townships of Thornton, Bremen, Calumet, Bloom, and Rich. The courthouse is at 16501 S. Kedzie Parkway, Markham 60426; *phone 596 8000*

JUVENILE COURT

Juveniles are treated differently from adults under the law, and the Cook County Juvenile Court, established in 1899, was the first court in the United States set up with the specific purpose of dealing with children. Children under 17 years of age may be brought to Juvenile Court if they are charged with a criminal offense, if they are runaways, habitually truant, or beyond the control of parents; if they are addicted to drugs; or if they are abused, neglected or dependent. A child may be declared a ward of the court if found to be a Minor Requiring Authoritative Intervention (MRAI); such a child is often called a "status offender" because of the child's status as a minor. A MRAI child is one who is under 18 and a habitual truant, a runaway, or beyond the control of parents in circumstances which constitute a danger to the child's physical safety. However, a minor who was at least 15 at the time of an offense and who is charged with a serious offense (murder, rape, deviate sexual assault, or armed robbery with a firearm) must be prosecuted as an adult in Criminal Court.

Chicago juvenile cases are heard at the Juvenile Court at 1100 S. Hamilton in Chicago. Suburban cases are heard by a juvenile judge in suburban branch courts in Markham (Mondays), Hanover Park (Tuesdays), Skokie (Wednesdays), Maywood (Thursdays), and Oak Lawn (Fridays).

COOK COUNTY JUVENILE TEMPORARY DETENTION CENTER
1100 S. Hamilton, Chicago 60612; *phone 738 7102*

The Juvenile Temporary Detention Center provides secure custody for delinquent children under 17 who are awaiting disposition of their cases by the Juvenile Court or (for those whose cases have been transferred; see above) the criminal court. The Chicago Board of Education conducts classes; medical and dental care is provided, as well as psychiatric and social services and recreation; religious programs are supplied by the Catholic Archdiocese, the Good News Mission, and the Moody Bible Institute.

The Detention Center is headed by a superintendent appointed by the president of the county board, at an annual salary of $61,919. In 1988 the center was budgeted for 318 employees and had a county corporate fund appropriation of $8,903,106.

Fig. 9. 1. Cook County Juvenile Temporary Detention Center
Source: Cook County Highway Department for 1973 President's Annual Report

BAIL

Adults arrested by the police are held temporarily in lockups in police stations, sheriff's police lockups, or suburban lockups. At a pretrial hearing defendants may be released merely on their signatures (individual bond or release on recognizance), or bail may be set to assure their return for trial. When bail is set, 10% of the amount of bail is paid to the clerk of the court; the minimum amount accepted by the courts in criminal cases is $25. After trial, 90% of the cash deposit is returned to the defendant; the 10% (1% of the total bail) kept by the court is used to pay court costs. Adults who cannot afford bail, or to whom bail is denied, are held at the facilities of the Cook County Department of Corrections to await trial.

COOK COUNTY LAW LIBRARY

2900 Richard J. Daley Center, 50 W. Washington St., Chicago 60602; *phone 443 5423*

The Cook County Law Library was opened in 1966 when the Chicago Law Institute donated its legal collection to the county. Its current collection of 240,000 volumes includes legal materials from 153 countries. References and bibliographic services are provided to lawyers and judges. It is open to the public, and copying facilities are available. The librarian cannot interpret legal materials or offer an opinion as to the applicability of materials to a particular situation, as this would constitute the illegal practice of law.

The library has branches at the following locations: 1340 S. Michigan Ave., Chicago; Criminal Court Building, 2650 S. California, Chicago; and at district court houses in Markham (16501 S. Kedzie Parkway), Maywood (1500 Maybrook Drive), and Skokie (5600 W. Old Orchard Road). By the end of 1988, branches are planned for Bridgeview and Rolling Meadows.

The library and its branches are supported by fees charged to litigants involved in trials in Cook County; its revenue for 1987 was $2,565,554. Its 1988 budget was $2,794,797; it had an executive law librarian appointed by the president of the county board at an annual salary of $55,995 and 58 other employee positions.

PSYCHIATRIC INSTITUTE

2650 S. California Boulevard, Chicago 60608; *phone 890 6100*

The county Psychiatric Institute is a separate agency from the Illinois Psychiatric Institute. This county agency gathers psychosocial histories of defendants and performs psychiatric, psychological, and brain wave examinations in order to report the results and recommendations based on these studies to the appropriate judge. Examining psychiatrists also give direct testimony in court on issues of competency to stand trial and on questions of sanity at the time of an offense. Other special examinations, such as for fitness for sentencing, need for mental treatment or involuntary hospitalization, or fitness for custody of children, are performed when requested by the judge. The 1988 budget for this agency was $1,583,957, with 53 positions.

SOCIAL CASEWORK SERVICE
2650 S. California Boulevard, Chicago 60608; *phone 890 6010*

The Social Case Work Service assists the Municipal Department by providing correctional casework services before and after the final disposition of the cases of misdemeanor offenders. The service has offices throughout the county and provides a program designed to handle court referrals and sentences of supervision and conditional discharge. The budget for 1988 from the county corporate fund was $5,761,967, with 240 positions.

ADULT PROBATION DEPARTMENT
Administration Building, 2650 S. California Blvd. (lower level), Chicago 60608; *phone 890 3280.* Offices also in all suburban courthouses.

The Adult Probation Department supervises adult offenders who have received a sentence of probation (which permits them to remain in the community subject to conditions imposed by the court). Through office and home visits, probation officers supervise compliance with the terms of probation and attempt to assist probationers in obtaining counseling, job training, and job placement. The department had approximately 24,000 probationers under supervision in 1987. In selected cases, the department conducts a report-by-mail program. In addition, the department conducts presentence investigations (about 9,000 in 1987) to help judges determine proper sentences and conducts criminal record investigations (about 120,000 in 1987).

The department is headed by the chief adult probation officer, who is appointed by the chief judge of the Cook County Circuit Court, at an annual salary of $60,000. In 1988 the department had 321 probation officers and 26 supervisory officers, with an additional 128 administrative and clerical personnel. The corporate budget for 1988 was $12,521,753.

PUBLIC ADMINISTRATOR
33 N. LaSalle St., Chicago 60602; *phone 726 4944*

The public administrator is appointed by the circuit court to administer estates of decedents in cases where there is no known next of kin living in the United States, or where the next of kin declines to administer the estate. The office also arranges for burial of indigent decedents.

The public administrator is appointed to the office by the governor with the consent of the senate for a four-year term. In 1988 there were 18 employees and a Cook County corporate fund budget of $615,088. Revenues generated by administrative fees in 1987 amounted to $548,331. In addition, the county receives money from estates in which heirs are not found. The administrator's salary is $20,000 from fees collected by the office.

OFFICE OF THE PUBLIC GUARDIAN
Disabled Adults Division, 221 N. LaSalle St., Chicago 60601; *phone 609 5300*
Juvenile Division, 1112 S. Oakley, Chicago 60612; *phone 633 2500*

The Office of the Public Guardian was established by legislation passed in 1979. Its disabled adults division serves adults who have estates of more than $25,000 and who, through mental or physical incapacity, advanced age, or senility, are unable to manage their own financial affairs or make responsible decisions about care of themselves. (On occasion the statutory amount of $25,000 is waived where an issue of advocacy is involved.) The office is charged with management and investment of the wards' estates and coordination of services to meet the wards' daily living needs.

The juvenile division is the court-appointed lawyer and guardian ad litem for neglected, dependent, and abused youngsters who are respondents in cases in the Juvenile Court. As such the division's responsibility is to represent these youngsters in legal proceedings and to advocate for them later if they become wards of the state.

The 1988 Cook County corporate budget for this office was $2,494,612, with 81 budgeted positions; the public guardian's salary was $70,308 a year.

DEPARTMENT OF SUPPORTIVE SERVICES
118 N. Clark St., Chicago 60602; *phone 443 4703*

The Department of Supportive Services, on order of the Circuit Court, conducts investigations and makes social studies of independent adoption placements, contested adoptions, and custody, commitment, probate, and domestic violence cases. It offers mediation services in contested custody and visitation matters, including disputes arising in paternity support enforcement cases.

In 1987 the department initiated a job training referral program in which (on order of the court) it refers eligible clients to training programs and reports to the court the client's participation; the program is directed toward child support cases in which the supporting parent is unable to find work. It also offers mediation services on post-adoption inquiries from adult adoptees for non-identifying information about their biological background and from birth parents about the adoptive family.

The department is headed by a social service coordinator at a salary of $46,248 a year; in 1988 it had 26 additional employees, and a corporate fund appropriation of $742,272.

PUBLIC DEFENDER

7th floor, Courts Administration Building, 2650 S. California Ave., Chicago 60608; *phone 890 3217*

The public defender acts as counsel for persons held in custody or charged with committing a crime if the judge finds them indigent and unable to pay a private attorney. In addition to handling misdemeanor and felony cases, the office represents indigents with respect to involuntary commitments to mental health facilities.

The public defender, who must be a licensed attorney, is appointed by majority vote of the judges of the Circuit Court of Cook County and serves at their pleasure. Assistant public defenders must also be licensed attorneys.

In 1988 the corporate fund budget of $21,613,679 provided for 439 assistant public defenders, 81 investigators, and 96 other personnel. The salary of the public defender was $70,308.

ILLINOIS JUDICIAL INQUIRY BOARD

State of Illinois Building, 100 W. Randolph St., Chicago 60602; *phone 917 5554*

The Illinois Judicial Inquiry Board is authorized under the state constitution to receive or initiate and investigate complaints against judges. If the board finds a reasonable basis for complaint, it must file and prosecute the complaint before the Courts Commission.

The board is composed of two circuit judges (appointed by the Supreme Court) and four lay persons and three lawyers (appointed by the governor). All serve four-year terms and may be reappointed to one additional term. Members who are not judges are paid per diem expenses of $100 per meeting by the state. In the state fiscal year 1987-88 the staff of six included the executive director and three investigators; the budget was $323,500, from state funds.

COURTS COMMISSION

The Courts Commision hears complaints filed by the Judicial Inquiry Board. It can take action if it finds a judge guilty of willful misconduct in office, persistent failure to perform judicial duties, or other conduct prejudicial to the administration of justice or that brings the judicial office into disrepute. It can censure or reprimand judges, remove them from office, or suspend them with or without pay. It can retire a judge who is physically or mentally unfit to perform judicial duties.

The commission consists of one Supreme Court judge (appointed by the Supreme Court), two appellate judges (appointed by the Appellate Court), and two circuit court judges (appointed by the Supreme Court). The state provides a budget of $100,000 a year, which is rarely spent, and the director of the Supreme Court Administrative Office acts as secretary.

JUDICIAL ADVISORY COUNCIL
Room 526, County Building, 118 N. Clark St., Chicago 60602; *phone 443 4450*

The five-member Judicial Advisory Council was established by state law and county ordinance to study the administration of the courts, propose measures for improvement, assist in planning and budget review, and monitor state and federal grants. The members are appointed by the president of the county board, with the consent of the board, and are not paid. Two must be members of the judiciary. There is a staff of three and a 1988 budget of $116,603.

CLERK OF THE CIRCUIT COURT
Richard J. Daley Center, 50 W. Washington St., Chicago 60602; *phone 443 5030*

The clerk of the Circuit Court is elected for a four-year term by the voters of Cook County at the general election in presidential years. The clerk is responsible for administration and maintenance of all court records for the Cook County circuit. Duties of the office include accounting for and distributing money paid to the court in fines, court costs, bonds, paternity and non-support payments, and other payments in trust. The clerk also supplies personnel for the county's more than 350 courtrooms.

The Circuit Court clerk receives a salary of $55,000 a year. The budget for the office in 1988 was $47,781,530 from the county corporate fund, with 2,055 employees under the direction of the clerk. Entry-level employees are tested, and promotions are from within the department. Grievances are taken to a personnel review board.

JURY SYSTEM
The Illinois Constitution guarantees the right of trial by jury in all criminal cases and most civil cases, including traffic cases. The only exceptions are in cases in chancery and those of mandamus (a court order commanding that a specific thing be done), prohibition, and habeas corpus (a court order requiring that a person be brought before a judge or court).

Jury Commissioners. In Cook County the circuit court judges appoint three Jury Commissioners to serve for staggered three-year terms. The commissioners compile a list of the names of all registered voters, and jurors are chosen by lot from this list to serve on grand or petit juries.

About 700,000 questionnaires a year are sent to prospective jurors. Those selected for duty must be physically sound, must meet standards of character, integrity, and judgment, and must be able to understand the English language. Legislation passed in 1987 removed occupational exemptions for jury service. A person who fails to return the jury service questionnaire, does not respond to a jury summons, refuses to testify, or gives false testimony is subject to penalty.

State Grand Jury. A grand jury hears witnesses in accusations against persons charged with criminal offenses. If it finds there is probable cause, it returns a bill of indictment (a formal list of criminal charges) against the accused, and the person is bound over for trial. A full grand jury panel consists of 16 persons, with 55 additional supplemental jurors. A grand jury may function with as few as 12 members, and concurrence of at least 9 jury members is needed for indictment. Jurors are chosen at random to serve on grand juries and receive the same pay and travel compensation as those serving on petit juries (see below).

In Cook County, a grand jury usually serves for 30 days. Its term can be extended for several 30-day periods, but no longer than 16 months. More than one grand jury may be serving at a time.

Petit Jury. A petit jury may consist of 6 or 12 persons, depending on the request of the lawyers involved in the case. The jury's function is to inquire into the truth of questions of fact raised and to reach a unanimous verdict for conviction or acquital. If such a verdict cannot be reached, a mistrial is declared. Under the "one-day-one-trial" system, a juror is dismissed if not assigned to a case within the first day. If assigned, the juror must serve until the case is finished. In 1988 jurors serving the Circuit Court of Cook County were paid $15 a day plus $2.20 transportation.

Federal Court Juries. Selection for service in the U.S. District Court is also made by lot from a list of registered voters. In 1988 jurors serving the federal court were paid $30 a day plus 21 cents per mile round-trip.

10 Government Services

Previous chapters of this book have described the responsibilities and organization of individual local governmental bodies. For many services of local governments, there is a single municipal department or governmental agency responsible; the reader of this book can refer to the index for those services. For other services, however, the responsibilities are divided among departments, governmental bodies, levels of government, and sometimes government-funded or government-licensed private bodies.

This chapter selects a number of services important to residents of the county and the city and shows how the responsibilities for those services are divided among the various levels of government. It includes brief descriptions of state agencies which provide important direct services not provided by local government in Chicago or Cook County, though such services may be provided by local government in other states. For sources of federal and state funds which help to support specific local agencies, see the descriptions of those agencies and chapter 4, Financing Local Governments. For addresses, telephone numbers, and more complete descriptions of services, see the descriptions of local government agencies and departments in chapters 2, 5, 6, 7, and 8.

Since the source of services often depends on where you live (Chicago, a suburban municipality or particular township, or the unincorporated area of Cook County), the presentation is divided where appropriate by geographic area. Some services depend on belonging to a particular category (senior citizen, disabled, veteran), and these are listed as well.

WELFARE AND EMPLOYMENT

Programs and funding for assisting people living in poverty or in need of jobs or job training involve federal, state, and local governments, a variety of departments within municipal governments, and independent agencies as well. Most of the funding for such programs comes from the federal government and so depends on Congressional appropriations and administrative guidelines set by federal agencies. The Social Security retirement and Medicare programs are administered by the federal Social Security Administration, and employment taxes and Medicare fees are paid to the federal government and payments are made by it. Other social security programs (such as Medicaid) may be funded by both state and federal governments. Programs may be administered by the state, or the state may delegate administrative responsibility to local government agencies. Still other programs are supported by local taxation and administered by local government. The local governments, in turn, may fund private for-profit and not-for-profit agencies to deliver the services.

Until the depression of the 1930s, assistance to those in need was considered to be the responsibility of local governments and private charity. The federal Social Security Act, originating in that depression, selected certain categories of grants (hence the name, categorical grants) for which the federal govenment would provide grants-in-aid to the states. The decision to operate a public assistance program which makes use of the federal grants-in-aid rests entirely with each state; the Illinois Department of Public Aid administers federal assistance programs which Illinois has undertaken.

A listing of services provided and agencies responsible for each should not be taken to mean that all those in need of the services are receiving them. The number reached depends on the funding provided relative to the needs and the success of outreach programs.

AGENCIES AND DEPARTMENTS

Responsibilities for providing services to low-income people, the elderly, the disabled, and veterans are spread over federal and state agencies, eight county agencies, eight city agencies, the townships, the schools, and two housing authorities (Chicago and Cook County). Part of the diversity is due to requirements of federal and state funding programs which may specify administrative agencies or procedures, part to the gaps in those programs filled by local funding, and part to administrative convenience or the initiative of agencies.

This section will attempt to categorize the services and then briefly describe the federal Social Security Act and the Job Training Partnership Act, General Assistance, and two state agencies which provide direct services to Cook County residents, the Illinois Departments of Public Aid and Children and Family Services.

Emergency Services. Emergency services to provide housing and food in Chicago are the responsibility of the city Department of Human Services in Chicago (chapter 5) and of the Community and Economic Development Association in suburban Cook County (chapter 8). Township supervisors (chapter 2) in suburban Cook County administer General Assistance, often temporary aid to those awaiting the start of state aid in the categorical assistance programs. For Chicago, General Assistance is administered by the Illinois Department of Public Aid (see below). Emergency care shelters for children are the responsibility of the Illinois Department of Children and Family Services (see below).

Longer-term Aid. In Cook County longer-term aid for low-income families with dependent children (AFDC) is the responsibility of the Illinois Department of Public Aid. For the aged, the blind, and the disabled, assistance is provided through the Supplemental Security Income program of the federal government and the State Supplemental Payments administered by the Illinois Department of Public Aid. The Cook County Veterans Assistance Commission (chapter 7) assists indigent veterans and provides burial benefits for indigent veterans and their families.

Food and Nutritional Assistance. A variety of agencies provide food and nutritional services. Emergency food supplies are provided, as indicated above, by the city Department of Human Services (DHS, chapter 5) and the suburban Community and Economic Development Association (CEDA, chapter 8). The Illinois Department of Public Aid is in charge of the food stamp program of the U.S. Department of Agriculture. A supplemental food program, WIC, for low-income women, infants, and children, is administered by the Department of Health in Chicago and by CEDA in suburban Cook County. School lunch programs are administered by the schools, and DHS provides meals for Chicago children in its day-care programs; CEDA does so for its suburban programs. The DHS Infant Mortality Reduction Initiative has a nutrition counseling program. Food service programs for the elderly in Chicago are conducted by the city Department on Aging and Disability (chapter 5), and in the suburbs by CEDA. DHS also administers a neighborhood farm program.

Child Support Laws. Agencies administering public aid programs are concerned with child support laws. The Illinois Department of Public Aid will assist single parents, on request, in collecting delinquent child support payments. The Cook County state's attorney takes legal action on paternity suits and child support orders, and the sheriff enforces child support orders.

Job Training and Finding. Participation in job training and finding is required as part of public aid and general assistance programs. The federal Job Training Partnership Act, through the Illinois Department of Commerce and Community Affairs, has a major job training and finding program (see below). The Illinois Department of Public Aid's Project Chance program helps recipients to find jobs and provides training. Township supervisors must set up work programs. The Illinois Department of Employment Services has nine Chicago and eight suburban job service offices listed in the blue pages of the Chicago telephone book. The city Department on Aging and Disability has an employment program for disabled persons and persons over 60 years of age. The Veterans Liaison

Advisory Committee of the Chicago Commission on Human Relations has programs to assist veterans in finding jobs and developing businesses. Employment training programs are described below, under Education.

Financial Advice and Assistance. Other programs in Chicago to assist people in financial difficulties include credit counseling, offered by the Department of Consumer Services; budgeting counseling and financial assistance in paying heating and utility bills, offered by the Department of Human Services; legal services, offered by the Department on Aging and Disability; and housing improvement loans and grants, provided by the Department of Housing. The Cook County clerk's Tax Redemption Division assists in redeeming property sold or forfeited for delinquent real estate taxes, and the Cook County assessor administers the Circuit Breaker grants to low-income senior citizen and disabled home owners and renters, the senior citizen real estate tax deferral program, and the homestead improvement exemption for disabled veterans.

Low-income Housing. The Chicago Housing Authority (chapter 6) and the Housing Authority of Cook County (chapter 8) are responsible for low-income housing funded by the federal and state governments. Health services for low-income persons are described in the Health section, below.

Reduced Fees and Charges. Assistance is also provided through reduced fees and charges, not necessarily related to income. Public transportation charges are reduced for senior citizens and students, and special services are provided for the disabled. In Chicago senior citizens pay reduced charges for motor vehicle licenses, and there is a sewer charge exemption for senior home owners. In unincorporated Cook County, the wheel tax is waived for the physically handicapped and disabled veterans and reduced for senior citizens. A senior citizen homestead deduction is allowed on Cook County property taxes (chapter 4).

Income Tax Reductions. Very-low-income persons pay no federal income tax. For individuals, the income tax begins at a taxable income of $2,480 (after a standard deduction of $2,450 for a single person), and those with a child and taxable income under $11,000 may be eligible for tax reduction or refund under the Earned Income Credit. (They still pay Social Security taxes, however.) As of 1988, federal tax forms provided additional tax deductions for senior citizens.

Illinois does not tax retirement and social security income. It also allows property taxes paid on a principal residence to be deducted from taxable income. Income of under $1,000 a year per person is not taxed.

Special Categories. The above listings make it apparent that certain groups of people receive governmental assistance not necessarily because of low income but because of membership in a category. Some of these are as follows (those with income eligibility requirements are marked with a dollar sign; others may have fees based on income):

Senior Citizens
  Social Security and Medicare
  Supplemental Security Income ($)
  Foster Grandparents
  Golden Diners Club
  Home-delivered meals
  In-home services
  Legal services
  Protective services
  Sewer charge exemption
  Housing ($)
  Home maintenance program (minor rehabilitation) ($)
  Reduced vehicle license taxes
  Reduced property taxes
  Reduced transportation fares
  Reduced federal and state income taxes

Disabled
  Supplemental Security Income ($)
  Employment services
  Reduced vehicle license taxes
  Special transportation services
  State grants to home-owners and renters ($)
  Reserved parking

Veterans
  Services provided by U.S. Veterans' Administration
  Emergency and funeral assistance ($)
  Employment and business assistance

SOCIAL SECURITY ACT
Social Security Information: north of Madison St., *phone 725 8838*;
  south of Madison St., *phone 636 8811*

The Social Security Act is divided into parts dealing with different aspects of the programs, called "Titles."

Title I provides for old age assistance and Medicare.

Title IV provides for aid and services to needy families with children (AFDC).

The Supplemental Security Income program was passed in 1974 and absorbed former titles X, XIV, and XVI; it provides for aid to the aged, the blind, and the disabled. These grants are made to the individual by the U.S.

Social Security Administration, but the state Department of Public Aid provides additional assistance and social services to SSI recipients.

Title XIX provides for essential medical care for people receiving public assistance or people who are medically indigent (Medicaid).

Title XX provides for the Social Service Block Grant, created in 1981 under the federal Omnibus Budget Reconciliation Act. The block grant combines funds of several previous categorical federal programs: it provides an overall total for support of such programs as child care, job training, adoption, homemaker services, transportation, and rehabilitation. The block grant eliminates most federal requirements, leaving rule making for eligibility and allocation to the states within general federal guidelines.

The Illinois Department of Public Aid administers the program. Funds are allocated through the state budget and appropriations process.

Donated Funds Initiative. In addition to the federal block grant, Illinois established the Donated Funds Initiative (DFI), a state appropriation funded through Title XX, to be matched by local private or public funds for service programs. As of the end of 1987, the structure of DFI was under reconsideration.

JOB TRAINING PARTNERSHIP ACT (JTPA)

The federal Job Training Partnership Act (JTPA) of 1982 established a federally funded program that provides job training for unskilled adults and youth who are economically disadvantaged and for others who face serious barriers to employment. The act assigns primary responsibility to the state, and the Illinois Department of Commerce and Community Affairs is the state agency which administers the program.

There are 26 Service Delivery Areas (SDAs), each with an appointed Private Industry Council (PIC) to provide direction and policy guidance. The majority of members must be private sector businessmen; other members represent education, labor, community-based organizations, public service employment, rehabilitation agencies, veterans, and the general population.

Locally developed plans and programs are intended to meet the needs of the local job market. They include teaching remedial reading, training in basic or vocational skills, assistance in preparation for jobs, on-the-job training, work experience programs (including development of work habits to enable participants to obtain and retain employment), and pre-employment skills training (including career awareness, job clubs, and vocational counseling).

Funds are distributed through the governor to each SDA by a formula which reflects the number of disadvantaged and unemployed in the SDA.

Percentages are set for expenditures: 70% must go to training costs (of the training costs, 40% must go for youth and 60% for adult programs), 15% for supportive services, and no more than 15% for administrative costs.

In Chicago the Mayor's Office of Employment and Training administers federally funded job training and placement programs; in suburban Cook County the President's Office of Employment Training administers them.

GENERAL ASSISTANCE

General Assistance provides funds for those who are in need but who do not qualify under categorical programs for federal or other state assistance. Among these groups are unemployed adults who are under 65 and who have no minor children; families with two parents in the home, one of whom is employed; children living with legal guardians who are not relatives; and pregnant women in the first five months of pregnancy. Clients are frequently people who have applied for and are awaiting the start of state aid.

Requirements for General Assistance. An applicant for general assistance must meet the following requirements; he or she must

be a U.S. citizen or legal resident
meet financial eligibility standards
have applied for all appropriate pensions and benefits
accept any suitable offer of employment
register with the work and training program (exceptions to this requirement are those under 16 or over 65, full-time students, those who are medically exempt, and those required to be in the home for care of a child under six or for full-time care of another member of the family)

Chicago. General Assistance for Chicago residents is administered by the Illinois Department of Public Aid. Applicants for General Assistance who are able to work must participate in the Project Chance program administered by the Illinois Department of Public Aid (see below). The caseload of the department for Chicago General Assistance in July, 1987 was 88,240. The cost amounted to about $200 million a year; about one-tenth of the support for the program came from the city's tax levy, at a rate of one mill per $100 equalized assessed valuation.

Suburban Cook County. The township supervisor is responsible for General Assistance in suburban Cook County. General Assistance is administered by the townships and funded by a township property tax. Supervisors must establish written standards and policies, which must include statements of confidentiality for the client and a policy of nondiscrimination. The supervisor establishes eligibility, refers applicants to appropriate categorical aid programs, keeps records and reviews them every five months, and informs applicants of their rights. These rights include freedom of choice, information about all services, and appeal of a supervisor's decision to the Hearing Officer for Suburban Townships, General Assistance Appeals. The supervisor may provide social services, such as child care and housekeeping services, education and training, day care, home and financial management, and housing improvements; health services which may be provided include a licensed drug abuse program and essential medical care, but not preventive care or psychiatric services.

All townships are required to institute a workfare program or a Job Search, Training, and Work Program, or both. In the workfare program, the client receives credit at the minimum wage for hours worked in a local taxing district, to offset the basic maintenance grant. In the Job Search, Training, and Work Program, the client receives more comprehensive assistance and may work for a private company or not-for-profit organization.

If a township receives state public aid funds, it must follow rules set by the Illinois Department of Public Aid, and the total of the township's tax levy and unobligated funds from the previous year's levy must be equal to 10 cents per $100 of the township's equalized assessed valuation. As of 1987, no Cook County township used state funds to administer its general assistance program.

ILLINOIS DEPARTMENT OF PUBLIC AID (IDPA)

Regions 1, 2, 3: 624 S. Michigan Ave., Chicago 60605
Region 4: 1308 W. 105th St., Chicago 60605.
phones, 1. Metro North, 793 2200; 2. Metro West, 793 4131; 3. Central, 793 3740; 4. Metro South, 881 2950

IDPA services in Cook County are administered through 4 regional offices. Within these regions are 26 district offices (districted by ZIP code), which provide services. Persons seeking assistance should telephone a regional office to find out which district office serves their ZIP code.

In 1974 the Cook County Department of Public Aid was transferred to the Illinois Department of Public Aid. Cook County government has no responsibilities for public assistance. In July 1987, the caseload of the AFDC program in Cook County was 154,495.

IDPA sets income standards, within limitations set by federal laws and regulations, for eligibility to receive its programs. In some programs state matching funds are required, and the state also supplements federal funds to provide additional assistance. The department administers the following programs:

AFDC: Aid to Families with Dependent Children. The Aid to Families with Dependent Children (AFDC) program provides a monthly cash grant to low-income families having dependent children. It is funded equally by the state and federal governments. Statewide, about 230,000 families receive AFDC grants each month.

MA: Medicaid and Aid to the Medically Indigent. The Medicaid and the Aid to the Medically Indigent programs provide coverage for medical care. More than one million persons in the state are eligible for services. Funding for Medicaid is split equally between the federal and state governments, and Aid to the Medically Indigent is funded by the state.

SSP: State Supplemental Payments. State Supplemental Payments may be made to aged, blind, or disabled persons who receive federal Supplemental Security Income benefits. About 29,000 persons statewide receive SSP.

FS: Food Stamps. Under the Food Stamp program of the U.S. Department of Agriculture about 416,000 families receive food stamps in Illinois.

GA: General Assistance. See above for General Assistance for Chicago residents.

Child Support Enforcement. Assistance is given to single parents in collecting delinquent child support payments; it is provided on request.

Work Requirements. Unless specifically exempt by law, all AFDC and Chicago General Assistance recipients must register and cooperate with the department's Project Chance program, instituted in 1985. Failure to comply with the work requirement may result in loss or reduction of the cash grant. Recipients who are exempt may volunteer to participate. The program helps recipients find jobs and also provides special training for those who need it. Persons who get jobs may qualify for a six-month extension of subsidized day care and medical benefits. (As of spring, 1988, state and federal legislation was introduced to extend this period to 12 months for persons who leave the welfare rolls to take low-paying jobs.)

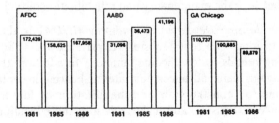

Fig. 10. 1. Applications received for assistance programs, 1981, 1985, 1986
Source: *Annual Report, 1986, Illinois Department of Public Aid*

ILLINOIS DEPARTMENT OF CHILDREN AND FAMILY SERVICES

Cook County Regional Office, 100 W. Randolph St., Chicago 60601; *phone 917 6800*

Information and Referral, 2020 W. Roosevelt Road, Chicago 60608; *phone 793 2100*

Child abuse and neglect, *24-hour toll-free phone 1 800 25 ABUSE*

Adoption information, *phone 1 800 572 2390*

Day Care Centers information, *phone 793 8600*

Day Care Homes information, *phone 793 8846*

Foster Parent Recruitment, *phone 1 800 624 KIDS*

The Illinois Department of Children and Family Services (DCFS) has statewide responsibility for child welfare services. It is mandated by law to investigate suspected cases of child abuse and neglect, and it provides foster care for such children and others who cannot stay with their parents. It operates three emergency care shelters in the Chicago area. It provides services for unwed parents and adoption services.

DCFS regulates licensed child care facilities, both day-care and residential. It contracts for counseling and for homemakers for families. Through a grant program, it encourages development of community-based programs to divert adolescents from involvement in the child welfare or juvenile justice systems.

Services are provided through area and field offices. Those seeking information or assistance should call the information and referral number listed above; they should call the abuse hotline to report child abuse and neglect.

HOUSING DEVELOPMENT

Individual builders are subject to the building, zoning, and sanitation codes of their municipalities or, in the case of unincorporated areas, of the county departments. Larger-scale housing developments may be subject to approval by municipal planning departments and to availability of water and sewer facilities. The development of low-income housing is dependent on funds available from the U.S. Department of Housing and Urban Development, as is the maintenance and rehabilitation of such housing.

The Illinois Housing Development Authority (IHDA) is the state unit authorized to administer rental subsidies to private owners and developers for providing rentals to low-income families. In addition, the authority makes mortgage loans, advances non-interest-bearing loans to nonprofit corporations for construction or rehabilitation of low-income and moderate-income housing, and makes advisory and educational services available to nonprofit agencies. Operations are financed by sale of tax-exempt revenue bonds.

The Housing Authority of Cook County (chapter 8) is the agency which administers public housing in suburban Cook County, and the *Chicago Housing Authority* (chapter 6) administers a very much larger program in Chicago.

The Chicago Department of Housing (chapter 5) administers 15 programs which provide loans and grants for maintenance, improvement, and development of low-income and moderate-income housing. Such programs are funded chiefly by federal block grant funds: Community Development Block Grants (CDBG), Urban Development Action Grants (UDAG), and (until eliminated in 1987-88) Housing Development Action Grants (HODAG). *The Chicago Urban Renewal Board* has the power to designate slum and blighted areas, to acquire such land and clear it, and to recommend redevelopment proposals to the city council.

ECONOMIC DEVELOPMENT

Northeastern Illinois Planning Commission. The Northeastern Illinois Planning Commission (NIPC, chapter 1) is designated by the state to be responsible for preparing comprehensive plans to guide the development of the six-county metropolitan area. Its powers are advisory only.

Property Tax Incentives. Changes in Cook County property tax assessments (see chapter 4) have been made in recent years to encourage development and rehabilitation, including reductions for commercial and industrial property (particularly those in enterprise zones), areas in need of commercial development, and slum and blighted areas. Taxing districts may abate property taxes on new or relocating industrial firms. Tax increment financing permits the financing of public improvements and other financial support to bring developers into blighted areas.

Enterprise Zones. Enterprise Zones are geographic areas designated as economically depressed, in which the state and local governments provide incentives for private business investment. Incentives include state income tax credits for hiring dislocated workers, property and sales tax reductions, and state and local loans and grants. The program is administered by the Illinois Department of Commerce and Community Affairs and, in Chicago's five enterprise zones, by the city's Department of Economic Development, which can modify building and zoning codes and issue city licenses within the enterprise zones. The Cal-Sag area, Chicago Heights, Cicero, and Elgin also have enterprise zones.

Suburban Cook County. The Cook County agency responsible for economic development is the Cook County Office of Economic Development within the county's Bureau of Administration. It conducts economic planning and research and publishes an annual program update.

Chicago. In Chicago a number of departments have responsibilities for economic development. Any development within Chicago by a public body must be reviewed by the Chicago Plan Commission. The Department of Planning is the planning and coordinating agency for development of the city and has particular responsibility for planning and implementing redevelopment projects in the Loop. The Department of Economic Development has responsibility for developing programs to retain existing businesses and help them to expand and to attract new business. It provides services for neighborhood economic development as well. The Economic Development Commission is charged with developing a long-range economic development plan for the city. The Commercial District Development Commission recommends the designation of Commercial District Development Districts and can acquire and dispose of land within those districts. The Commission on Chicago Landmarks affects development by requiring that property designated as a landmark be preserved and protected. The Office of Film and Entertainment Industries in the city's Department of Cultural Affairs is charged with encouraging and assisting film and television productions.

PUBLIC HEALTH

Public health involves prevention as well as treatment of disease. It includes provision of health services directly to individuals, as in clinics and hospitals, and control of communicable diseases, as in compulsory vaccination, a clean water supply, food inspection, sanitation regulations, pollution control, and waste management.

In the Chicago metropolitan area, public health protection is provided by some federal agencies, the state, the county, the Metropolitan Sanitary District, mosquito abatement districts, and Chicago and a few other municipalities.

HOSPITALS AND CLINICS

The federal government provides hospitals for veterans, and there are four of these hospitals in the Chicago metropolitan area: Lakeside and Westside in Chicago, and North Chicago and Hines in the suburbs. There are several state agencies concerned with health matters.

The Illinois Department of Public Health oversees the administration of health care facilities in Illinois and enforcement of state and federal laws regulating licensing and operating of long-term care facilities, hospitals, and ambulatory care centers.

The Illinois Department of Mental Health and Developmental Disabilities supports programs to provide residential care, sheltered workshops, day treatment, and outpatient and crisis services for mentally ill and developmentally disabled persons. Statewide, it operates 20 inpatient facilities and 3 research and training institutes.

The department is organized into two divisions: Mental Illness and Developmental Disabilities. Services are organized by seven geographical regions, four of which are in the Chicago metropolitan area. Regions 5A and 5B cover the city of Chicago, 5A the northern part of the city and 5B the southern part.

In Region 5A, Chicago-Read Mental Health Center provides inpatient care for mentally ill adult patients. A special program for patients who have been readmitted several times is run by Chicago-Read, Edgewater Community Mental Health Center, and Northwestern University. Henry Horner Children's Center serves children and adolescents.

Region 5B includes the Illinois State Psychiatric Institute (ISPI) and the Institute for Juvenile Research. Patients from Region 5B are also sent to Madden Mental Health Center, located in Region 2 but administered by Region 5B, and to Tinley Park Mental Health Center, in Region 6.

Region 2 serves north suburban Cook County and the counties of Lake, McHenry, Kane, and Kendall. Elgin Mental Health Center provides care for adults of the area.

Region 6 serves south and southwest Cook County and the counties of DuPage, Will, Grundy, and Kankakee. Its mental health hospital is Tinley Park Mental Health Center, serving adults. Children and adolescents from the region are sent to Madden Mental Health Center.

The Illinois Department of Rehabilitation Services serves disabled persons through vocational rehabilitation, home services, schools for the visually impaired, the deaf, and disabled youth.

The Medical Center Commission was created by state law to foster development of the medical center district in Chicago, in the area bounded by Ashland Boulevard, the Eisenhower Expressway, Oakley Boulevard, and the Chicago and Northwestern Railroad. Medical facilities in that area include Cook County Hospital, the University of Illinois Hospital and Medical Schools, Rush Presbyterian St. Luke's Medical Center, a Veteran's Administration Hospital, and state mental health facilities. The commission has seven members, serving unpaid staggered five-year terms;

four are appointed by the governor, one by the president of the county board, one by the mayor, and one by the president of the Park District. The commission is empowered to borrow money to buy land, which is in turn sold to hospitals, medical schools, and allied health organizations. Operating costs are paid by the state.

Cook County is responsible for a major part of hospital care, particularly for the medically indigent. The Cook County Health Facilities (see chapter 7), supported by a tax levy separate from that of the rest of county government, include Cook County Hospital, Oak Forest Hospital, Cermak Health Services at the county Department of Corrections, the Cook County Department of Health, and the Office of the Medical Examiner. The Cook County Department of Health provides clinics serving suburban Cook County except for Evanston, Skokie, Oak Park, and Stickney Township; these (like Chicago) have their own state-recognized health departments. As part of their General Assistance programs, township supervisors may provide essential medical care but not preventive care or psychiatric services.

The Chicago Department of Health (see chapter 5) operates neighborhood health clinics, school clinics, community mental health centers, and the Chicago Alcoholic Treatment Center. It inspects and licenses medical and health care facilities.

The Suburban Cook County Tuberculosis Sanitarium District provides suburban residents with cost-free care for tuberculosis and complications associated with tuberculosis.

ENVIRONMENTAL PROTECTION

The Illinois Department of Nuclear Safety is charged with protecting Illinois residents from potential health hazards caused by radioactive materials and radiation-producing devices. It also advises on the hazards of radon build-up in homes and on how to reduce this risk.

The Illinois Department of Energy and Natural Resources conducts research to solve problems of the management of hazardous waste and promotes alternatives to landfills for solid waste disposal.

The Metropolitan Sanitary District (chapter 8) is responsible for collection, treatment, and disposal of wastewater from most of Cook County and is charged with protecting the quality of Lake Michigan water.

The Cook County Department of Environmental Control enforces the county air pollution and noise and vibration ordinances in suburban Cook County.

The Cook County Department of Public Health inspects septic tanks, seepage systems, water supply, and solid waste disposal in suburban Cook County.

The Chicago Department of Consumer Services enforces the city's environmental protection codes for air, water, noise, solid waste, and hazardous materials.

HEALTH INSPECTION SERVICES

Inspection of restaurants and food suppliers and food and insurance of clean water and air are all part of public health care. The state Department of Agriculture inspects meats, fruits, and vegetables. In suburban Cook County, the Department of Public Health inspects restaurants, food establishments, and water supplies, and the Cook County Department of Environmental Control enforces air quality and noise pollution ordinances. In Chicago the Department of Health inspects food, dairy products and meat sold in the city, and the Department of Consumer Services enforces regulations on food and dairy products and environmental codes on air pollution, noise, solid waste, and hazardous materials. The Chicago Water Department provides purified water to Chicago and 94 suburbs.

LAW ENFORCEMENT

Law enforcement and the administration of justice are basic functions of government carried out by local, state, and federal agencies. Law enforcement includes prevention of crime and disorder, preservation of the peace, and protection of life, property, and personal liberty. The law enforcement agencies, the courts, and the correctional institutions are separate entities but closely related in their functioning. They form a series in the criminal justice system in which those accused proceed from arrest to court, and then either to release or, if found guilty, to probation or incarceration, and in most cases to eventual return to society.

In Cook County and the many municipalities within it, a number of independent agencies have roles in law enforcement. Their responsibilities are described in previous chapters on the courts, Cook County government, and Chicago government; this section will attempt to give an overview.

Federal law enforcement is an entirely separate system from those of the state and municipalities. Various federal agencies and departments are charged with enforcing federal laws, among them the Federal Bureau of Investigation, the Treasury Department, the Immigration and

Naturalization Service, and many others. The U.S. attorney general is the chief federal law enforcement officer. The federal court system is briefly described in chapter 9. The federal prison system and probation and parole system is separate from that of the state. Since this book is about local government, we cannot attempt a description of the federal system in any detail.

The federal constitution contains no specific provisions relating to local police forces. The state legislature, within the limits of the state constitution, specifies the powers and authority of all officers operating within the state. County, city, and village police are considered officers of the state and are regulated by state statutes as well as by municipal or county ordinances.

The courts which adjudicate matters falling under state law or municipal ordinances are part of the state court system. The incarceration system is divided between the state and the county: the state correctional system is responsible for those sentenced for felonies, and the county Department of Corrections under the county sheriff is responsible for those convicted of misdemeanors.

Illinois Attorney General. The chief law enforcement officer of the state is the attorney general, who is elected. The office of the attorney general is responsible for prosecution of violations of consumer fraud and environmental protection laws and for collection of monies owed to the

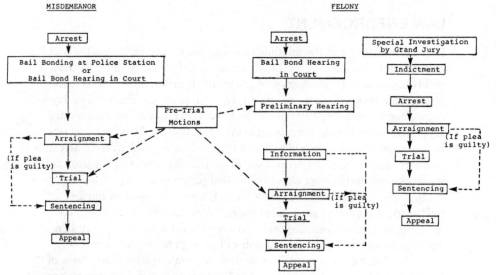

Fig. 10. 2. Steps in a criminal prosecution
Source: Cook County Court Watchers, Inc.

state. It also administers awards to individual victims of violent crimes and grants money to agencies that provide services to crime victims.

Department of State Police. The Department of State Police assists local law enforcement agencies and provides technical assistance to them. Among its programs is the I SEARCH Program, which seeks to recover missing children. The Division of State Troopers patrols state highways and recently has been assigned responsibility for traffic law enforcement on state expressways within the city of Chicago (formerly a responsibility of the Chicago police).

Cook County Sheriff's Police Department. The Cook County Sheriff's Police Department serves warrants for arrest in criminal fugitive cases, and the sheriff's Court Services Department serves eviction notices, carries out seizure of property under court order, and serves wage garnishment orders and summonses to appear in court. It is also responsible for maintaining order in the courts.

Municipal Police. Every community has some form of police protection. If the force available to a municipality is inadequate, it is supplemented by the county sheriff's police (chapter 7). Unincorporated areas are the responsibility of the sheriff. The Chicago Police Department is described in chapter 5.

Adults arrested by the police are held temporarily in lockups in police stations in Chicago, in sheriff's police lockups, or in suburban police lockups. Juveniles taken into the custody of the police are placed in the care of their parents, if possible, until the court hearing. If detention is considered advisable, they are sent to the Juvenile Detention Center, which is maintained by the county. There is a separate court for hearing juvenile cases (see chapter 9).

Nonmunicipal and Private Police. The police forces of a municipality may be supplemented by extra police hired by other agencies or institutions. Sometimes these are off-duty regular police hired, with the consent of the municipal police department, to do additional police work.

Special Police. Special police are regarded as deputized for a specific purpose and are subject to the same rules as public police, with certain restrictions. Chapter 173 of the Chicago municipal code gives the Chicago police superintendent power to appoint special police; examples are police officers for Illinois state colleges and universities, for sanitary districts, and for private universities which are authorized by local ordinance to maintain a police force. Special police have the power of arrest, must follow rules of search and seizure, and must inform suspects of their constitutional rights.

They may carry guns only within their area of duty and may not take them to and from work.

In Chicago, by city ordinance, any person who for hire guards and protects property or persons within the city must be appointed by the city superintendent of police with full police investigation. Uniforms for such special police must be approved by the superintendent, and special police must wear a badge but not a star. Special police must conform to all rules and regulations governing city police officers.

Chicago Public School Security Officers. In addition to officers detailed to serve in and near schools which need extra security, the school system employs off-duty police officers for 4-hour-a-day tours of duty. These officers have all the powers of regular police. In addition, the school system's Bureau of Safety and Security hires safety and security officers for full-time and part-time work. Such officers are directly under the supervision of the principal of the school, work only within the boundaries of the school, and are charged with maintaining order and preventing harm to persons and damage to property. They are unarmed and must wear a Bureau badge. They are trained by the Bureau of Safety and Security with the cooperation of the district police superintendents and the school principals. In 1987 there were about 800 civilians and part-time police officers working in the schools. Some schools have volunteer parent patrols as well.

Campus Police. The City Colleges of Chicago also hire off-duty Chicago police officers for part-time duty within their colleges. Like those serving in the public schools, these officers have the power of regular police.

Community colleges and state colleges and universities may appoint police officers who have the powers of municipal police. They may make arrests in the course of upholding the laws of the state, county, or municipality.

Private colleges and universities may appoint persons to be members of a campus police department. Northwestern University in Evanston and Chicago appoints them under state law which permits certain private universities to appoint peace officers. The University of Chicago appoints its police force under the Chicago ordinance. Campus police have the power to make arrests for violations of law.

All appointees to campus police forces must, by state law, meet state training requirements: this includes firearms training and a training course established under the Illinois Police Training Act.

Federal Agency Guards. The Post Office and certain interstate carriers are authorized under federal regulations to have guards.

Private Security Guards. There are a large number of private agencies offering security guard services listed in the business telephone directory. The state licenses the agencies, but not the individual guards. Guards may wear uniforms and badges, but most municipalities require that these be easily distinguished from those worn by the municipal police. Armed guards are required to undergo a 40-hour training course approved by the state and may carry their guns to and from work. Unarmed guards are required to undergo a 20-hour training course. Guards do not have police powers of arrest but hold suspects for police arrest.

Complaints. Police departments have procedures for receiving and reviewing complaints about police behavior. In the Cook County Sheriff's Police Department there is an Internal Investigation Unit (chapter 7). In the Chicago Police Department (chapter 5) complaints about police use of excessive force are investigated by civilian personnel of the Office of Professional Standards, and other types of complaints are investigated by the Internal Affairs Division. Complaints about nonmunicipal and private police and security guards should be made to the agency employing them. All complaints should be specific as to time, place, witnesses, and identification of the officer if possible.

CODE ENFORCEMENT

Municipal code enforcement and county code enforcement for unincorporated areas are generally assigned to various departments which have the power to take code violations directly to court through the municipal legal department. In cases of criminal negligence, the Cook County State's Attorney prosecutes. In Chicago the departments in charge of inspection are the Department of Inspectional Services (building, electrical, heating and ventilating, housing, and plumbing), the Fire Department (fire hazards), Consumer Services (fraudulent businesses practices, food and dairy products, condominium ordinances, environmental protection), Health (food inspection, medical and health facilities), the Department of Zoning (zoning ordinance), the Housing Department (landlord-tenant ordinance, housing discrimination), the Commission on Human Reations (antidiscrimination ordinances except housing), the Commission on Animal Control (inspection of animal-related businesses). Other municipalities have similar divisions of responsibilities.

The Superintendent of the Educational Service Region is responsible for compliance with laws concerning school and school bus safety regulations. The Cook County Department of Environmental Control enforces air pollution and noise and vibration controls in suburban Cook County. The Cook County Department of Public Health provides inspectional services for 130 Cook County municipalities (not including

Chicago and other areas with state-recognized health departments); the services include inspection of day-care centers, restaurants and food establishments, mobile home parks, motels, septic tanks and septic tank cleaners, seepage systems, water supply, solid waste disposal, and swimming pools.

For unincorporated areas and some suburban municipalities, the county Department of Animal Control enforces leash laws. For unincorporated areas, the county Department of Building and Zoning enforces zoning and building standards.

EDUCATION

Education, recreation, and cultural programs, including libraries, are grouped together in the following sections because they are interrelated. Schools offer athletic and cultural programs, and many of the programs conducted by recreational agencies also include educational programs. Museums, libraries, botanical gardens, zoos, and cultural events all contribute to the educational process for children and adults. There are a multiplicity of separate agencies providing these services.

Headstart and Day-Care Programs. Head Start programs may be funded by federal grants from the U.S. Department of Health and Human Services passed through the state. In low-income areas of Cook County, the program of the Community and Economic Development Association (CEDA, a private not-for-profit corporation) includes Head Start. Day care is among the services which township supervisors may provide as part of their general assistance programs.

The Chicago public schools provide prekindergarten, for three- and four-year-olds in programs funded by the state and federal governments. Churches and private agencies also provide Head Start programs through funding received through the city Department of Human Services (DHS), and DHS provides child-care programs. All DHS child-care programs have income-eligibility requirements.

Public Schools. There are 144 separate school districts in Cook County, of which the Chicago Public Schools is the largest. They are described in chapters 2 and 6; the responsibilities of the county Superintendent of the Educational Service Region are described in chapter 7. School libraries may be part of multilibrary systems described in chapter 2.

Supplementary Services. Public libraries, such as the Chicago library branches, offer homework and study centers, and literacy and General Educational Development (GED) classes. The Forest Preserve District (chapter 7) offers courses for teachers in outdoor science education and maintains education centers for children and adults. Most museums conduct special programs and guided tours for school groups. The Chicago Park District has sports education and arts and crafts programs and special activities for mentally and physically handicapped children.

State Schools for Disabled Children. The state Department of Rehabilitation Services offers residential schools for the disabled, the visually impaired, and the deaf.

Employment Training Programs. In addition to programs in the schools and public libraries, economic development agencies provide job training for those who are unemployed and need such training. The President's Office of Employment Training (POET) administers federally funded training programs in suburban Cook County, and the Mayor's Office of Employment and Training administers them in Chicago. Applicants to the Illinois Department of Public Aid for Aid to Families with Dependent Children and General Assistance are given job training when needed. Township supervisors may provide training programs for General Assistance applicants.

Community Colleges. There are seven suburban community college districts supporting one community college each (described in chapter 2), and a community college district in Chicago -- City Colleges of Chicago -- including eight colleges (described in chapter 6). All require tuition payments, which vary from one district to another and are less for students who live within the district. If students' home institutions do not offer courses they want, they may take courses in other community colleges.

State Universities. The University of Illinois at Chicago includes what were formerly called Chicago Circle Campus and the Medical Campus. The campus areas are located on the near west side of Chicago, roughly bounded by Van Buren Street, Roosevelt Road, the Dan Ryan Expressway, and Ogden Avenue (not including the area between Ashland and Racine Avenues). The administration building is at 601 S. Morgan St., Chicago 60607. The university is administered by the elected Board of Trustees of the University of Illinois. Northeastern Illinois University is at 5500 N. St. Louis Avenue, Chicago 60625; Chicago State University is at 95th Street and Martin Luther King Drive, Chicago 60628; and Governors State University is at Governors Highway and Stunkel Road, University Park 60466. These three universities are governed by the Board of Governors of State Colleges and Universities. All state universities charge tuition, less for Illinois residents than for out-of-state residents.

There are many privately supported universities and colleges in the Chicago area. These include the University of Chicago and the Illinois Institute of Technology on the South Side of Chicago; Northwestern University in Evanston, with professional and evening schools on the Near North Side; Roosevelt University downtown; and DePaul and Loyola Universities on the North Side.

RECREATION

The chief public agencies which provide recreation and sports facilities are the Forest Preserve District (chapter 7), the Chicago Park District (Chapter 6), suburban municipal and special district parks, and the Metropolitan Fair and Exposition Authority (chapter 6). The city of Chicago's Department of General Services is responsible for a nature preserve and study area in North Park Village, on the site of the former Municipal Tuberculosis Sanitarium. The Metropolitan Sanitary District dedicates some land not in immediate use to nature preserves and shares the use of other land with local park districts.

The Forest Preserve District, almost entirely in suburban Cook County, has a large number of sports facilities, nature centers, and the Botanical Gardens and the Brookfield Zoo. The Chicago Park District has both indoor and outdoor sports facilities, including the stadium at Soldier Field, beaches, and yacht harbors. On Park District grounds are the Adler Planetarium, the Art Institute, the Chicago Academy of Sciences, the Chicago Historical Society, Du Sable Museum, the Field Museum of Natural History, and the Museum of Science and Industry. The Illinois Sports Facilities Authority (chapter 6) is authorized to build a sports stadium in Chicago.

A number of suburban lakefront municipal parks have beach facilities, some of which require proof of local residence for use.

CULTURAL FACILITIES AND PROGRAMS

In addition to the museums and other cultural facilities (listed above) on the grounds of the Forest Preserve or the Chicago Park District, the yellow pages of the Chicago phone book list 30 privately funded museums. Public institutions which have art exhibits include the State of Illinois Building and the Cultural Center of the Chicago Public Library.

Libraries. A state network of library systems provides Cook County residents access to materials throughout the country (see chapter 2). The Chicago Public Library, a separate taxing body, is described in chapter 6; suburban district libraries (also separate taxing bodies) and municipal libraries are described in chapter 2. The Cook County Law Library is a specialized library serving the court system and funded by the county (chapter 9). The Chicago Municipal Reference Library (chapter 5), a resource for information on local government, is located in City Hall and funded by the city. Schools and colleges and universities have their own libraries, and some trade and industrial associations have libraries. The Chicago Art Institute has a library on art, which is open to members.

Concerts and Events. The Chicago Department of Cultural Affairs sponsors a series of events, including lakefront festivals and concerts, a program of free exhibits and lunch-time concerts, dance exhibits, and other events at the Daley Center, and provides grants to neighborhood groups for neighborhood events. Libraries often conduct discussion groups, lectures, and special exhibitions. Notable among these are the exhibits and concerts sponsored by the Department of Cultural Affairs and the Chicago Public Library at the Cultural Center, 78 E. Washington St. The Chicago Park District sponsors free concerts during the summer at Grant Park and sponsors events in neighborhood parks.

TRANSPORTATION

Public Transportation. In the Chicago Metropolitan area public transportation is provided by the Chicago Transit Authority, Metra, and PACE, all funded and overseen by the Regional Transportation Authority (chapter 8) and supported by sales taxes, fares, and state and federal grants. Planning for public transportation is assigned to the Chicago Area Transportation Study (chapter 1).

Taxi Service. The state requires all taxicabs to be licensed and to carry appropriate insurance. The state issues drivers' licenses. Municipalities have the right to regulate and license cab companies, including rates, hours of service, and regulations on passenger service and on shared riding. Municipalities may restrict the number of cabs operated through issuing a limited number of medallions (municipal licenses). A Chicago ordinance of January 1988 set the maximum number of taxicab licenses to be issued (including renewals) at 4,800 in 1988, increasing by 100 each year to 5,700 in 1997. The Yellow Taxi Company and the Checker Cab Company, which at one time held 80% of the Chicago medallions, must relinquish and not renew 1,300 licenses: 400 in 1988 and 100 a year through 1997. Livery services are separately licensed; the maximum number of livery licenses is set at 445 for 1988, to be increased each year to 745 in 1992. An individual or company is not permitted to hold both a livery and a taxicab license, and no one may hold more than 25% of the authorized livery or taxicab licenses.

Airport Limousines. The Chicago Commissioner of Aviation (subject to city council approval) may contract with operators of public transportation systems to provide ground transportation to and from the airports. The ordinance requires that 10% of the gross receipts from transportation of passengers be paid to the city. In 1988, the department had a contract with Continental Air Transport, a privately owned company. By regulation, the department assigns curb sites to bus and livery services and taxis.

Highways and Roads. Responsibility for highways and roads is shared by federal, state, and local governments. Federal funds pay most of the costs for the interstate highway system and a smaller portion of the costs for roads providing interconnections for interstate, statewide, and regional travel. Federal funds come chiefly from the federal tax on gasoline.

The Illinois Department of Transportation, through its Division of Highways, plans, designs, constructs, rehabilitates, and maintains federal and state routes and some local roads. Funds come from the federal government with a requirement that the state provide matching funds. State highway funds are derived from the sale of bonds and from the State Road Fund, which is supported by motor vehicle license fees and the state motor fuel tax. District I is responsible for operation of the Chicago metropolitan area expressway system, including snow and ice removal, lighting, and maintenance. The Illinois State Toll Highway Authority is responsible for the tollway system; funds to pay for the tollways come from revenue bonds and tolls.

Municipalities are responsible for building and maintaining streets which are not federal or state routes. Township road districts (chapter 2), construct and maintain about 500 miles of roads in 21 Cook County townships having at least four miles of roads in unincorporated areas. The Cook County Department of Highways is responsible for design and improvement on 600 miles of roads which constitute the county highway system. The Chicago Department of Public Works is responsible for designing and building highways, streets, and bridges in the city. It has a joint program with the city Department of Economic Development to upgrade streets in certain industrial areas, and it has a New Street Construction Program under which property owners may pay for part of the costs of replacement of unimproved streets (chapter 5). The Bureau of Streets of the city's Department of Streets and Sanitation maintains 3,677 miles of streets, including, by agreement with the state, 200 miles of state routes.

Funds for highways, roads, and streets come from motor fuel taxes levied by the federal, state, and local governments, and from vehicle license fees levied by state and local governments (see chapter 4).

Index